LIVING *a* THEOLOGY *of* GENDER

LIVING *a* THEOLOGY *of* GENDER

How to Love Our Gendered World

Fellipe do Vale

Baker Academic
a division of Baker Publishing Group
Grand Rapids, Michigan

Published by Baker Academic
a division of Baker Publishing Group
Grand Rapids, Michigan
BakerAcademic.com

Printed in the United States of America

Library of Congress Cataloging-in-Publication Data
Names: Do Vale, Fellipe M., 1994– author
Title: Living a theology of gender : how to love our gendered world / Fellipe do Vale.
Description: Grand Rapids, Michigan : Baker Academic, a division of Baker Publishing Group, [2026] | Includes bibliographical references and index.
Identifiers: LCCN 2026021406 | ISBN 9781540968883 paperback | ISBN 9781493454556 ebook | ISBN 9781493454563 pdf
Subjects: LCSH: Theological anthropology | Gender identity—Religious aspects—Christianity | Love—Religious aspects—Christianity
Classification: LCC BT701.3 .D68 2026
LC record available at https://lccn.loc.gov/2026021406

Cover design by Paula Gibson

Baker Publishing Group publications use paper produced from sustainable forestry practices and postconsumer waste whenever possible.

26 27 28 29 30 31 32 7 6 5 4 3 2 1

To Karla

For your friendship, love, wisdom, care, and understanding.

No one knows me like you do.

Contents

Introduction

What in the World Is Gender?

On any ordinary day, human beings interact with a host of gendered goods. You wake up; is someone lying beside you? Perhaps a spouse or a child rests peacefully at your side. You make your way to the bathroom to have a shower; notice the products that line your sink and shelves. Are there cosmetics to help you meet beauty standards expected of you at work, shampoos and conditioners made for balding men, or beard trimmings on the sink? After showering, you get dressed. What clothing options are available to you? Do you feel that you can wear what you wore last week without being perceived negatively? Is your clothing comfortable? Does it have pockets? Can you accessorize it? From what kind of store did you buy it? Is it a uniform, or do you pick out clothing in order to communicate something? You make your way to the kitchen for breakfast. Do you cook, or does someone else cook for you? In fact, how are household responsibilities divided between you and those with whom you live (if you live with anyone)? Will there be a "second shift" after work, or is that someone else's burden?

After breakfast you head to work (if you indeed have a position outside the home). What do you listen to on the way there? A lifestyle podcast, or maybe Taylor Swift? Do you have to drop off any children for childcare on the way, and how are you perceived for doing so? You finally arrive at work. What is the nature of your duties? Do you find it difficult to ascend the ranks and gain promotion? What kinds of virtues are associated with your work? Are you praised for your hard-edged competence or for your warmth and compassion? In fact, which of your superiors take the time to praise you? Are you paid less than those who do the same work as you?

Finally, it's your lunch break. What's for lunch? A salad and a yogurt because they are approved by your weight-loss program? Or perhaps you go out for something more oriented around meat, like a burger or tacos? As you mindlessly scroll through social media on your break, you see news of yet another politician accused of sexual assault (is he male?), and then you are saddened by the hateful comments made by internet trolls about your favorite Instagrammer—some are truly gruesome, threatening to rape her. You should probably get off Instagram anyway; just looking at the highly polished photos makes you feel like you need to update your wardrobe, get in better shape, and buy that missing item from that targeted ad that will finally make you look the way you want. You finish your workday and head home; what does your most comfortable space look like? Is it decorated with thrifted items sensitive to color palettes, or do you share a messy home with friends who invite you to watch sports the moment you walk in? What sport is it, and what kind of people participate? If you wanted to watch a particular sport (say, women's soccer), could you do so easily with your streaming package? Or perhaps a family is waiting for you at home. If so, what is your place in that family, and what makes this group of people family?

Before you end your day, you go to a service at your church. Maybe it is a women's ministry event, or a men's ministry event, or one of those "post-college" events for singles to meet a potential spouse (despite their best efforts to say that these are *not* events for singles). What do they do at this ministry event? If it is a women's or a men's event, what do you talk about? Is it an environment focused primarily on learning and theology, or one focused primarily on relationships and sharing? What key themes and challenges are addressed? What is assumed about your life and the kind of help and guidance you need? And if you *did* go on a date with someone from that group, what would you do? What are the expectations you would have, and would you trust them right away?

Before bed, you watch a few minutes of your favorite movie. What is that movie? Does it have violence, adventure, and action? Or does it display someone whose life is like yours, just trying to make their way through the various challenges of balancing work and relationships? Do you anxiously review the day, scrutinizing every interaction? Are you planning tomorrow's errands? Eventually you drift off to sleep, only to negotiate the messiness of a gendered day all over again tomorrow.

The Otherworldliness of Theologies of Gender

It seems to me that much that is written about gender in contemporary theology is oddly abstract and otherworldly. Typically, debates about gender held among theologians tend to operate at a distance from the present concerns of ordinary gendered people who live through ordinary gendered days like the one described above. Work being done at the intersection of gender and theology seems to forget its responsibility to help individuals think theologically about the fact that they have to get dressed in the morning, navigate sexist workplaces, and sort out what they will have for lunch.[1] Or, in the words of Lauren Winner, theologies of gender seem to have forgotten that they are accountable to what happens on "an ordinary Tuesday."[2]

I will shortly provide more precise terminology about just what has gone wrong, but the problem is not difficult to discern. If all I know about gender is that I stand in a relationship of either authority, submission, or equality with regard to someone else (the evangelical version of this problem) or that gender is either a binary or a spectrum (the version of this problem familiar to the academy), then I have not gained much clarity on how to buy clothes online, which granola bars to purchase, or whether I should have kids after getting married. In other words, there is a common problem this book aims to address: *Theologies of gender, as they are currently articulated, are impracticable*. That is, they are often sophisticated attempts at asserting visions for being women and men that leave one puzzled as to how to practice these visions in one's ordinary gendered life. As a result, when it comes to making those decisions in practice, some alternative script will be followed, some way of living with no operative connection to the theology of gender.

This book attempts to rectify this problem largely by showing and not telling. After this introductory chapter articulating the theology of gender needed to perform our duties well, each chapter investigates how gender is implicated

1. Ephraim Radner makes a similar observation at the outset of his work on theological anthropology and sexuality: "Part of the frustration of these debates, outside of their purely destructive force within the Christian community, is the strange lack of living context they assume" (*A Time to Keep: Theology, Mortality, and the Shape of a Human Life* [Baylor University Press, 2016], vii). For Radner, this context includes the day-to-day events of human life *and* the broader canonical context of time as it is defined by Christ.

2. Lauren F. Winner, *Wearing God: Clothing, Laughter, Fire, and Other Overlooked Ways of Meeting God* (HarperOne, 2016), 15. For a broader summary of the ordinary in relation to Christian ethics, see Brent Waters, *Common Callings and Ordinary Virtues: Christian Ethics for Everyday Life* (Baker Academic, 2022).

by a variety of domains in our day-to-day experiences, domains that largely make up our gendered worlds and will hopefully feel very real to those of us navigating our human existence amongst the complexities and pressures of life. These include, but are not exhausted by, goods like politics, bodies, marketing, clothing, food, friendships, and dating. By situating a theology of gender in conversations about each of these concrete goods, I hope to avoid the impracticability so common to theologies of gender.

In my previous book, *Gender as Love: A Theological Account of Human Identity, Embodied Desire, and Our Social Worlds*, I argued that gender is about the organization of social goods pertaining to a sexed body to form an identity by means of our loves.[3] In other words, I argued that one's gender is an identity like the identity of being a professor. If someone were to ask me, "What does it mean to be a professor?" I would have to make recourse to a variety of social goods that I organize in my life to make sense of that identity, goods like the laptop I use to prepare lectures, the students I teach, the institution that employs me, the books that I own, and so on. If someone were to encounter my laptop at the table of a coffee shop, they would not be able to conclude from it alone that it is a *professor's* laptop. To arrive at such a conclusion, one also needs the broader organizational context in which the laptop is integrated. Gender is like this—it is about encountering a variety of social goods in our worlds and organizing them to make sense of an identity. Furthermore, I argued that we must theologically understand our efforts at organizing social goods by means of our loves, for it is through our loves that we integrate the goods in our life into a coherent narrative and identity.

I intend to build on these arguments here. What are the social goods organized to form a gender identity? Most theologies treating gender are silent on this issue. Their reasons for remaining silent are, of course, related to the fact that gender is expressed in a variety of cultural contexts throughout the world and throughout history, making it impossible to state, in a simple list, what clothes, food, and so on are appropriate for all women and all men. But this does not mean that there are *no* gendered goods; it means that there are *too many* gendered goods for the theologian to say once and for all which of them make up our genders. It does not mean that theologians can get away with *no* analyses whatsoever of the gendered goods that populate our worlds.

3. Fellipe do Vale, *Gender as Love: A Theological Account of Human Identity, Embodied Desire, and Our Social Worlds* (Baker Academic, 2023).

Something between a universal statement about gendered goods ("men should always wear *x*; women should always eat *y*") and silence must be possible. In this introduction, I shall argue that this is in fact possible and that it consists largely of two tasks that enable us to discover our true selves. Through these two tasks, I maintain, we can engage in a form of moral analysis that enables us to identify the gendered goods that already populate our worlds and how best to live with them practically.

The True Self and the Gendered Self

A helpful place to begin in thinking about gender in a manner reflective of its actual practice is with an investigation regarding what our *true selves* amount to. This is a concept used fairly widely, especially in psychological circles, and it should be familiar as a name for the struggle between the elements characterizing us that we accept and the elements that we wish were different. Perhaps we are proud of having kicked a destructive habit, of the way a certain haircut frames our face, or of the fact that we come from a country whose story and cultural identity represent some lovely aspects of our personality. Alternatively, we might dislike the way we regularly respond harshly to those we love, how quickly we gain weight or how we are unable to keep it on, or the number of regrets we bear about our lives. There is a gap, it seems, between *who we are* and *who we would like to be*, and bridging that gap is often described as an attempt to discover our true selves.

Importantly, the notion of a true self is commonly appealed to when individuals try to express the clarity or difficulty they have experienced with respect to gender. For instance, trans author Kate Bornstein describes her experience in such terms:

> I mapped out the recurring pattern of several crises I've experienced in my life: first I question an identity I have, then I see all its bad qualities, and eventually I lose it or give it up. Then I get what seems to be a new, more pure, more unshakable identity—maybe I call it my authentic self—and I go through learning the ropes about what it means to be that new identity. Then, once I'm comfortable in the new identity, I question that, and the identity crisis starts all over again. It's what I did with gender; it's what I'm still doing with gender.[4]

4. Kate Bornstein, *Gender Outlaw: On Men, Women, and the Rest of Us*, rev. ed. (Vintage, 2016), 150–51.

The true self (or here the "authentic" self) seems to be a very helpful tool for individuals thinking through the complexities of gender identity and how gendered terms and goods should fit within their lives. But what is a true self? Can we say anything theologically about such an important concept?

Christian theology also recognizes the gap that generates a need for a true self, typically calling the process of aligning who we are with who we are meant to be *sanctification*, *deification*, or some other term associated with the work God performs to take us from the way we are to the way we ought to be. Theologically, therefore, the true self is indexed to the array of divine actions that constitute a coherent narrative about what God is doing to create, redeem, sustain, and perfect us. Eleonore Stump has recently developed a theological account of the true self with which I have great sympathies. She defines one's true self as "the condition of that person when he has what he most cares about in both an objective and a subjective sense and when his deepest heart's desires converge with his thriving."[5] Stump's proposal makes two concepts central to the true self—namely, a person's deepest loves and a person's thriving.[6] When these two align, one has arrived at one's true self. For Stump, and for the overwhelming majority of Christian history, this desired alignment is found when one's deepest loves are ordered to union with God: "A person will therefore be her true self only in relationship; and on Christian doctrine, the ultimate relationship required for thriving is union with God."[7] Although this true self is perfected only eschatologically,[8] Stump emphasizes that the full sweep of a person's life narrative and care for particular goods are woven into it: "The notion of the true self should reflect the human condition as an embodied particular; the particularity of a human being should be mirrored in the particularity of the person's true self. It should turn out that the true self of a person has particular attachments to particular places, things, and people."[9] Stump, in her analysis of a true self, adequately balances both sides of the equation: It is "true" insofar

5. Eleonore Stump, *The Image of God: The Problem of Evil and the Problem of Mourning* (Oxford University Press, 2022), 51.

6. Stump defines love as consisting of two desires, the desire for union with the beloved and the desire for the good of the beloved, which is why I transition from her language of "care" and "deepest desire" to "love." For her, they are the same thing. See Stump, *Image of God*, 106–10.

7. Stump, *Image of God*, 83.

8. Stump, *Image of God*, 30.

9. Stump, *Image of God*, 22.

as it has obtained that for which it was made—namely, union with God—and insofar as it is a real "self," entangled in the ordinary processes of life.

Taking Stump's proposal as a point of departure, we can ask: How do we discover our true selves? What does it take to unify our love for God, the one in whom we thrive, and our loves for particular goods, those necessary for us as the kind of creatures that we are? And how does that unification help us better understand our gendered selves? I want to argue here that our discovery of our true selves requires at least two tasks, a *descriptive* task and a *normative* task.[10] Performing these two tasks allows us both to offer a theologically robust account of the true self and to articulate a model of gender that remains workable even in the midst of cultural particularity.

The Descriptive Task

Christian ethics ordinarily begins with an attempt to describe the world in which one finds oneself; the possibilities for engaging in some moral project require knowing the context in which one will act and the avenues available for action. It does little practical good to stipulate what *ought* to be done before taking stock of what *can* be done. This is why, for instance, H. Richard Niebuhr states that someone concerned with responsible moral action must ask the question "What is going on?" in "every moment of decision and choice."[11] An awareness of context is necessary for knowing how best to act

10. This is a development of a claim I made in *Gender as Love*, 165–66: "We do not have to *try* to be gendered, nor do we have to wonder which are those social goods that make up our genders. We walk out of our doors in the morning and encounter them directly, often with force. The goods are right there to be loved, and this is why I am not taking any time to specify *which* gendered goods constitute masculinity and femininity. Such a task would be impossible, for those goods will differ contextually. Rather than imagining the theological task as one in which we draw up gender from the ground up, theologies of gender instead have a two-fold task: first, they must be *descriptively* accountable, making sense of the gendered lives we already live. What are the gendered goods encountered by the individuals in these contexts? . . . Second, they must be *normatively* accountable, telling us not just what gender *is* but what it *ought* to be, or how to engage these goods *rightly*, as we encounter them simply by living our lives. . . . The normative task is not completed by providing definitions of gender that are not descriptive. Rather, the normative task must take into account the descriptions already provided and work *within those* to love rightly. So, turning to the normative task, we must ask, As we are encountered by these goods, how *should* we love them?" What follows here is an elaboration of this statement into a fuller methodology. For a parallel statement of this methodology from feminist theory, see Sally Haslanger, "Gender and Race: (What) Are They? (What) Do We Want Them to Be?," in *Resisting Reality: Social Construction and Social Critique* (Oxford University Press, 2012).

11. H. Richard Niebuhr, *The Responsible Self: An Essay in Christian Moral Philosophy* (Harper & Row, 1963), 60.

in a given circumstance. For example, we might have a moral responsibility to be honest, but knowing *when* to be honest and *in what ways* might make the difference between speaking a truthful word and inappropriately exposing someone's vulnerabilities.

Theological approaches to gender, therefore, must begin with what I am calling "the descriptive task." If they are to be morally helpful contributions, theologies of gender must confront the questions, difficulties, and puzzles that human beings face in the lives they actually live. They must inquire about what is going on in the lives of women and men in order to know what demands theological attention. When is gender puzzling or difficult? What is going on in the life of someone when they struggle with gender? What goods played a part in the struggle? How can the theologian prayerfully contribute something of use to those who are struggling to make their way through life's complexities? What kinds of contributions are needed? Luke Bretherton has recently employed the metaphor of "listening" to make clear that description is the starting point of Christian ethics. Listening is a way to be lovingly attuned to what is happening in the places and times in which one finds oneself so that one can act in the best ways possible.[12] The moral importance of doing so is significant, according to Bretherton:

> Listening is not just a theologically pregnant act. It is also a moral gesture. It is a refusal to treat others merely as *biology* that I make us of for my own benefit and instead responds to others as having a *biography*. Those before me are people who have meaning and purpose, a story to tell, and a voice independent of me that needs to be heard and responded to. In sum, listening is vital to deepening our moral conversion in relation to God and neighbor and thus our ability to discover the right or just judgment made with these people, at this time, in this place.[13]

Listening in order to describe well allows us to remain aware, grounded, and sensitive to those whose lives make up the subject matter of our study. Christian theology must be done gently and with compassion. When bearing witness to the open wounds of God's people, listening must be the starting point. A sign that one has engaged in the right kind of listening is that one is

12. See Luke Bretherton, *A Primer in Christian Ethics: Christ and the Struggle to Live Well* (Cambridge University Press, 2023), 22.

13. Bretherton, *Primer in Christian Ethics*, 23. Unless noted otherwise, all italics throughout this book are original to the quoted author.

able to describe well what one has just heard. The descriptive task, therefore, is necessary for theologies of gender looking to encourage virtue.

Description is also necessary for theologies of gender to conform well to the standards of Christian ethics. We have already seen how the notion of a true self requires a gap between who we are and the eschatological conditions under which we thrive, and this gap mirrors the broader gap between the world as it is and the world as it should be. The dogmatic location[14] of Christian ethics is found precisely in that gap. Christian ethics emerges from our attempts to find faithful, hopeful, and loving ways to live in the tension between the way the world is and the way the world ought to be, the tension between who we are currently and who we will be eschatologically. To appreciate that tension, we must first describe the world as it is in terms that are honest about the effects of sin and domination currently on display. Bretherton states, "Ethical descriptions should situate us within and help us respond morally to the world in which we find ourselves. Inherent in ethical description is a determination of the gap between the world as it is and a vision of the world as it should be if we are to live well."[15] This is especially important for a topic like gender; if we fail to describe the particular goods of our contexts, we will not be speaking about the gendered lives we actually live.

This is precisely why, as stated above, so many theologies of gender are problematically otherworldly and impracticable: Many of them ignore the task of description altogether. There are, of course, many works in other disciplines that perform the descriptive task quite capably.[16] The trouble is that those doing normative work tend to operate in isolation from those doing descriptive work, and those doing descriptive work tend to think that normativity is beyond their remit.[17] If theologians concerned with gender engage in the work of description at all, it is usually to denounce the "cultural confusion" ostensibly

14. An inquiry's "dogmatic location" specifies the place or places in the divine economy or biblical story in which it is found or which are most relevant for its understanding. Where in the Bible must I look to find Christian ethics (or any other doctrine), and what parts of that story are relevant for its construction? For more on a doctrine's dogmatic location, see John Webster, "On the Theology of Providence," in *God Without Measure: Working Papers in Christian Theology*, vol. 1, *God and the Works of God* (Bloomsbury T&T Clark, 2016).

15. Bretherton, *Primer in Christian Ethics*, 129.

16. I will be drawing on many of these throughout the course of this book, but for just one example of a work on gender that operates purely in the descriptive mode, see Celina Durgin and Dru Johnson, eds., *The Biblical World of Gender: The Daily Lives of Ancient Women and Men* (Cascade Books, 2022).

17. The division between theology and biblical studies is partly to blame for this, but so is the general isolation of the disciplines.

holding us all captive.[18] At most, treatments of gender of this kind tend to rely on superficial genealogical accounts of historical decline, blaming whatever expressions of gender are deemed most problematic on some past bogeyman.[19] These decline narratives have their problems—not the least of which is their inability to make clear the causal connections between the bogeyman and the gender expressions[20]—but, for our purposes, we need only to notice how genealogical narratives of decline are not sufficient for reliable description. At most, they provide a broad and generic story that obscures complexities and assumes too much about the motivations of the individuals they describe.[21]

The descriptive task, if performed well, must accomplish more. It must describe gender in the world as it is, in the world of clothing, food, money, politics, families, cars, and so on. It must be willing to get its hands into the dirt of ordinary life to know exactly what is demanded of the theologian. Only then is the true self a *real* self, grounded in the lives we actually live and reflecting the gender identities by which we live. But theologians cannot stop there. After describing gender, they must then move on to the normative task.

The Normative Task

It seems to me that one of the unique features of Christian ethics is its ability to listen well to the contributions of various disciplines while emphasizing the importance of normativity alongside the work of listening. Thus Bretherton: "Ethics does not live by description alone. It also necessitates a

---

18. Notice the subtitles of two recent theological books on gender: Katie J. McCoy, *To Be a Woman: The Confusion over Female Identity and How Christians Can Respond* (B&H, 2023); David Dockery and Lauren Green McAfee, *Created in the Image of God: Applications and Implications for Our Cultural Confusion* (Forefront Books, 2023).

19. There are "conservative" and "liberal" versions of this. For the former, see Carl R. Trueman, *The Rise and Triumph of the Modern Self: Cultural Amnesia, Expressive Individualism, and the Road to Sexual Revolution* (Crossway, 2020); for the latter, see Adrian Thatcher, *Redeeming Gender* (Oxford University Press, 2016). On both accounts, cultural and historical decline have led to ubiquitous expressions of gender they deem problematic. Perplexingly, they make opposite claims about these ubiquitous expressions of gender, leading one to wonder just how ubiquitous they actually are.

20. For more on this, see Fellipe do Vale, review of *The Rise and Triumph of the Modern Self: Cultural Amnesia, Expressive Individualism, and the Road to Sexual Revolution*, by Carl R. Trueman, *London Lyceum*, April 27, 2021, https://www.thelondonlyceum.com/book-review-the-rise-and-triumph-of-the-modern-self/.

21. For instance, Trueman reduces the motivations for contemporary expressions of gender to a desire for sexual fulfillment derived from Freud (Trueman, *Rise and Triumph of the Modern Self*, 391), while Thatcher reduces them to the insistence on sustaining binaries that betray the continued influence of Aristotle (Thatcher, *Redeeming Gender*, 82).

movement from description to action."[22] Once we have a grasp of gender as it is lived, we must then ask ourselves whether this is the way things ought to be, so that we may live well as gendered people. Should it be the case that work in the home is inequitable? Should it be the case that maternity-leave policies are vague and often not easily accessed? Should it be the case that survivors of abuse are discredited in their testimonies? Should it be the case that men die by suicide three to four times more often than women? It is not difficult to feel a lingering malaise when taking stock of our gendered world; the normative task turns its attention to the states of affairs and the diagnoses provided by the descriptive task.

The success of the normative task is measured by its ability to bring to light a way of life that approximates our true selves. Recall that our true selves, on Stump's account, emerge when our love and our thriving align. Moreover, recall that our thriving is first and foremost an eschatological fulfillment of the relationship of love we ought to have for God, for whom we have been made, and that this love does not preclude our loving particular creaturely goods. So, if we want to know what our true selves *ought to* look like, we need to attend to (a) the nature of human love and (b) the nature of eschatology as it relates to our present moral endeavors.

Gender and Human Love

In *Gender as Love*, I argued at length that we organize the social goods that make up our gender identities by means of our loves.[23] I adopted an Augustinian theology of human love according to which love is both natural to human beings and the means by which humans engage their social worlds in a manner that is morally evaluable. While I did not endorse Augustine's views of gender, I found his perceptive analysis of human love of immense value for breaking deadlocks in gender theory and theology, particularly in its ability to bridge what is typically held to be natural over against what is social. For Augustine, "one becomes conformed to that which one loves"; this is a fact that is hardwired into human nature and guides human beings to their proper place of rest—namely, life with God.[24] Earthly goods must

22. Bretherton, *Primer in Christian Ethics*, 129.
23. See do Vale, *Gender as Love*, chaps. 4 and 5.
24. Augustine, *The Catholic Way of Life and the Manichean Way of Life*, in *The Manichean Debate*, trans. Roland Teske, The Works of Saint Augustine: A Translation for the 21st Century 1/19 (New City, 2006), 1.21.39.

be *referred* to God, or loved as gifts from God, a fact that alters both our appreciation of creaturely goods and the way we engage them. Put simply, knowing that something is a gift from God imposes new and unexpected constraints on its use, constraints that are usually not intuitive to human beings under the conditions of sin. Augustine thought that *all of creation* was good and a gift from God, a God who is necessarily good and could not make bad things. As a result, Augustine considered evil to be a privation,[25] holding that the primary way human beings sin in their loves for earthly goods is by using them improperly: "Sin consists *not in the things themselves*, but in the unlawful *use* of them. Now the use of things is lawful when the soul remains within the bounds of God's law and subject to the one God in unqualified love and regulates other things that are subject to it without greed or lust."[26] In no uncertain terms, Augustine is affirming that "the earth is the Lord's and all that is in it" (Ps. 24:1), and as a result, creation can be nothing but good. Created things are put to evil use by disordered loves, and that is ultimately the difference between vice and virtue. In other words, the goodness of a particular object *depends on the use to which it is put*, which is a matter of the quality of one's loves and one's ability to receive the earth as a gift from God.[27] There is a wrong way to love anything, and the Christian's pursuit of her true self requires attention to these misuses.[28]

---

25. See Augustine, "Catholic Way of Life," 2.2.2, 2.4.6, along with the discussion in do Vale, *Gender as Love*, 123–29.

26. Augustine, *The Literal Meaning of Genesis*, in *On Genesis*, trans. Edmund Hill, The Works of Saint Augustine: A Translation for the 21st Century 1/13 (New City, 2002), 1.1.13. See further Augustine, *On Free Choice of the Will*, trans. Thomas Williams (Hackett, 1993), 26: "The very same things are used in different ways by different people; some use them badly and others use them well. Someone who uses them badly clings to them and becomes entangled with them. . . . But one who uses these things rightly shows that they are good, although not good for himself. For those things do not make the one who uses them good or better; in fact, they become good by being put to good use." I defend this claim in greater detail in "'Sin Consists Not in the Things Themselves, but in the Unlawful Use of Them': An Approach to the Moral Analysis of Contextual Goods," in *Receiving Redemption: Explorations in Constructive Dogmatics*, ed. Fred Sanders and Uche Anizor (Zondervan Academic, 2026), 108–24.

27. Christopher Bobonich calls this the "Dependency Thesis" and claims that Plato held to such a view. See *Plato's Utopia Recast: His Later Ethics and Politics* (Oxford University Press, 2004), 32. Joseph Clair summarizes Augustine's perspective nicely: "He claims that the virtuous person displays the goodness (*bonus esse*) of these temporal things. . . . Exterior goods are a constituent part of the happy life, for Augustine, insofar as one learns to recognize and cling to the source of these goods through well-ordered desire and appropriate use of them" (*Discerning the Good in the Letters and Sermons of Augustine* [Oxford University Press, 2016], 30, 32–33).

28. In dogmatic terms, this is seen most clearly in how Christians think about idolatry. On Christian doctrine, anything can be an idol through a person's particular attachment to the

This is a crucial insight for the purposes of this book, for, as we have seen, the estrangement of theologies of gender from concrete gendered goods lies in the fact that we cannot give a specifiable list, for all places and all times, of how all women and men dress, what they eat, what jobs they must perform, and so on. To take seriously the need to engage gender in its particularity, we need a way of thinking about ethics that is sufficiently open-textured and pliable to allow both for the variety of contextually specific goods *and* for their moral evaluation. I believe Augustine's theology of human love does this. For any evaluation of a gendered good, we must ask, To what use is it being put, and in what context? For instance, we cannot answer whether it is wrong or right for women to wear men's clothing if we possess only that information. Some instances of this practice are good, such as when women's suffrage advocates began wearing trousers (or "bloomers," named after Amelia Bloom, who was one of the first to do so publicly) to promote the social and political equality they sought. Or again, no one would make a case that it was wrong when female slaves escaped their captivity by dressing as men.[29] Some instances of this practice are not good, such as when it is done in a manner that flaunts wealth or superficiality, or in a way that is insufficiently critical of how clothing is produced. The point is that context is almost always needed to know whether the use to which something is being put is virtuous or vicious.[30] As Paul Griffiths has articulated, "If the earth and all that is in it belongs to the Lord, . . . then its contents cannot, in principle, be divided into clean and unclean things. . . . The task of moral theology is to discriminate [clean uses] from [unclean uses]. That task is prosecuted by descriptive analysis of the

---

idol. William Cavanaugh's work on the subject highlights this helpfully: "The key question underlying the matter of idolatry is not what people believe about the metaphysical status of gods but how people organize their lives and loves around what they worship. Idolatry is primarily a matter not of error but of betrayal. . . . In other words, the idolatry of improper attachment to created things is caused by the person's response to those things, not by the things themselves" (*The Uses of Idolatry* [Oxford University Press, 2024], 123, 169).

29. Several such instances are recorded in William Still, *The Underground Railroad Records: Narrating the Hardships, Hairbreadth Escapes, and Death Struggles of Slaves in Their Efforts for Freedom*, ed. Quincy T. Mills (Modern Library, 2019). Clarissa Davis, for instance, "arrived dressed in male attire" (64–65). I am grateful to Daniel Lee Hill for these references. For discussion, see his *Bearing Witness: What the Church Can Learn from Early Abolitionists* (Baker Academic, 2025).

30. I say "almost always" because some things may be intrinsically good or evil. On Christian doctrine, God is intrinsically good and is the source of all good, so the "Dependency Thesis" would not apply there. More complicated is the question of whether certain creaturely goods are intrinsically evil. I prefer to leave the question open, assuming that most things are not intrinsically evil on the grounds of the doctrine of creation just outlined.

extent to which, and the ways in which, particular patterns of action diminish those who perform them by distancing them from the Lord who has cleaved them to Jesus."[31] There is no Christian uniform, diet, or political party; the rightness or wrongness of our attachment to clothing, food, or politics will depend on the qualities of our loves. So it is with gendered goods. We cannot specify in advance what gendered goods make up Christian masculinity or femininity. But we can specify the way Christians ought to love the goods they find before them as they walk the aisles of the grocery store, peruse the clothing racks at the department store, or scroll through Instagram. Even the most "acceptable" gendered goods can become instruments of sin. Just because someone shops in the section of the clothing store designated for their gender does not mean they are free of sin.

In what I have just argued, I have tried to uphold what Paul mentions in Romans 13:8–10, a text I take to be central to a biblically oriented ethic: "Owe no one anything, except to love one another, for the one who loves another has fulfilled the law. The commandments, 'You shall not commit adultery; you shall not murder; you shall not steal; you shall not covet,' and any other commandment, are summed up in this word, 'You shall love your neighbor as yourself.' Love does no wrong to a neighbor; therefore, love is the fulfilling of the law." According to Paul, the sum of the moral life is captured in the command to neighbor love, and every command to which Christians are accountable is "recapitulated" (*anakephalaioō*, v. 9) in the command to love rightly. That command, however, must be exercised in particular ways in particular places, as the discussion of dietary practices in Romans 14 makes clear, and this can be seen in the various contexts discussed in each of the following chapters. Whether an act of love for a particular good is a covetous love cannot be discerned until the person doing the loving is observed either to be loving their neighbor or not. In this sense, an Augustinian theology of human love provides a pliable and context-sensitive component of the moral vision necessary to analyze gendered goods as they are encountered in the lives of individuals.

Eschatology

Our true selves are eschatological selves, for it is only in the eschaton that our thriving in God will be complete. Only when we are resurrected will we

31. Paul J. Griffiths, *Christian Flesh* (Stanford University Press, 2018), 72, 74.

be like God, seeing God as God is (1 John 3:2). This is when our lives will be truly revealed in Christ (Col. 3:4). By extension, only at the resurrection of the dead will we know gender without the stains of sin.[32] Knowing the ways Christian eschatology and its promise of resurrection shape our expectations for gender now will therefore be crucial to undertaking the normative task.

Already we have seen that the dogmatic location of Christian ethics is in the gap between the world as it is and the world as it should be, a gap in which we find ourselves continually. The descriptive task provides the theologian with clear pictures of the world as it is; eschatology provides the theologian with a vision for the world as it should be. Kelly Brown Douglas articulates the gap well in relation to racial violence: "On the one hand, there is no clearer indication of the breach between the world as it is and the world as God has called it to be than the fact that Black life continues to be 'worth a half-cent.' Yet, on the other hand, there is no clearer indication of the hope that Black life will one day matter than in the resurrection."[33] Eschatology depicts the world as it should be, where injustice is no longer possible and every tear is wiped away (Rev. 7:17; 21:4), something for which God's people strive in hope. As Frederick Ware states, "Eschatology is vision not only of a certain end but also of a people's true humanity. This vision inspires people to moral and ethical action."[34] In other words, appeals to eschatology in Christian theology imply normativity.

There are important theological reasons for my decision to prioritize eschatology and resurrection for the moral analysis of gender, especially in a theological context where appeals to creation are far more frequent.[35] Biblically,

---

32. I have already argued at length that gender will be present in the resurrection; I will not repeat those arguments here. My interest now will be on the moral implications of such an affirmation. For the aforementioned argument, see Fellipe do Vale, "Cappadocian or Augustinian? Adjudicating Debates on Gender in the Resurrection," *International Journal of Systematic Theology* 21, no. 2 (2019): 182–98; do Vale, "Gender Identity: To Infinity and Beyond," *Pro Ecclesia* 32, no. 1 (2023): 24–46; do Vale, *Gender as Love*, chap. 7; do Vale, "Our Gender on Earth as in Heaven," *Christianity Today*, April 2024.

33. Kelly Brown Douglas, *Resurrection Hope: A Future Where Black Lives Matter* (Orbis Books, 2021), 189. The internal citation is a reference to Frederick Douglass's observation of the impunity with which one may kill someone racialized as black. For the quote, see Douglass, *Narrative of the Life of Frederick Douglass, an American Slave: Written by Himself*, ed. John R. McKivigan et al. (Yale University Press, 2016), 28.

34. Frederick L. Ware, *African American Theology: An Introduction* (Westminster John Knox, 2016), 171.

35. For suggestive summaries of eschatological doctrine, see Susannah Ticciati, "Resurrection of the Dead," in *St. Andrews Encyclopaedia of Theology*, ed. Brendan N. Wolfe, April 20, 2023, https://www.saet.ac.uk/Christianity/ResurrectionoftheDead. For examples of theological

the trajectory of the divine economy leads not back to the first state but forward to an eschatological surplus in which the true meaning of creation is fulfilled. In eschatology, we get all that creation was meant to be and then some. According to theologians like Irenaeus and Augustine, creation was *good* (made precisely according to God's intent) but it was not *perfect* (in the sense that it had already fulfilled the telos for which it was made).[36] Because time moves forward to history's conclusion, we are called not to restore the original created state but to approximate the promises of resurrection joy. In this sense, the moral function of eschatology is to create an anticipation for the way things were meant to be. Imagine going to a friend's home for a special dinner. When you arrive, your friend is still preparing the food, but you can smell its aromas from where you wait. Periodically, your friend emerges from the kitchen with a spoon to have you taste the food before it is presented. These tastes build your excitement for what is to come, and the rumbling in your stomach does not feel quite so bad in light of what you know is ahead. Christian eschatology functions something like this.[37]

With Janet Soskice, therefore, I wish to emphasize an "eschatological anthropology," the key features of which are that "we are loved, we will love, and will be made lovely in our Lord Jesus Christ."[38] She summarizes my claims in this section nicely: "Anthropology in the Bible is never wholly separate from eschatology, nor creation from redemption, because 'what we will be' is not separable from what we were made to be and what we now are."[39] Soskice's emphasis on love helpfully unites the claims of the previous section regarding love with those made here. Love and eschatology belong together, for out of

---

work that unevenly appeal to doctrines of creation, see Glen G. Scorgie, *The Journey Back to Eden: Restoring the Creator's Design for Women and Men* (Zondervan, 2005); Dennis P. Hollinger, *Creation and Christian Ethics: Understanding God's Designs for Humanity and the World* (Baker Academic, 2023).

36. See do Vale, "Gender Identity"; do Vale, *Gender as Love*, chap. 7.

37. Some important feminist theologians have criticized attempts to emphasize eschatology. Their main worries surround the ways in which eschatology can be used to legitimize oppression and the portrait of divine power that it assumes. For a helpful summary, see Emily Pennington, *Feminist Eschatology: Embodied Futures* (Routledge, 2017), chap. 2. For a feminist response to such worries, see Valerie A. Karras, "Eschatology," in *The Cambridge Companion to Feminist Theology*, ed. Susan Frank Parsons (Cambridge University Press, 2002). Because my emphasis on eschatology is designed precisely to provide moral impetus for action, I do not think these objections apply here.

38. Janet Martin Soskice, *The Kindness of God: Metaphor, Gender, and Religious Language* (Oxford University Press, 2007), 181.

39. Soskice, *Kindness of God*, 181.

the theological virtues, love alone endures without end. Faith, while crucially necessary for our earthly pilgrimage, helps us because we do not *now* see Jesus (1 Pet. 1:8), though we will see him one day, at which point faith will no longer be necessary (2 Cor. 5:6–7). This contrast to sight is also applicable to hope, for we can only hope in what we do not see (Rom. 8:24; Heb. 11:1). The Christian promise that we will see and enjoy full union with God renders the eschatological presence of faith and hope unnecessary, even as it increases the perennial need for love. Because "love never ends," it enables us to enjoy the thriving that we were promised without end (1 Cor. 13:8).[40] Augustine offers an important summary of this insight: "When we ask whether somebody is a good person, we are not asking what he believes or hopes for but what he loves. For one who rightly loves without doubt rightly believes and hopes, and one who does not love believes in vain, even if the things he believes are true; he hopes in vain, even if the things for which he hopes are those which, according to our teaching, belong to true happiness, unless he also believes and hopes that if he asks he may also be given the ability to love."[41] If love is the means by which we engage our social worlds and form our gender identities, then we should expect our love to be eschatologically grounded.

"Our world," writes Katherine Sonderegger, "must strike us as *incomplete*. We can state it as simply as that. For the Christian, the earth we dearly prize and fear must tell out in unmistakable tone its fragmentary and unfinished nature. A proper doctrine of creation must set out a world that implies—no, insists upon—a completion elsewhere; everything must say and show: we are incomplete."[42] The exclusive focus on creation in contemporary theologies

---

40. John Thiel articulates the governing relationship of love to faith and hope helpfully: "God not only loves but is love itself, which makes love the most deeply theological of the theological virtues. Love is the very essence of God's own divine life. It is both what God is and who God is. By comparison, faith and hope are thoroughly creaturely dispositions. They are not possessed by God, nor do they flourish as the divine being itself. . . . Love is the graceful energy of faith and hope" (*Now and Forever: A Theological Aesthetics of Time* [University of Notre Dame Press, 2023], 29).

41. Augustine, *Enchiridion*, in *The Augustine Catechism: The Enchiridion on Faith, Hope and Charity*, ed. Boniface Ramsey, trans. Bruce Harbert (New City, 1999), 31.117.

42. Katherine Sonderegger, "Towards a Doctrine of the Resurrection," in *Eternal God, Eternal Life: Theological Investigations into the Concept of Immortality*, ed. Philip G. Ziegler (T&T Clark, 2016), 119. Sonderegger continues: "The doctrine of Last Things cannot do real work in the Christian life, its gears cannot engage, so long as the very colour of Heaven is not made vivid before our eyes. We must peer into Divine Things and long for them; we must greet the Promise, even from afar, and yearn to enter into It. The doctrine of Resurrection and Eternal Life must set forth a reality we deeply desire; we must know its shape—even if beyond our comprehension—in order to hope for it" (119).

of gender is puzzling for the very reasons Sonderegger has just articulated; creation is good, but its goodness lies precisely in the fact that it points forward to its eschatological completion. We must remember that "the doctrine of creation is not the whole of Christian teaching, nor can it exhaust the Ways and Works of God *ad extra*."[43] I intend, therefore, to operate with a sufficiently vivid eschatology that grounds our practices now. The love with which we love the world now is the same love that will endure in the new heaven and new earth. Therefore, the cultivation of love now is precisely the means by which we can, in Wendell Berry's words, "practice resurrection."[44]

Love and eschatology, therefore, will serve as two crucial pillars for the normative task. To know whether our organizations of gendered goods reflect our true selves, we must examine the quality of our loving attachments to those goods and measure them up against the world as it will be, as it is eschatologically disclosed. These two concepts will have recurrent roles to play throughout the book, but it suffices to observe now that the vast variety of gendered goods across times and places should not cause the theologian to refrain from normative evaluations. We must also note, finally, how these two elements combine. I believe the normative impulses of love and eschatology place the emphasis of our moral evaluations of gendered goods on *compassion*.[45] As I will attempt to highlight and demonstrate in the chapters that follow, if love is the fulfillment of the law, and if our selves are incomplete until we are resurrected, then our normative lead must be characterized by a compassionate response to our attempts to organize gendered goods. We know that "every high priest chosen from among mortals"—that is, from among the frail who experience the effects of death—"is able to deal gently with the ignorant and wayward, since he himself is subject to weakness" (Heb. 5:1–2). This must also be the case for Christians learning to love as they practice resurrection. Because we are still struggling with sin, ignorance, and death, the primary moral response to others should be *gentleness*, demonstrated primarily in compassion. I will look to clarify that claim in relation to a variety of gendered goods, and tie up the loose ends in the conclusion, but

43. Sonderegger, "Towards a Doctrine of the Resurrection," 121.

44. Wendell Berry, "Manifesto: The Mad Farmer Liberation Front," in *The Peace of Wild Things* (Penguin, 2018), 55.

45. For a defense of this view, see Jesse Couenhoven, "The Justice in Mercy: A Hopeful Pessimist's Account," *Journal of Religious Ethics* 48, no. 3 (2020): 399–417. Throughout this book, *mercy* and *compassion* can be understood interchangeably, as both come from the Latin term *misericordia*.

the idea is that the normative impulse for gender must begin from a compassion that recognizes the incompleteness of love as well as the fact that love is patient and kind.

At our disposal, then, is a sufficiently flexible and contextually sensitive set of moral parameters ensuring that the "true" of "true self" retains its moral content. With it we can approach our two tasks, a task of description and a task of normativity. We must first say what gender is before we can say something about what gender ought to be. Contemporary theology's inability to perform these two tasks concurrently is precisely what has made it so otherworldly and impracticable. Before going on to engage the gendered goods of our world, therefore, it will be instructive to examine two case studies—one from so-called conservative theology and one from so-called liberal theology—for their failures to be descriptive *and* normative. (I insist that the terms *conservative* and *liberal* are rather useless in theological work. All the same, they proliferate within conversations about gender, so I use them for expediency. We must remember, however, that "theology is not a matter of being liberal or conservative but a matter of truth.")[46] Examining these case studies will helpfully distinguish my proposal from both of these approaches and illustrate just what I think is necessary for doing a theology of gender well.

The Absence of the Two Tasks in Contemporary Theology

For a theology of gender to succeed—for it to capture adequately the true self, which so many individuals hope to find illuminating for gender identities—it must be both descriptive *and* normative. Methodologically, the theologian will therefore listen well to what is going on, which will often require attending to the data that sociology, history, anthropology, cultural history, fiction, material culture, and the like are bringing to our attention in addition to the recognizable virtues of systematic and moral theology. A frequent temptation in theologies of gender, however, is to perform the normative task without taking into account any descriptive material. Normative projects, when undergone in this way, fail to operate in the world as it is, opting instead to see only the world as it should be. They therefore become unworkable for ordinary people seeking to live faithfully.

46. Stanley Hauerwas, *The Peaceable Kingdom: A Primer in Christian Ethics* (University of Notre Dame Press, 1991), xviii.

In "conservative" theology, conversations about gender have tended to orbit around debates between "complementarians" and "egalitarians." Roughly, complementarians hold that to be a man is to bear the roles of leading, providing for, and protecting women, roles expressed in a variety of ways in churches and homes.[47] To be a woman, then, is to bear the roles of affirming, receiving, and nurturing the leadership of men in homes and churches.[48] There is some diversity among complementarians about how to parse the precise application of such terms, but these definitions go on to shape how life is understood within families and in churches, and they are largely based on texts like Ephesians 5:21–33, 1 Timothy 2:12, and 1 Corinthians 14:34–35.[49] This latter claim is precisely what is denied by egalitarians, who claim that what obtains between men and women is an unqualified relationship of equality, with no barrier placed before women on ministerial roles.[50]

Recently, however, sociological work has shown that whether one is an egalitarian or complementarian does little to guide one's actual gendered practice. One's belief about gender roles, observes Brad Wilcox, is not the most important indicator of the well-being of one's marriage, as even some complementarians have agreed.[51] If that is the case, then whether a family is egalitarian or complementarian is not the most sociologically important sign of its health. Additionally, since the beginning of these debates in the 1980s, rates of women clergy have generally remained roughly the same (10.6

---

47. John Piper, "A Vision of Biblical Complementarity: Manhood and Womanhood Defined According to the Bible," in *Recovering Biblical Manhood and Womanhood: A Response to Evangelical Feminism*, rev. ed., ed. John Piper and Wayne Grudem (Crossway, 2021), 41: "At the heart of mature masculinity is a sense of benevolent responsibility to lead, provide for and protect women in ways appropriate to a man's differing relationships."

48. Piper, "Vision of Biblical Complementarity," 41: "At the heart of mature femininity is a freeing disposition to affirm, receive and nurture strength and leadership from worthy men in ways appropriate to a woman's differing relationships."

49. For the most sophisticated explanation and defense of this family of views, see Gregg R. Allison, *Complementarity: Dignity, Difference, and Interdependence* (B&H Academic, 2025).

50. See Ronald W. Pierce et al., eds., *Discovering Biblical Equality: Biblical, Theological, Cultural, and Practical Perspectives*, 3rd ed. (IVP Academic, 2021). Some have also tried to blend complementarian and egalitarian perspectives as applicable in different domains. See Gordon P. Hugenberger, "Complementarian at Home, Egalitarian at Church? Paul Would Approve," *Christianity Today*, March 18, 2024, https://www.christianitytoday.com/2024/03/complementarian-home-egalitarian-church-paul-hugenberger/.

51. See Brad Wilcox, "Evangelicals and Domestic Violence: Are Christian Men More Abusive?," *Christianity Today*, December 11, 2017, https://www.christianitytoday.com/ct/2017/december-web-only/evangelicals-domestic-violence-christian-men-domestic-abuse.html; Nancy R. Pearcey, *The Toxic War on Masculinity: How Christianity Reconciles the Sexes* (Baker Books, 2023), 38–39.

percent of churches were led by women in the United States in 1998, while 13.5 percent were led by women in 2018), leading some to conclude that an institution's position about women in ministry, especially if that institution is evangelical, does little to alter, let alone increase, the number of women who actually lead churches.[52] Most recently, Lisa Weaver Swartz's sociological study of two seminary campuses—one explicitly complementarian, one explicitly egalitarian—reveals how such convictions did very little to shape the concrete gendered practices of the communities, practices still acutely felt by the student body. After summarizing her fieldwork, Swartz concludes that the egalitarian institution "struggled to consistently practice egalitarianism in real life," while the on-the-surface theological consistency of the complementarian institution "belies the complexities of social life."[53] The complementarian school, for instance, entreated men to carry guns to church, associated masculinity with eating meat, sold knives for men on campus, and cared so much about the personal grooming and adornment of a pastor that for a time it housed a store on campus that sold suits, ties, personal accessories, leather satchels, and bottles of craft beard oil.[54] My point here is not to evaluate the associations of these gendered goods with masculinity; it is simply to observe that the connection between a particular reading of Ephesians 5 and the promotion of men with thick, full beards is at best opaque. In fact, what is likely occurring is that a *stated* theology of gender is misaligned with a *practiced* theology of gender. Or, in terms of the argument of this chapter, the theology of gender is impracticable.

The egalitarian institution did not fare any better. The term Swartz (and some students) uses to describe the culture of this seminary is "genderblind," deliberately invoking "colorblind" language in parallel discussions of race.[55] The idea here is that gender is "an individual reality isolated from structural forces that affect people as collectives. It supposes that [at institutions] where

---

52. For the numbers, see Ryan P. Burge, "America Elected a Female Vice President: Now Will It Put Women in the Pulpit?," Religion News Service, December 9, 2020, https://religionnews.com/2020/12/09/congrats-america-you-elected-a-female-vice-president-now-put-a-woman-in-your-pulpit/. For the conclusion that one's position does not alter practice, see Mark Chaves, *Ordaining Women: Culture and Conflict in Religious Organizations* (Harvard University Press, 1997).

53. Lisa Weaver Swartz, *Stained Glass Ceilings: How Evangelicals Do Gender and Practice Power* (Rutgers University Press, 2023), 15, 73.

54. Swartz, *Stained Glass Ceilings*, 53, 62, 64, 61 (respectively).

55. For Swartz's diagnosis, see Swartz, *Stained Glass Ceilings*, 86. One student is quoted as saying, "Why can't we just be colorblind? Why can't we be genderblind? . . . I wish everything was done blind" (139).

official policies do not limit individual women from assuming positions of authority and influence, gendered barriers do not exist."[56] The trouble, of course, is obvious: *Stating* that gender barriers do not exist is not the same as gender barriers *not existing*. The barriers were not encoded in the stated theology, but it turns out that they were still present in the practice of community, and this goes a long way to explain why the number of women pastors has not increased despite the best intentions of egalitarians. There is, effectively, a gap left by the rejection of complementarianism, and it is filled either with vague affirmations of the importance of the difference-in-equality between women and men or with a reversion to old patterns of gendered practice that were ostensibly rejected. Thus Swartz: "While many . . . students have rejected their hierarchical teachings, they seem to have little to replace them with save the lingering sense that difference, somehow, *matters*. . . . Many seemed satisfied with the vague but firm affirmation that difference is, somehow, vitally important. . . . Even students who adhere to genderblind convictions in theory sometimes revert to deeply gendered assumptions when it comes to the practical realities of social life. . . . While allowing for the presence of difference, it nonetheless serves to diminish more than accentuate gender's salience."[57] Egalitarianism, it seems, remains defined far more by what it rejects than by what it affirms, and it leaves those looking for theological guidance uncertain how to pursue their desire to live as women and men before God. This was especially detrimental to the women on campus: They were left to themselves to decide whether to wear lipstick while preaching, whether they should have kids, or how to relate to one another in ways that promoted women's well-being in ministry and beyond.

It is my opinion, therefore, that both complementarianism and egalitarianism are impracticable theologies of gender. This is largely because they engage in the normative task without engaging in the task of description. Both rush quickly to the question of whether or not there should be a relationship of authority and submission between women and men without pausing to consider the people who will actually practice their recommended theological positions. They do not speak to men and women as they pick out their clothes, decide whether they should apply for a concealed carry permit, or debate between

56. Swartz, *Stained Glass Ceilings*, 104.
57. Swartz, *Stained Glass Ceilings*, 106–7, 90–91.

a meaty sandwich or a salad for lunch *because they do not include theologies of clothing, politics, food, and so on*. But these are precisely the gendered goods we must discern as we describe and engage our worlds. As a result, if complementarianism and egalitarianism are actually concerned with gender, they remain at such a distance from the lives of Christians that they result in baptizing whatever cultural norms are preferred by their congregations, institutional leadership, and the like.

Some of these "conservative" authors have doubled down, however, and have appealed to natural law theory to ground a view that gender should not be about these social goods after all; in fact, "gender" is a meaningless term that only serves to obscure the potential that males and females possess to reproduce. This is often defended by "gender critical" thinkers, and it has garnered large appeal among Catholics and evangelicals.[58] The most notable of these recent proposals comes from Abigail Favale's book *The Genesis of Gender*.[59] Favale's central contention in this book is that "the concept of gender has driven a wedge between *body* and *identity*," with the result that gender has become "an empty signifier, a word that is only a shell, conveniently waiting to be filled with whatever meaning is most useful."[60] That gender theologies are impossible to carry out is not a problem for Favale, for it is precisely the concept of gender that is problematic. It is not surprising, in other words, that a concept "at odds with reality" should fail to guide lived practice.[61]

On Favale's view, we are faced with two necessarily incompatible paradigms, the "gender paradigm" and the "Christian paradigm"; affirming one

58. For gender-critical feminism, see Holly Lawford-Smith, *Gender-Critical Feminism* (Oxford University Press, 2022), chap. 3. For some recent evangelical proposals to ground a gender-critical view in natural law, see Patrick Schreiner, "Man and Woman: Toward an Ontology," *Eikon* 2, no. 2 (2020): 68–87; Steven Wedgeworth, "Good and Proper: Paul's Use of Nature, Custom, and Decorum in Pastoral Theology," *Eikon* 2, no. 2 (2020): 88–97.

59. Besides Favale, another Roman Catholic thinker who has defended a similar proposal is J. Budziszewski, *On the Meaning of Sex* (ISI Books, 2014).

60. Abigail Favale, *The Genesis of Gender: A Christian Theory* (Ignatius, 2022), 149, 153. There is an irony here with regard to Favale's gender-critical stance—namely, the degree to which she agrees with one of the chief antagonists of her book, Judith Butler. Like Favale, Butler maintains that gender is a problematic concept and wishes to see it undone. Butler desires to see "the subject of 'women' . . . nowhere presumed" (Judith Butler, *Gender Trouble* [Routledge, 1990], 8). Ostensibly, Butler inhabits the gender paradigm while Favale inhabits the Christian paradigm, and these two paradigms are necessarily incompatible. One would think it, therefore, impossible for them to argue for the same view, but this is precisely what they do.

61. Favale, *Genesis of Gender*, 101.

requires denying the other.[62] The "gender paradigm," from which the concept of gender was initially introduced,

> affirms a radically constructivist view of reality, then reifies it as truth, demanding that others assent to its veracity and adopt its language. According to the gender paradigm, there is no creator, and so we are free to create ourselves. The body is an object with no intrinsic meaning; we give it whatever meaning we want, using technology to undo what is perceived to be "natural." We do not *receive* meaning from God or our bodies or the world—we impose it. What we take to be "real" is merely a linguistic construct; ergo we should consciously wield language to conjure the reality we want. To be free is to transgress limits continually, to unfetter the will. "Woman" and "man" are language-based identities that can be inhabited by anyone. Because truth is just a story we tell ourselves, all self-stories are true.[63]

For Favale, the gender paradigm is godless, assumes a radically constructionist metaphysics, and cannot escape "the denigration of the body."[64] Christians "operate from different foundational assumptions about reality, and most versions of Christian feminism have their roots in the feminist worldview rather than the Christian one. So-called 'Christian feminism' is, too often, secular feminism with a light Jesus glaze on top, a cherry-picked biblical garnish."[65] To the degree that one insists upon terms like *gender* having content and utility, therefore, one is beholden to the gender paradigm at least to some degree.

We are faced with two mutually exclusive paradigms; if we are to maintain our Christian commitment, we must reject the "gender paradigm" and its way of thinking. We must turn instead to the "Christian paradigm." It begins with an affirmation of creation and the order it provides, an order that discloses "the sacramental function" of the body.[66] This means that the body discloses

---

62. See Favale, *Genesis of Gender*, 29: "Embracing Christian orthodoxy means rejecting certain feminist dogmas. Accepting those dogmas entails betraying some Christian beliefs." I make the interpretive assumption here that the feminist dogmas she has in mind are those contained in the gender paradigm. What aspects of Christian orthodoxy she has in mind is mysterious to me if orthodoxy is assumed to be equivalent to the creedal affirmations of the catholic church in places such as the Nicene Creed and Chalcedonian definition.

63. Favale, *Genesis of Gender*, 30–31.

64. See Favale, *Genesis of Gender*, 82–83.

65. Favale, *Genesis of Gender*, 55. Favale does not provide any examples of Christian feminists to substantiate this assertion.

66. Favale, *Genesis of Gender*, 40. Here Favale is drawing from John Paul II, *Man and Woman He Created Them: A Theology of the Body*, trans. Michael Waldstein (Pauline Books, 2006).

a further meaning about the person, just like the bread of the Eucharist (in Roman Catholic doctrine) discloses a further meaning about itself. That further meaning about the body lies in the potential such a body possesses for gestating new life. So, for Favale, "a woman is the kind of human being whose body is organized around the potential to gestate new life," whereas a man "has the [potential] capacity to transmit life outside of himself."[67] Or again: "'Man' and 'woman' refer to our generative potentiality."[68] Favale is clear that this potentiality is not the mere *fact* of reproductive capacity but also includes the associations related to these capacities. Thus, for women, the potential to gestate new life also signals "creation, nourishment, and primal compassion," bringing about a unique signaling of "feminine self-gift, the capacity and call to nourish the souls and bodies—the full personhood—of those who come under our care."[69] Favale, then, summons Christians to abandon the gender paradigm and its constructionist metaphysics in favor of a sacramental vision of the body according to which women and men are defined by gestational potential and the character associations related to those potentials.

There is much that could be said about Favale's proposal. Its forthright theological commitment is admirable in an academic and ecclesial context where such things are often kept separate from gender. Nevertheless, there are some serious faults that I believe make it just as unworkable and detached as other theologies of gender that have preceded it. There are some issues with its argumentation; it relies on heavy-handed caricatures of views in order to support its broad-brush generalizations of the paradigms,[70] and we can question whether analyzing these movements in terms of paradigms is the right procedure when there are so many clear counterexamples. For instance, where should one classify the large number of feminist theorists, many remarkably well-known, who deny a constructionist understanding of the world?[71]

67. Favale, *Genesis of Gender*, 120–21, 237.

68. Favale, *Genesis of Gender*, 144.

69. Favale, *Genesis of Gender*, 174–75.

70. For instance, Brown biologist Anne Fausto-Sterling is referred to as "the fairy godmother of the intersex gambit," while Favale speculates that pioneering feminist theorist Simone de Beauvoir simply "hates being female" (Favale, *Genesis of Gender*, 126, 64). Judith Butler's views are introduced by pointing out that she won an award for bad writing (71). So far as I can tell, none of these designators are relevant to their arguments, and pointing them out is plainly incompatible with the Christian commitment to the love of enemy, which requires presenting an opposing view in its most charitable framing.

71. See Sally Haslanger, *Resisting Reality: Social Construction and Social Critique* (Oxford University Press, 2012); Martha C. Nussbaum, "Human Functioning and Social Justice: In Defense of Aristotelian Essentialism," *Political Theory* 20, no. 2 (1992): 202–46; Martha C.

There are even feminist critiques of the social construction of gender itself; apart from disparaging comments that these theorists are speaking from both sides of their mouths, Favale's categorizations are silent about these figures.[72] Some further issues are intrinsic to her constructive proposal; she is clear that she is looking to reject gender in order to emphasize biological sex, but biological sex is not the same thing as reproductive or gestational potential. Biological sex would also include nonreproductive elements of our bodies, like the amount of body and facial hair one possesses, vocal patterns, the allocation of body fat, whether one possesses an Adam's apple, and so on. Favale refers to biological sex as though it were *only* reproductive potential, but such a move confuses which bodily aspects are actually involved in each sex. (One might ask, for instance, whether there is a sacramental meaning to one's Adam's apple.) Additionally, Christian doctrine has traditionally cast significant doubt on the naturalness of reproductive potential. For something to be natural, it must define (in the sense of being a necessary condition for) all instances of the natural kind. Being brown is not part of a dog's nature, for instance, because being brown is not necessary for being a dog; some dogs are yellow. But is potential reproductive capacity of a certain sort a necessary condition for being a man or a woman? On traditional Christian doctrine, we will still be men and women at the resurrection, but we will not have the potential to reproduce or be given in marriage.[73] It is possible, therefore, to be a woman or a man and *lack* the reproductive potential Favale favors, just as it is possible to be a dog and not be brown.[74] This is not the same as saying that some people cannot reproduce or are barren (that some lack a capacity

Nussbaum, *Women and Human Development: The Capabilities Approach* (Cambridge University Press, 2001). Nussbaum is particularly salient here, for she adopts Favale's own Aristotelean metaphysics to defend feminist conclusions.

72. For a close examination of two such theorists, Charlotte Witt and Mari Mikkola, see do Vale, *Gender as Love*, chap. 2.

73. There are exceptions to this consensus teaching in the thought of figures like Gregory of Nyssa and Maximus the Confessor. Given her commitment to Roman Catholic doctrine, I am assuming that Favale would be inclined to follow the trajectory established by Augustine that maintains that we will be resurrected as men and women.

74. This is a point perceptively made by Brian Brock in *Disability: Living into the Diversity of Christ's Body* (Baker Academic, 2021), 132: "In Mark 12:19–25 Jesus suggests that people will be resurrected male and female but 'like the angels'—that is, not engaging in reproduction. To be a man or a woman in the resurrection will mean having parts that will not function reproductively. So in Jesus's anthropology, it seems that every body part does not have to have a function in order to be beautiful and good." If something lacks a function, it does not potentially perform that function.

that would in ordinary circumstances be there). It is rather to say that there are some women and men who lack the potential to reproduce, but we would not describe them as *lacking* something that ordinarily would be there (i.e., the potential for reproduction is not something that picks out all women and all men). Reproductive potential, therefore, cannot serve as the definition of manhood and womanhood because—according to the main lines of development within Christian doctrine—when we are raised as women and men, we will not have the potential to gestate new life.

These issues aside, Favale's proposal remains impracticable. If all I know about my manhood is that it amounts to a generative potentiality of a certain sort, I do not know how to buy clothes on the internet, whether to buy the "men's soup" at the grocery store, or how to discern concrete practices about parenting (such as how long leave should be after the birth of a child). Favale operates strictly at the normative level—it is wrong to see reality as constructed; we must see our bodies sacramentally—and dismisses any descriptive accountability by placing all considerations of gender into a single paradigm that, she then argues, needs to be abandoned. But gender does not go away so easily. I might reject the gender paradigm, but I will still inhabit a world that thrusts its gendered goods upon me. I will still live in a world of Disney Princesses, of women having to work a "second shift" when they get home, and of men who are told that their mental-health issues are weaknesses. Dismissing the gender paradigm does not make these realities disappear, and we leave Christians rudderless to navigate the detrimental effects of sinful structures when we ignore the world as it is in the mistaken assumption that we can deal simply with the world as it should be. Surprisingly, expecting gender to disappear because we have rejected a paradigm commits one to the same constructionist metaphysics adopted by theorists like Judith Butler.

But perhaps Favale is not doing this. In several places, she also seems to celebrate the diversity and vulnerability of sexed bodies, summoning us to appreciate the rich variety in which masculinity and femininity can express themselves. So she calls us to "witness firsthand the diversity of the female form" and admits to the ways Christians and others have rigidly defined women and men according to "cartoonish understandings of femininity and masculinity" that are "regressive."[75] Here she has in mind disapproval of boys who like pink and other such superficialities. In this tone, Favale's argument is

75. Favale, *Genesis of Gender*, 163, 158.

much more suggestive. Yet one is left wondering how her prior commitments to a gender-critical stance restricted to procreative potential furnish Christians with theological tools to challenge such shallow gender associations. Favale's normative tools cannot be applied to patterns of gendered dress unless some story is told about how our adornment practices facilitate our procreative potential. I suspect that, once again, we are left with a theological gap waiting to be filled by whatever cultural practices are already persuasive to the community in question, practices that have no obvious theological warrant.

"Conservative" theology is not alone in its neglect of the two tasks required of theologies of gender. Adrian Thatcher[76] has recently defended a proposal for a "liberal" theology of gender that is liable to the same critiques. In his *Gender and Christian Ethics*, Thatcher makes a sustained argument that understanding gender as a binary established between men and women is a mistake that theologians should avoid. Sharing surprising similarities with Favale, Thatcher maintains that terms like "'man' and 'woman,' at least without some open qualification, are no longer serviceable (at least for a Christian theology of gender)."[77] Unlike Favale, however, Thatcher suggests that familiar gender terms be replaced by a continuum in which gender differences are "a matter, not of kind, but of degree."[78] In other words, Thatcher wants to offer theological resources for maintaining that gender is a spectrum, not a binary.

Thatcher's reasons for rejecting a binary approach to gender are profoundly theological. He asserts, "I found my understanding of equality in the Trinity, and for a theologian there is no better or higher or more authoritative place to look."[79] Thatcher's argument hangs on a correspondence that, he argues, obtains between the divine essence and human essences. Because "God has a single essence," it follows that humans "are one kind—humankind—not two or more kinds, male and female."[80] Since this correspondence is so strong, moreover, the only essence that should characterize our understandings of

76. Thatcher introduces his work as self-avowedly "liberal." See Adrian Thatcher, *Gender and Christian Ethics* (Cambridge University Press, 2021), xii, where he understands himself to have a "commitment to progressive theology more generally."

77. Thatcher, *Gender and Christian Ethics*, 195. For more detail on Thatcher's argument, see Fellipe do Vale, review of *Gender and Christian Ethics*, by Adrian Thatcher, *Anglican Theological Review* 105, no. 1 (2023): 108–9.

78. Thatcher, *Gender and Christian Ethics*, 11.

79. Thatcher, *Gender and Christian Ethics*, 197.

80. Thatcher, *Gender and Christian Ethics*, 46.

human beings is a human essence, and every other aspect of human identity should be seen as existing on a spectrum.[81]

Thatcher's central contention is that "human difference is best understood as mirroring *divine* difference. . . . Just as theology can illuminate human difference by modelling it on divine difference, so theology can illuminate human nature by modelling it on the nature of God."[82] Thus, just as there is *one* divine essence, we must affirm that there is only *one* human essence. But there is also diversity in the Trinity, and the "similarity of concepts" that obtains between divine threeness and gender theory allows for gender identities to be appreciated as a spectrum.[83] Such a similarity is applicable to trans identities, gay identities, bisexual identities, and all other forms of gender expression that display the porousness of categories once taken to be rigidly binary.

Remaining committed to theological resources throughout, Thatcher makes a case for understanding gender as a spectrum that results in God's image being honored and Jesus Christ being exalted. Despite these strengths, it leaves us in the same place of impracticality as before. Thatcher's detection of a similarity of concepts between God and humanity moves far too quickly. In the presence of Karen Kilby's strong objections to trinitarian projection and Kathryn Tanner's incisive resistance to the use of the Trinity in political questions,[84] application of trinitarian concepts requires much more argument than Thatcher provides. We shall have occasion to return to this argument in a later chapter, but today's theological landscape requires more argument when making trinitarian applications to social issues. One might also wonder about the operative theory of religious language Thatcher employs to detect the similarity of concepts between God and gender. Even proponents of univocity emphasize that sameness of terms does not entail sameness of concepts.[85] Most important for our purposes, however, is the fact that Thatcher provides a normative proposal with no descriptive analysis. Even if we were to accept

81. See Thatcher, *Gender and Christian Ethics*, 105.

82. Thatcher, *Gender and Christian Ethics*, 101, 104.

83. Thatcher, *Gender and Christian Ethics*, 139.

84. See "Perichoresis and Projection: Problems with Social Doctrines of the Trinity," in Karen Kilby, *God, Evil and the Limits of Theology* (T&T Clark, 2021), 5–16. See Kathryn Tanner, *Christ the Key*, Current Issues in Theology (Cambridge University Press, 2010), 216: "Trinitarianism can be every bit as socially and politically dangerous as monotheism. Everything depends on how that trinitarianism (or monotheism) is understood and applied."

85. See Thomas Williams, "The Doctrine of Univocity Is True and Salutary," *Modern Theology* 21, no. 4 (2005): 575–85.

his claim that gender is a spectrum, such knowledge provides remarkably little in terms of concrete practice. Certainly, *some* gendered goods are best appreciated in terms of a spectrum, like clothing preferences. Others, however, are best seen as a binary: Biological females have certain reproductive rights that biological males do not.[86] Still others are neither a spectrum nor a binary; in some cases, our best moral response is to say that this or that particular aspect of our world *should not be gendered*. Such was the case with debates regarding women's suffrage in the United States: There was a gendered good in the world prior to 1920 that *should not have been gendered*. Applying a spectrum there would not have helped.

Once again, we are left at a place of impracticality because we are given normative arguments lacking descriptive bases. Often, appeals to spectrums are made because of rigid stereotypes regarding clothing, food, politics, and the like that poorly describe the lives of gender minorities. But there is no one-size-fits-all approach to these domains, so that goods such as clothing, food, and politics might enrich the lives of God's people rather than dominate them. Claims regarding these domains, and their gendered implications, must be analyzed on their own merits, and a simple trinitarian application is not enough for this task.

The Road Ahead

What in the world is gender? Whatever it is, gender must be something *in the world*. That is, it must be practicable by ordinary people living their lives. Contemporary theologies of gender, whether "conservative" or "liberal," have failed to deliver on this. They do not offer guidance to human beings navigating the ordinary gendered goods that populate their days. This is because they have largely operated at the register of the normative task *to the exclusion of the descriptive task*. If description is performed at all, it is either a vague appeal to a narrative of decline or a strategy to avoid normative claims. Yet Christian ethics does not allow us this division. If we live only in the mode of description, seeing only the world as it is, the only option available to us is despair. Taken on its face, the world is a remarkably difficult place to be. Description alone offers nothing but this "present evil age," in Pauline terms

86. Even prima facie "progressive" views affirm this. See Rebecca Todd Peters, *Trust Women: A Progressive Christian Argument for Reproductive Justice* (Beacon, 2019).

(Gal. 1:4), or life "under the sun," in the terms of the Teacher of Ecclesiastes (1:3). Alternatively, if we live only in the mode of normativity, we offer God's people theologies of gender that are deeply impracticable, that lack any guidance about the gendered activities performed on a Tuesday evening. At worst, we fall into a different kind of despair as we witness to norms that are beyond the reach of frail sinners.

If gender is all about the organization of social goods by means of our loves to form an identity, then we must first understand what those goods are before we can say what gender should be. So we must listen, describe, and remain alert to the dynamics of the world as we make our way through it on our pilgrimage back to our home with God. Once we have listened well, we can ask, "But is this how things ought to be?" I have suggested that love and eschatology give us sufficiently flexible tools for answering this question, no matter where we find ourselves. While it is impossible to say, for all times and all places, what Christian men and women should wear, eat, and do, it is possible to think through the goods we find before us and test whether our attachments to them are rightly calibrated to the love of God. Gender, in other words, might be more about *how* we relate to the goods in our world than about *what* goods should be locked into our definitions of manhood or womanhood for all time. The goodness of creation and its subsequent devastation require no less.

This book will be an attempt to keep these tasks in balance. Each chapter will be devoted to a particularly salient gendered good encountered by individuals today. We will address politics, bodies, the market, clothing, food, and friendships in their association with dating. Each of these will draw on love and eschatological normativity, but they will do so while remaining accountable to the actual conditions in which God's people find themselves, keeping an eye on compassion. While the divisions between the two tasks will not be formulaic, they will form the spine that supports each sounding in the domains in which gender is found. The goal will be to articulate a *living* theology of gender, one attentive to the dynamics of the world as it is, in its tension-filled distance from the world as it should be. In the end, that is the only world in which gendered individuals can live, so it must be the world theologians deal with.

1

Who Is My Neighbor?

Gender and Politics

> Even now, late as it is, nobody can really believe that it didn't work after all. The U.S.A. didn't work! Is it even possible that from the beginning it never did work? That the thing always had a flaw in it, a place where it would shear. . . . And yet—here's the wonder of love—even as I bend shivering over the glittering mound of grits, love revives! Love is always possible, even here in the ashes of my forty-five-year-old life.
>
> —Walker Percy, *Love in the Ruins*[1]

The novel *Fight Club*, by Chuck Palahniuk, was released in 1996, and it shortly thereafter became the basis for the recognizable 1999 film of the same title. "Recognizable," however, does not adequately describe the impact of *Fight Club*, especially among men. *Fight Club*, for a great many men, has become something of a metanarrative that explains what has gone wrong in their lives and what it would take to change those lives.[2]

---

1. Walker Percy, *Love in the Ruins: The Adventures of a Bad Catholic at a Time Near the End of the World* (Farrar, Straus & Giroux, 1971), 56–57, 176.

2. Sociologists and cultural theorists have been surprised by the influence *Fight Club* has generated among men. Thus, sociologist Michael Kimmel has noted, "I was . . . constantly struck by how strongly so many young men identified with Tyler Durden, the antihero and doppelganger of the unnamed narrator and protagonist in *Fight Club*. . . . The movie quickly became a cult classic among young men, who saw in it a touchstone text of Gen Y gendered ennui" (*Angry White Men: American Masculinity at the End of an Era* [Bold Type Books, 2017],

Fight Club is the story of an unnamed narrator who is deeply discontented with his life on account of its monotony and complacency, captured by the IKEA furniture that he meticulously collects but also cares nothing about. The narrator describes it thus: "I was tired and crazy and rushed, and every time I boarded a plane, I wanted the plane to crash. I envied people dying of cancer. I hated my life. I was tired and bored with my job and my furniture, and I couldn't see a way to change things."[3] As he begins to suffer from insomnia, he looks for ways to cope. He tries attending various support groups for illnesses that he does not have, and for a time he has reprieve. But one day there is an explosion at his apartment. With the loss of the identity-defining furniture, the narrator begins to see that the life to which he was so devoted was really no life at all.

It turns out that he is not alone. Many men like him similarly feel that "their lives end one hour at a time": "Advertising has these people chasing cars and clothes they don't need. Generations have been working in jobs they hate, just so they can buy what they don't really need."[4] These men realize that they lead what feel to them like underfulfilled lives: "We are the middle children of history, raised by television to believe that someday we'll be millionaires and movie stars and rock stars, but we won't. And we're just learning this fact."[5] In losing everything, the narrator learns that he never really had anything to begin with. One day, he meets Tyler Durden (who turns out to be an alter ego he has subconsciously created, the person he's always wished he could be), and Tyler asks the narrator to hit him in the face. Thus began "fight club," a place where men (and only men) gather to brawl in the basements of bars. Fight clubs do for their participants what their humdrum existences could never deliver. They bestow a purpose upon men who needed to be redeemed from a specifically masculine form of discontent. The problem they look to address through their pugilism is gendered: "What you see at fight club is a generation of men raised by women."[6] There is a release, but there is also a

219–20). Angela Nagel notes that 4chan, an online gathering place for aggrieved men, based its "50 rules of the internet" on the book. *Fight Club*, she notes, "constructs a rebel masculinity that rejects both traditional male roles and pro-feminist new ones as its anti-conformist antidote" (*Kill All Normies: Online Culture Wars from 4Chan and Tumblr to Trump and the Alt-Right* [Zero Books, 2017], 114).

3. Chuck Palahniuk, *Fight Club* (Norton, 1996), 172.

4. Palahniuk, *Fight Club*, 120, 149.

5. Palahniuk, *Fight Club*, 166.

6. Palahniuk, *Fight Club*, 50.

sense of brotherhood and liberation from a feminine environment through shared purpose.

Tyler Durden does not rest content with fight clubs, however. As interest grows, Durden launches Project Mayhem, a domestic terrorism effort made up of committees who give their members homework assignments that include assault, arson, mischief, misinformation, and the like. Project Mayhem achieves a greater purpose: "When Tyler invented Project Mayhem, Tyler said the goal of Project Mayhem had nothing to do with other people. Tyler didn't care if other people got hurt or not. *The goal was to teach each man in the project that he had the power to control history*. We, each of us, can take control of the world."[7] Through acts of murder and destruction, Project Mayhem instills in its participants the sense that they can effect historical change. Forget buying IKEA furniture; try blowing up a building or murdering your horrible boss. Through fight clubs and Project Mayhem, men learned a credo: "As long as you're at fight club, you're not how much money you've got in the bank. You're not your job. You're not your family, and you're not who you tell yourself. . . . You're not your problems. . . . You're not your age."[8] Fight clubs and Project Mayhem offer their masculine participants freedom, and through their exertions of violence and destruction, they also recover the masculinity that society promised but never allowed them to express. *Fight Club* ends with its promise of hope through a newfound ability to control history: "We are going to break up civilization so we can make something better out of the world."[9]

Fight Club is an extended argument that masculinity is in a politically and theologically bad place: Men, in the words of Susan Faludi, have been "stiffed."[10] The nation-state had promised men that if they kept their heads down and worked hard, they could provide for their families and live lives worth being proud of. Instead, they are stuck with IKEA furniture and depression, with jobs outsourced, factories shut down, and children sent off to fight in the nation-state's wars that never seem to end. They want to seize history for themselves and set it back onto the proper trajectory. The narrative, in their eyes, is in decline, and the time has come to restore it to its proper calibration. But is this the right way to intersect theology, politics, and gender?

7. Palahniuk, *Fight Club*, 122 (emphasis added).
8. Palahniuk, *Fight Club*, 143.
9. Palahniuk, *Fight Club*, 208.
10. Susan Faludi, *Stiffed: The Betrayal of the American Man* (William Morrow, 1999).

This chapter engages that intersection. It argues that combining masculinity with a narrative of decline is not a Christian approach to politics, history, and their connection with gender. When gender is united to politics, it too often arranges history as either a narrative of decline or a myth of progress in the service of promoting some cause of aggrievement. But this results in expressions of gender that misconstrue the proper nature of politics, which is instead about finding ways to live with those with whom we have fundamental disagreements and cultivating the necessary virtues for negotiating life before Christ's return. Or, as Luke Bretherton expresses it, politics "refers to . . . forming, norming, and sustaining some kind of common life between friends, strangers, enemies, and the friendless amid their ongoing differences and disagreements and as they negotiate asymmetries of various kinds of power."[11] The span of time during which politics is necessary, which this chapter will refer to as the "saeculum," is resistant to simplistic narratives that obscure its complexity. Attempts to seize control of history will be shown to be attempts to deny this theological account of history. Additionally, such an approach to history's perceived decline is descriptively inadequate, again looking to build normative platforms on shaky descriptive foundations. Politics, as an activity suited for the mortal life of sin, serves a particular purpose related to the cultivation of a temporary peace for human beings' earthly pilgrimage.

According to this political theology, gender cannot be utilized to secure the meaning of history, as it looks to do in *Fight Club*. Rather, gender's place within politics is to identify the conditions necessary for women and men to live a common life anticipatory of the peace of Christ. This will require, I shall argue, a resistance to a simplistic understanding of history as either a decline narrative or a myth of progress and an emphasis on local, organizational forms of politics. To illustrate this, I will return to the example of masculinity and political decline to show that at its heart is a deeply unchristian understanding of history and politics. All the same, these men are naming the ways in which promises have been made and not kept, resulting in injustice and harm. There is a kernel of hope in their responses should they turn not to violence, in the name of wresting control of history from their enemies, but to local organizational efforts where neighbors act to care for one another. A Christian account of political hope requires such broad-based communal

11. Luke Bretherton, *Christ and the Common Life: Political Theology and the Case for Democracy* (Eerdmans, 2019), 445.

care, with neighbors (and enemies) forging surprising alliances for the sake of penultimate goods.

The Nature of Politics: Forging and Organizing a Common Life During the Saeculum

To see how gender and politics are best united, it is useful first to develop a theological account of politics,[12] but there is always a worry that such an inquiry attempts to unite "the political" and "theology," two things that cannot come together appropriately. It is important to note, however, that in "political theology," "political" should remain the adjective while "theology" should remain the noun. We are doing theology insofar as we are responding to the dynamics already native to Christian confession, and many of those dynamics are political. This is notably different from "theological politics," where some external political agenda is in search of theological justification. Oliver O'Donovan summarizes the difference well: "Theology is political simply by responding to the dynamics of its own proper themes. . . . It is not a question of adapting to alien requirements or subscribing to external agenda, but of letting theology be true to its task and freeing it from a forced and unnatural detachment."[13] Developing theology's familiar political commitments helps one know the difference between "political theology" (where theology is in the driving seat) and "theological politics" (where politics has usurped control of one's commitments).

Additionally, we must be clear about what we mean by the word *politics*. Although the political realm is typically identified with legislative bodies, presidencies, and elections, such a reduction of politics to the practices of statecraft is resisted here. Luke Bretherton makes the distinction clear: "Alongside statecraft, politics also refers to the participatory and collaborative social practices through which a common world is cultivated. Politics as an informal, relational craft takes place in multiple settings and is not coextensive with control of the state or even dependent on there being a state."[14] Informal

12. For an exemplary introduction into this theological discipline, see Elizabeth Phillips, *Political Theology: A Guide for the Perplexed* (T&T Clark, 2012).

13. Oliver O'Donovan, *The Desire of the Nations: Rediscovering the Roots of Political Theology* (Cambridge University Press, 1999), 3.

14. Luke Bretherton, *A Primer in Christian Ethics: Christ and the Struggle to Live Well* (Cambridge University Press, 2023), 325.

political organization occurs when individuals assemble to achieve shared goals with power available to them only when they are gathered.[15] In other words, statecraft operates by means of top-down coercive measures, while organizing opts for bottom-up forms of collective agency.[16] It is the latter that is badly evidenced among aggrieved men, but it is also the most promising and redemptive way for gender and politics to unite in a hopeful, faithful, and loving manner, and so I will place the emphasis of this chapter on it.[17]

Humanity Is Naturally Social, but Sinful Humanity Is Prone to Conflict

A helpful place to begin in developing a political theology is with the claim that it is not good for human beings to be alone (Gen. 2:18). In light of this, God makes Eve from the side of Adam. Augustine takes up this biblical figure and interprets it to show that there is "nothing more social by virtue of its nature" than a human being.[18] Humanity is social because, says Augustine, a single individual was not enough. This is meant to show us that while we are many, hardwired into human nature is a tendency to organize itself into communities.

What is it about human beings that compels them to do this? Alongside their natural tendency toward sociability is humanity's natural capacity to love, and their loves are the driving force of their social organization.[19] Augustine is famous for his affirmation that a community is defined as "a multitude of rational beings joined together by common agreement on the objects of

15. For a vivid depiction of organizational politics, see Jeffrey Stout, *Blessed Are the Organized: Grassroots Democracy in America* (Princeton University Press, 2010).

16. It was Saul Alinksy, one of the founders of broad-based political organizing, who said in 1946 that we ought to be "interested in social planning but just as deeply suspicious of, and antagonistic to, any idea of plans that work from the top down. Democracy . . . is working from the bottom up" (*Reveille for Radicals* [Vintage, 1989], 17).

17. For a sustained argument displaying the promise of such political activity among religious groups, see Luke Bretherton, *Christianity and Contemporary Politics: The Conditions and Possibilities of Faithful Witness* (Wiley-Blackwell, 2010), chap. 2.

18. Augustine, *City of God*, trans. William Babcock, ed. Boniface Ramsey, The Works of Saint Augustine: A Translation for the 21st Century 1/6 and 1/7 (New City, 2012–13), 12.28. See also 19.12: A human being "is drawn by the laws of his nature, so to speak, to be social and to maintain peace with all human beings, so far as it lies in his power."

19. For the claim that we are created with a natural capacity to love, see Fellipe do Vale, *Gender as Love: A Theological Account of Human Identity, Embodied Desire, and Our Social Worlds* (Baker Academic, 2023), 118–23. For an elaboration on love's propulsion toward communities, see do Vale, *Gender as Love*, 135–40.

their love," for it is love that "joins many hearts into one."[20] A community's common objects of love, therefore, bring it together and forge it into a new social entity; this is an entirely natural process for human beings. Human beings are naturally social because they are made to be creatures who love and share loves in common.

As mentioned in the introduction, we are no longer in the garden, nor do we look to return to it. Between us and the garden stands the devastation of all things. All that has been made is now futile, fragile, and frail, subject to the powers of death, including our natural love for sociability. Such a love, when embroiled in sin, becomes what Augustine calls the *libido dominandi*, or "lust for domination."[21] What once motivated humanity to form bonds of relationship that fostered health and mutual benefit has now become "a dark drive to control, to appropriate and to turn to one's private ends, all the good things that had been created by God to be accepted with gratitude and shared with others."[22] Left to itself, human sociability now distorts into a feverish desire to control and dominate one's neighbor.

It goes without saying that operating by the *libido dominandi* necessarily leads to conflicts of varying intensity. Human history is marked by everything from petty squabbles between neighbors to intercontinental wars between nations. Given the reality of conflict, how are we to live? Luke Bretherton summarizes our options helpfully: "When I meet someone I disagree with, dislike, find strange or threatening, I can do one of four things. I can kill them. I can create a structure of domination so I can control them. I can make life so difficult that they run away. Or I can do politics. That is to say, I can form, norm, and sustain some kind of common life—amid asymmetries of power, competing visions of the good, and my own feelings of fear or aversion—without killing, dominating, or causing them to flee."[23] Bretherton alludes to the fact that human history is littered with examples of killing, systemic domination, and fleeing conflicts. If we find these solutions unacceptable, then we are left with one option: Do politics by finding a way to live a common life amid conflict in the effort to promote compassion amid death and destruction.

---

20. Augustine, *City of God* 19.24 and 15.3.

21. For more on the *libido dominandi*, see do Vale, *Gender as Love*, 134–35.

22. Peter Brown, *The Body and Society: Men, Women and Sexual Renunciation in Early Christianity*, 20th anniversary ed. (Columbia University Press, 2008), 418.

23. Bretherton, *Primer in Christian Ethics*, 317.

Politics Is for the Saeculum

While our sociability is a natural attribute, our need for statecraft politics is not. Because it is contingent on the ways sin distorts our sociability, statecraft is best seen as a merciful *response* to the introduction of sin into the divine economy.[24] Statecraft, in short, is a creaturely provision for sinful tendencies toward conflict. There is a parallel here with Israel's demand to Samuel for a king "like other nations" (1 Sam. 8:5). This is clearly a sinful request that amounts to a rejection of God (8:7), yet God nevertheless grants a king—a form of statecraft—to Israel (8:22). This is both a judgment on the sinfulness of Israel and a mercy on God's part. God grants certain *provisional* goods in view of human sin, and statecraft politics is one of them. It is God's provision for our survival under deathly conditions.

One way to understand this claim theologically is to say that statecraft is confined to the *saeculum*, which is a term used by classical theologians like Augustine to denote the span of time between the creation of all things, their devastation, their redemption in Christ, and their consummation at the return of Christ.[25] Theologically, the saeculum is derived from texts like Matthew 13:24–30, or the parable of the wheat and the tares. Here, all of history is compared to a field in which good seed is sown. During the night, "an enemy" (v. 25) creeps in and sows weeds among the wheat. Surprised, the workers of the field ask the owner of the field if they should gather the weeds, but he replies, "No; for in gathering the weeds you would uproot the wheat along with them. Let both of them grow together until the harvest" (vv. 29–30). Verses 38–40 clarify that the harvest is when Christ returns, which means that, until that time, just and unjust necessarily live together. This parable played an important role in Augustine's development of the saeculum,[26] and

---

24. For a helpful way to unpack the debate between those who claim that politics is natural and those who hold that it is a response to sin, see Eric Gregory and Joseph Clair, "Augustinianisms and Thomisms," in *The Cambridge Companion to Christian Political Theology*, ed. Craig Hovey and Elizabeth Phillips (Cambridge University Press, 2015). Often the distinction between statecraft and organizing is not made in these debates. Bretherton is again helpful: "Politics is a creational good, the goal of which is a just and loving common life, embodying as it does the good of association. Statecraft, which entails the use of coercive, unilateral power, is a post-lapsarian endeavor that at its best inhibits evil" (*Christ and the Common Life*, 25). Organizing is mixed on this point: Some forms are responses to evil; others obtain basic human goods.

25. Note that the meaning of *saeculum* here is quite different from what the English word *secular* has come to mean: a theologically neutral space that is absent of religion.

26. See especially his "Sermon 73," in Augustine, *Sermons 51–94*, trans. Edmund Hill, The Works of Saint Augustine: A Translation for the 21st Century 3/3 (New City, 1991), 291, 293.

he summarizes its implications for a Christian understanding of the course of history: "In this world [*saeculo*], in fact, these two cities remain intermixed and intermingled with each other until they are finally separated at the last judgment."[27] It can be no other way; the saeculum is and will remain a mixed time during which attempts to distinguish between wheat and tares remain premature. It is both gracious and grievous, beautiful and belligerent.[28]

Secularity is a necessary condition for politics as it makes our starting point a blended, complex, and unpredictable state of affairs. Thus Bretherton: "Theologically understood, the secular, noneschatological order is a deeply ambiguous and paradoxical one in which the world is complexly faithful and unfaithful, loving and idolatrous, in which political authorities may both participate in the reordering of creation to its true end and be anti-Christic (i.e., utterly opposed to God's good order)."[29] One's construal of history, it turns out, matters deeply to one's political expectations. The theological affirmation of the saeculum is an affirmation that history is irreducibly complex, able to surprise us with inbreakings of grace and to wreck our lives with inbreakings of tragedy and loss, often in the places we least expect. Because the saeculum is a swirling mix of positivity and negativity until Christ returns, those of us who remain in the field of wheat and tares must resist temptations to separate wheat from tares ourselves before the harvest. Our call is to form "*mutual* rather than *neutral* ground" with others,[30] not in spite of them, thereby forming bonds of unity to achieve a penultimate peace "during the world."[31]

There is one final element of a secularity relevant to our purposes—namely, a stubborn resistance to "myths of progress" and "declension narratives." Bretherton makes a crucial observation about the implications of the saeculum:

> History does not bear within itself its own resolution and so while the order of things can be improved in incremental ways, there is no inherent direction to history: things will not always get better (or worse). The non-progressive nature of history means that a perfect or true order of things is not realizable

27. Augustine, *City of God* 1.35.

28. See further Paul J. Griffiths, "Secularity and the Saeculum," in *Augustine's City of God: A Critical Guide*, ed. James Wetzel (Cambridge University Press, 2012), 34.

29. Bretherton, *Christ and the Common Life*, 235.

30. Bretherton, *Christ and the Common Life*, 254.

31. Charles Mathewes, *A Theology of Public Life*, Cambridge Studies in Christian Doctrine (Cambridge University Press, 2007), 3.

> within history, so any human system or ideology that claims to provide the means of bringing about this order is a denial of the fallen and contingent nature of historical existence. . . . Attempts to overturn a political system in the name of an ideological blueprint or set of abstract principles will be inherently destructive as they are an attempt to step outside of history or circumvent historical conditions and thereby deny the goodness and the limits of creation reaffirmed in the Incarnation and falsely realize the eschaton by sinful means.[32]

If history is secular, if it is really a mixed field of wheat and tares until the harvest, then it cannot account for itself from within. History's meaning is given to it from its Alpha and Omega (Rev. 1:8) and makes sense of what can only appear to us as perplexing and defeating. And yet, attempts to narrate history simplistically as either progress or decline abound, especially in application to gender.

Myths of progress usually take the form of arguments that one should be on the "right side of history," where such a claim is understood to imply that history has a discernible positive trajectory, and responsible political conduct requires one to act in line with this trajectory.[33] With respect to gender, these usually take the form of observing the unprecedented rights granted to gender minorities in comparison to the past, followed by a claim that this trajectory should continue.[34] Decline narratives are frequently associated with promises to "make America great again" or with Jerry Falwell's attribution of the 9/11 terrorist attacks to an increasing number of abortions, feminists, and gay individuals. However, Andrew Murphy, in his history of religious declension narratives, concludes, "Narratives of decline aren't limited to the political right. . . . The idea of American messianism has never been the sole possession of one political party."[35] Persons of all kinds of political persuasion employ a rhetorical tool commonly referred to as a *jeremiad* to convey a narrative of decline. It has three crucial

32. Bretherton, *Christianity and Contemporary Politics*, 85–86.

33. For a perceptive analysis of such arguments, see Nicholas Smith, "Making Sense of the Right Side of History," *Think* 21, no. 62 (2022): 103–15.

34. For examples of this approach, see David A. J. Richards, *The Case for Gay Rights: From Bowers to Lawrence and Beyond* (University Press of Kansas, 2005); Richard Mohr, *The Long Arc of Justice: Lesbian and Gay Marriage, Equality, and Rights* (Columbia University Press, 2007).

35. Andrew R. Murphy, *Prodigal Nation: Moral Decline and Divine Punishment from New England to 9/11* (Oxford University Press, 2009), 7, 12.

components:[36] It begins with an identification of some contemporary issue that makes life miserable and also illustrates a decline from how things used to be. It then locates the key catalysts of the history of decline, including those most deserving of blame for it. And, finally, it concludes with calls to repentance and renewal. These basic elements allow the modern Jeremiah to "evoke a dynamic tension between despair and hope," mobilizing hearers into action with a "powerful narrative of imperiled national promise and a yearning for national renewal."[37] The decline narrative places its finger on the pains that its hearers are feeling and also calls them back to a time when they did not feel (or at least would not have felt) them.

Countless examples of jeremiads have been voiced throughout history. Murphy, for instance, surveys how both the North and the South rendered their causes during the American Civil War as a recovery of the nation's original mission and destiny.[38] The latter has resulted in an enduring narrative often referred to as the Lost Cause, according to which the South was actually fighting to preserve values true to both God and the nation, supposedly evidenced by the South's explicit (even if nominal) recognition of God in its Confederate Constitution of 1861.[39] This is a "conservative" expression of a jeremiad, but "liberal" expressions are not hard to find either.[40] Today, "liberal" jeremiads lament the loss of communal cohesion and the rise of individualism,[41] but they also turn their attentions to gender. Hillary Clinton, for instance, claims that in the 1960s America took legitimate steps forward in advancing gender equity but that these advances were halted by ideologues

36. I derive these components from Murphy, *Prodigal Nation*, 7–10. The term *jeremiad* gestures toward the prophet Jeremiah, who can be read as observing Israel's decline and summoning them to repent. For another perceptive study of decline narratives, see Mark Stephen Jendrysik, *Modern Jeremiahs: Contemporary Visions of American Decline* (Lexington Books, 2008). For the landmark study on jeremiads in American political life, see Sacvan Bercovitch, *The American Jeremiad* (University of Wisconsin Press, 1978).

37. Murphy, *Prodigal Nation*, 12.

38. See Murphy, *Prodigal Nation*, 63–64.

39. See Murphy, *Prodigal Nation*, 70–71, 60. For more on the Lost Cause as a jeremiad, see Charles Reagan Wilson, *Baptized in Blood: The Religion of the Lost Cause, 1865–1920*, 2nd ed. (University of Georgia Press, 2009).

40. Again, such labels are used in quotations to recognize their inadequacy. Much of what I am attempting to do here is show how divisions between "conservatives" and "liberals" are artificial, especially given that they employ the same problematic rhetorical tools.

41. Witness the influential works of Robert Putnam, *Bowling Alone: The Collapse and Revival of American Community* (Simon & Schuster, 2020); and Robert Bellah, *Habits of the Heart: Individualism and Commitment in American Life* (University of California Press, 2007).

on the right.[42] Whereas "liberals" view the sixties as a lost era of progress, "conservatives" view it as that time during which family life as it should be lived was replaced by misguided understandings of gender. Pat Robertson's claim is emblematic of this sense of doomed decline: "There was a time not long ago that the Christian view of sexuality prevailed."[43] The "conservative" jeremiad, when applied to gender, usually states that there was a time when men were men and women were women, but this time has been forgotten. Whether "conservative" or "liberal," the jeremiad is and has always been an attempt to make sense of the present in light of the past for the sake of the future. This is usually in service of an ideological and political end. Gender is a frequent target for such narratives.

Although they are usually presented as straightforward history, jeremiads should really be seen as the strategic assemblage of historical data to facilitate "the formation and maintenance of communal identity."[44] The identity of a community is shaped by its objects of love. Very often, those objects need a compelling narrative in order to be loved. Thus, narratives of decline and myths of progress both arrange historical data to tell stories that clearly display a community's objects of love. If a particular expression of gender is desired, telling a compelling story about how gender *used to be* this way before things went wrong (or how it *will be* this way if we just stay the course) is a remarkably powerful way to organize individuals to make it possible to shift gender expression in the desired direction. However, we should not confuse myths of progress or decline narratives with neutral history; they are species of moral argumentation. They are fruits of the normative task often masked as the descriptive task. Because "narrators simply *must* ignore or hide elements of that social reality that do not comport with their plots to be persuasive," these must be seen as "moralized tales": "Only the relevant data made it into the story, and that data was presented in ways consistent with the larger story of decline."[45] This should already be a warning to those hearing a jeremiad: Is this is a

42. For a close analysis of Clinton's use of the jeremiad, see Jendrysik, *Modern Jeremiahs*, chap. 8. For a similar argument that the 1960s were a missed opportunity from which we have fallen, see James A. Morone, *Hellfire Nation: The Politics of Sin in American History* (Yale University Press, 2003), 494, 496.

43. Pat Robertson, *The Turning Tide* (Thomas Nelson, 1995), 21, quoted in Murphy, *Prodigal Nation*, 97.

44. Murphy, *Prodigal Nation*, 38.

45. Murphy, *Prodigal Nation*, 120–21.

moral argument disguised as objective history? Is it an appeal to a sense of fear, confusion, and loss when it should make its case more honestly, transparently, and clearly?

This fact usefully highlights the central theological weaknesses of myths of progress or narratives of decline. In light of the comments in the preceding chapter, we should be suspicious of the selectivity of jeremiads. If by design they omit important evidence, they are not likely describing the state of affairs at hand in an adequate way. For instance, one might think that gender today is more problematic than it has ever been in the past, but such a claim forgets the fact that not much more than one hundred years ago, women could not vote, hold bank accounts in their name, or sue their sexual assailants. Once again, we see the rush to make normative claims without describing well. Moreover, jeremiads are attempts to circumvent the saeculum, to use interpretations of history to make an untimely separation of the wheat from the tares for short-lived comfort. Living during the saeculum requires the ability to say, "I cannot make sense of history for myself, my attempts *always* omit relevant evidence, so I must resist judgment until sufficient clarity is provided at the harvest." Ecclesiastes 7:10 captures the idea well: "Do not say, 'Why were the former days better than these?' For it is not from wisdom that you ask this." Failing to show such restraint results in a species of moral argumentation that goes beyond the bounds of wisdom. History is always more complex than it appears, and Christians are tasked with discerning the light of Christ in history, not supplying external narratives to dilute the complexity. Decline narratives may be comforting, but they are not faithful.

Politics is for the saeculum, and the saeculum is an irreducibly complex time during which grace and devastation are both felt. Things are always better than they seem to be during the saeculum, and they are also always worse than they promise to be. We can expect no less; yet, when we try to join gender and politics, myths of progress and narratives of decline are often the first tools for which we reach. They facilitate the political organizations that channel our disappointment at statecraft politics. If we are frustrated with the direction in which the state is headed, we can reach for a jeremiad to help bring others together to make things "right." This, however, comes at the expense of the saeculum and positions one as able to discern the meaning of history. To conclude, we shall turn now to a concrete example of political acts performed in the interest of gender.

Aggrieved Men and Gendered Political Acts

In the previous section, I argued for a constructive understanding of political theology. It distinguishes between the various senses of the word *politics* and favors an approach that sees politics as navigating a common life with others in the attempt to avoid violence and coercion. Such political theology is done during the saeculum, an ambiguous time trending neither upward nor downward but Christ-ward. During the saeculum (i.e., before the harvest), attempts to separate wheat from tares are misguided, and decline narratives are one such attempt. As discussed in the introduction, however, this is precisely what has occurred among some contemporary men who find themselves aggrieved by the economic and political developments of their generation.

In roughly described terms, many present-day men have been told that if they work diligently, keep their heads down, establish a family in a good neighborhood, and generally stay out of trouble, the system in place will reward them for their efforts and take care of them. That system, moreover, was largely established by the market and the nation-state. But the check has bounced; these men have done their part, but they have been abandoned. Sociologist Michael Kimmel captures the phenomenon well. Contemporary men

> believed that there was a contract between themselves, and guys like them, and the government "of the people" that is supposed to represent us. They believed in the corporations that they worked for, confident in the knowledge that they could support a family, enjoy a secure retirement, and provide for their families. That contract was the stable foundation for several generations of America's working men—an implied but inviolable understanding between businesses and workers, between government and employers. They had kept the faith, fulfilled their part of the bargain. And somehow their share had been snatched away by faceless, feckless hands. They played by all the rules, only to find the game was rigged from the start. . . . There's a painful sense of betrayal from their government, from the companies to whom we give our lives, from the unions. There was a *moral* contract, that if we fulfill our duty to society, society will fulfill its duty to us in our retirement, taking care of those who served so loyally. . . . [These men] are filled with rage at the disappearance of the America into which they believe they were born and to which they feel entitled.[46]

---

46. Kimmel, *Angry White Men*, 202–3, 229. Kimmel is here describing the beliefs of Joe Stack, an IRS agent, and Patrick Sherrill, a postal worker. Stack flew a private plane into an IRS office in 2010, killing his manager and himself; Sherrill killed fifteen of his coworkers in

In the past, these men believed, hard work was rewarded according to a mutually beneficial compact between working men, their places of work, and the state. Yet something happened; the compact has been broken. Now, even though they have kept up their side of the bargain, these men believe they have been betrayed: They have lost their families, their children in divorce proceedings, their jobs, their pensions, or some other element of the security that was promised to them.[47] As one man Kimmel interviewed stated, "I think there are a lot of people who sorta feel like they're at the end of their rope and don't know what to do. They're panicking, freaking out, you know? Back in the day, *if you got screwed by your company, you could go to the government, get unemployment, get food stamps, whatever, get some help. Now there's nowhere to go*. The government does nothing; the corporations—they're the problem. Nowhere to go."[48]

Men have differed in their responses to this state of affairs. Rates of depression and completed suicide among men are quite high,[49] but others turn in a more outward direction. Some men blame, and therefore direct violence toward, women—men like George Sodini, George Hennard, and Marc Lépine.[50] Lépine, after being rejected by the University of Montreal in 1989, walked into a classroom, separated the men from the women, and opened fire randomly at the women while shouting, "You're all feminists! I hate feminists!" He killed fourteen women that day and explained his rationale thus: "I have decided to send the feminists, who have always ruined my life, to their Maker. . . . They want to keep the advantages of women (e.g., cheaper insurance, extended maternity leave preceded by a preventative leave, etc.) while seizing for themselves those of men. . . . They are so opportunistic they do not neglect to profit from the knowledge accumulated by men through the ages."[51] In Lépine's anger and aggrievement, he separated wheat from tares and took history into his own hands.

1986, targeting supervisors, before taking his own life (this is the event from which the phrase "going postal" is derived).

47. For a poignant analysis, see Jocelyn Elise Crowley, *Defiant Dads: Fathers' Rights Activists in America* (Cornell University Press, 2008).

48. Quoted in Kimmel, *Angry White Men*, 209 (emphasis added).

49. For one of the first to associate depression and masculinity, see Terrence Real, *I Don't Want to Talk About It: Overcoming the Secret Legacy of Male Depression* (Scribner, 1997).

50. Sodini opened fire on an aerobics class in 2009 after making public his sexual frustration, killing five young women. Hennard drove his car into a restaurant in 1991, killing fourteen women, after being rejected by two sisters with whom he was obsessed. See Kimmel, *Angry White Men*, 169–70.

51. Quoted in Kimmel, *Angry White Men*, 171.

I do not want to misrepresent the men who feel this way. It is clearly true that not all men who feel "stiffed" open fire on those who have the advantages they believe should be theirs. There is a spectrum of responses, and one end of that spectrum represents men who quietly suffer, especially in their mental health and quality of relationships.[52] *What places all these men on this spectrum, however, is a shared perception of historical decline.* Kimmel writes that the diagnoses offered by aggrieved men "reflect a somewhat nostalgic longing for that past world, when men believed they could simply take their places among the nation's elite, simply by working hard and applying themselves."[53] In the spirit of the jeremiad, these men see the cause of their suffering in a decline of masculinity, usually brought about by shifting attitudes about gender. What is the cause of the position men have found themselves in, believing the state and the market no longer hold up their ends of the bargain? The blame is usually placed on feminism, and so feminists are the tares to be burned.

In recent years, online culture has facilitated the spread of these decline narratives and enabled them to take new forms.[54] There are two examples of this: the emergence of the "manosphere" and the enormous influence of Jordan Peterson. The "manosphere" is the name given to an aggregate of websites, memes, forums, and other forms of online organizing committed to the "shared belief that feminism is a major cause of civilizational decline."[55] Men should not be content with their losses, claims the manosphere, but, through collective action, they must reclaim what has been lost. The manosphere provides a new form of political organization whereby gendered grievances can be identified, set within a coherent story of decline, and generate a basis for collective action against enemies with whom one no longer wishes to be intermingled. Peterson similarly provides a story for men that can serve as a "rejoinder to the feminization . . . of modern life."[56] His overarching mes-

52. See, for instance, John Ibson, *The Mourning After: Loss and Longing Among Midcentury American Men* (University of Chicago Press, 2018).

53. Kimmel, *Angry White Men*, 112; see also 264.

54. See Nagle, *Kill All Normies*, 41, 64, 96. She notes how "masculinist and neomasculinist antifeminist online subcultures" are "typically concerned with the decline of Western masculinity" (18). For more on online culture and the development of aggrieved masculinity, see Christa Hodapp, *Men's Rights, Gender, and Social Media* (Lexington Books, 2017).

55. Nagle, *Kill All Normies*, 89. For more detail on the manosphere's gendered dimensions, see Debbie Ging, "Alphas, Betas, and Incels: Theorizing the Masculinities of the Manosphere," *Men and Masculinities* 22, no. 4 (2019): 638–57.

56. Tara Isabella Burton, *Strange Rites: New Religions for a Godless World* (PublicAffairs, 2020), 212.

sage is that human beings are wired to shape chaos into order, but his appeal largely comes from the *kind* of order he proposes to the men who watch his videos and read his books. Peterson is known for telling them to stand up straight, make their bed, speak precisely, tell the truth, and live purposefully.[57] Doing these things is an antidote to what he perceives as the chaos of identity politics—a perception he demonstrated concretely when he resisted Canada's C-16 bill, which made conformity with "gender identity and expression" a matter of law. Living by order is how today's men recapture what was lost, but "contemporary culture is in decline because it has devalued the trappings of order: institutional structure, regimented discipline, and masculine heroism."[58] Peterson and the manosphere provide men who feel as though something is missing with a narrative that explains why men have fallen so far from where they were, a vision for organizing themselves into political structures to regain power, and a common enemy to blame and conquer as they reclaim what they take to be a lost promise.

While it is tempting to dismiss and disregard these men for their misguided accusations of feminists, a more nuanced critique of their views is required. Kimmel puts it well: "They may have some legitimate gripes, though they are delivering their mail to the wrong address. . . . It hasn't been black people who have foreclosed on their farms, or feminist women who have outsourced their jobs and closed the factories, or gay people who have sunk their mortgages underwater, or immigrants who opened the big-box store with massive tax breaks and spectacular local government initiatives that forced them to close the small hardware store their family had been operating for generations."[59] Their narratives of decline, like most jeremiads, have oversimplified the historical developments to allow for an enemy that is easy to identify. To separate out the wheat from the chaff, these men place their pain within a story that misdirects it. Remember that the broken compact was not between men and feminists but between men and *the market* and *the state*. In the premature effort to separate themselves from the tares, the story misses the mark on who is actually to blame for any legitimate suffering these men experience. They forget that there are just as many feminists who critique the market and the state for its shortcomings. On display here are all of the faults we should

57. See many of the rules in Jordan B. Peterson, *12 Rules for Life: An Antidote to Chaos* (Random House Canada, 2018).

58. Burton, *Strange Rites*, 217.

59. Kimmel, *Angry White Men*, 276.

expect from jeremiads: a lack of proper appreciation for the way we remain intermingled during the saeculum, a premature attempt to separate wheat from chaff, historically misguided narratives that misattribute blame for the harms done, and an inability to see that the explanations for the evils faced will not actually help the problem, much like an unhelpful theodicy. Blaming feminists will not bring back jobs.

All the same, it should not be hard to see why declension narratives (and myths of progress) are so attractive. When one is facing loss and disappointment—when a father who used to have a relationship with his daughter now feels like a stranger to her because after the divorce her mother moved across the country with her—it is an understandable impulse to reach for a narrative that makes sense of it all. As Murphy noted, the power of a jeremiad is its ability to blend despair with hope. Yet, the impulse comes at a cost; this is not how politics and gender should go together. During the saeculum, the complexity cannot be explained away. In any case, these jeremiads are actually less about hope and more about a vacuous optimism. In a distinction he developed from James Cone, Cornel West confesses, "I'm never optimistic. From that angle, the evidence always looks undetermined. But I am full of hope. . . . When you're optimistic, you can stand apart to see how things are going. But when you're full of hope, you're in the midst of the muck. You're working it out with love power and a commitment to justice."[60] A jeremiad will construe historical data so we have some evidence for optimism. But the saeculum is not for optimism; it is for *hope*. In the words of J. R. R. Tolkien, we might not "expect 'history' to be anything but a 'long defeat'—though it contains . . . some samples or glimpses of final victory."[61]

So what might political hope look like for these men (and everyone else) while we endure the grief, loss, and betrayal of contemporary life? The solutions will be as diverse as the issues they face, but these men already have something of a basis on which they can build healthy political action. They must continue to organize for bottom-up collective action to address the harms they have faced, but not with jeremiads as their structuring narratives. What might it look like to take their appropriate impulses for organization and join them with the true source of hope, the resurrected Christ, who will

60. Cornel West, *Hope on a Tightrope: Words and Wisdom* (Hayhouse, 2008), 41, 15.

61. J. R. R. Tolkien, *The Letters of J. R. R. Tolkien: Revealing Insights into the Life of Middle-Earth's Creator*, expanded ed. (William Morrow, 2023), 368.

one day return to wipe away all tears?[62] How can these men act in such a way that God "will make [their] vindication shine like the light, and the justice of [their] cause like the noonday" (Ps. 37:6)? Such a vindication is an eschatological reality, for it comes only when the one with authority to separate wheat from chaff finally arrives. Until then, the pilgrimage of this life will be difficult, but small steps in hope can be taken through collective action.

In practical terms, this will require *unity* rather than separation before the harvest. Collective political action requires broad-based collaboration for its success: Neighbors must be willing to work with one another to bring about penultimate goals, even if their ultimate interests differ.[63] So, if the state and the market are truly to blame for the plight of these men, what might a critique of the state and the market look like when it is made jointly by *both* feminist authors *and* members of the father's rights movement? What exactly stands in the way of such a critique coming about? When the saeculum and its Savior guide the narratives we employ to understand history, I suggest, such creative solutions become possible because we focus less on amorphous and abstract problems and more on immediate, concrete issues, on features and situations within the community that can be changed. In Saul Alinsky's terms, "an issue is something you can do something about," whereas a problem feels so overwhelming that the only thing we can do is tell a story to dilute it.[64] Issues are found in a community, and if you face an issue, a neighbor who cares is likely to notice it too. As Bretherton puts it, "Impatient endurance means addressing issues even while we endure problems."[65] These men sought optimism by focusing only on problems disclosed by their decline narratives; hope, however, can be found when neighbors and enemies link arms against oppression in unified political action that takes small steps to rectify identifiable and fixable issues.

Conclusion

This chapter has been an exploration of gender and politics with normative and descriptive dimensions. Descriptively, special attention has been paid to

---

62. For a political theology oriented around hope, see Michael Lamb, *A Commonwealth of Hope: Augustine's Political Thought* (Princeton University Press, 2022).

63. On this point, see Stout, *Blessed Are the Organized*, 7–8.

64. Saul Alinsky, *Rules for Radicals: A Pragmatic Primer for Realistic Radicals* (Vintage, 2010), 119.

65. Bretherton, *Christ and the Common Life*, 270.

men who find themselves aggrieved. In the words of Tyler Durden quoted in the introduction, "We are the middle children of history, raised by television to believe that someday we'll be millionaires and movie stars and rock stars, but we won't. And we're just learning this fact."[66] But instead of blaming television and those who are in charge of what is shown on it, these men have adopted a decline narrative according to which it is "feminists" who are to blame. Normatively, however, this falls short of how gender and politics ought to be united on theological terms. Theologically, politics is meant for the saeculum, the time from the creation to Christ's return. The saeculum does not disclose its own meaning from within; its Alpha and Omega is Christ, and Christ has told us that we cannot separate the wheat from the tares prematurely. This is why declension narratives fall so far short: They tell a story of a fall where one side is unequivocally bad and the other good in order to provide an explanation for contemporary sorrows. But political theology must resist these temptations in order to forge common lives with others.

The above has been both an investigation into a particular set of gendered goods and a basis for the chapters to come. The summons to live well in common during the saeculum implicates all of our other domains of life—how we dress, how we eat, our families, and so on. As we proceed, we will see how the call of Christ to live faithfully, hopefully, and lovingly in this secular time shapes our gendered lives in more ways than one.

66. Palahniuk, *Fight Club*, 166.

2

Your Closest Neighbor

Friendship with the Body and Trans Identities

> The sense of being inhabited by warring impulses or parts is common to all of us. . . . Exploring—even befriending—those parts is an important component of healing. . . . Self-regulation depends on having a friendly relationship with your body.
>
> —Bessel van der Kolk[1]

> This long struggle to be at home in the body, this difficult friendship.
>
> —Jane Kenyon, "Cages"[2]

It is difficult to look in a mirror and love what is reflected back. Though Christian doctrine confesses the body to be good, such goodness is not always obvious or easily accepted. Our bodies, more often than not, are very difficult to love. With a lifetime of increasing pain, our bodies die, and their death announces itself in slow and agonizing ways, with nothing we can do to avoid it. Yet, despite all this, Saint Paul makes a surprising claim: "No one ever hates his own body" (Eph. 5:29). How can this be so? What prevents us from reading this passage as the naive assertion of someone unacquainted

1. Bessel van der Kolk, *The Body Keeps the Score: Brain, Mind, and Body in the Healing of Trauma* (Viking, 2014), 278, 97.
2. Jane Kenyon, "Cages," in *The Best Poems of Jane Kenyon* (Graywolf, 2020), 10–11.

with bodily tragedy? How could *Paul*, a man who describes himself as outwardly "wasting away" (2 Cor. 4:16), make such a claim? This theological tension between the affirmation of the body's goodness and its present tragedy must indicate something: We still "wait . . . for the redemption of our bodies" (Rom. 8:23). Bodies that were created as good are now devastated by sin and death, requiring a deliverance that can come about only through resurrection.

These observations are succinctly captured in the following statement preached by Saint Augustine in 419 CE: "Take away death, and the body is good. Let death, the last enemy, be removed, and my flesh shall be forever my friend."[3] According to Augustine, what stands in the way of our proper love for our bodies is *death*. On Christian doctrine, death is far more than the cessation of biological life. It encompasses the full range of corruption introduced to humanity as a consequence of sin. Those moments of difficulty with our bodies—when the summons to love our bodies feels more like a summons to love an enemy than a friend—are symptoms of the deeper ailment of death. Worse still, no amount of self-improvement or technological advancement can heal us from death. *Only resurrection cures death*. Christians now must live in tension with their bodies, engaging in the backbreaking project of cultivating friendship with them as a form of testifying against death. This is true both for those who might claim not to have any discomfort with their bodies (and such a theological picture should lead them to reconsider) and those whose bodies are enormously heavy burdens.

In light of these considerations, what does it mean to cultivate a "difficult friendship" with our bodies, in the words of the poet Jane Kenyon? More specifically, how might we think theologically about trans identities against the backdrop of these theological affirmations? Present debates about trans identities tend to be theologically reductive, assuming that the question is whether one ought to prioritize the body or one's felt gender identity in the presence of conflict between the two. The result is an inadequately Christian picture of human beings in which it is supposed that bodies must conform to minds or vice versa. To think well about trans identities, we will have to resist such lopsided tendencies, and the metaphor of friendship will serve us

3. Augustine, *Sermons 148–183*, trans. Edmund Hill, The Works of Saint Augustine: A Translation for the 21st Century 3/5 (New City, 1992), 93. Augustine immediately follows this quote by citing Eph. 5:29. For the mature Augustine, this text primarily operates as a statement about the goodness of the body against those who see it as an obstacle. See Tarsicius Jan van Bavel, "'No One Ever Hated His Own Flesh': Eph. 5:29 in Augustine," *Augustiniana* 1, no. 2 (1995): 45–93.

well here. Friendships, in the midst of the deepest conflict of death, must find constructive relationships of love that honor both sides of the relationship. To think theologically about trans identities, some alternative must be found that honors bodies *and* gender identities. I will argue that we misdescribe trans experiences and misunderstand the nature of the conflict when we are forced into a decision to prioritize either the body or the mind. Using the lens of friendship, we will see that compassion is the best response to life lived while enduring death.

Thus, the argument of this chapter begins with a theological analysis of the human body as we know it under the reign of death before proceeding to make a contribution to discussions about trans identities. Before we begin, a word about terminology is necessary. Ordinarily, the word *trans* refers to someone whose gender identity does not correspond with their natal sex, and for ease of reference, I will use the term in this sense. There are, of course, many more nuances necessary for a proper understanding of trans identities.[4] However, we must be clear at the outset that trans identities are not captured by one experience or definition. As trans actress Laverne Cox says, "There's not just one trans story. There's not just one trans experience."[5] My argument—that we must think of trans identities in terms of the organizing of social goods related to sexed bodies—is intended to accommodate precisely this dynamic: Because the particular gendered goods relevant to a trans person's identity will differ, we should expect experiences and stories to differ in important ways too. Without attention to the particular gendered goods in question, we cannot know what is ostensibly in tension with the body. Additionally, this insight must shape our normative understanding of trans identities. Rather than casting the choice between bodies or minds, trans identities, like all gender identities, must navigate the gendered world as we encounter it and make morally wise attachments to goods like clothing and food. The normative

---

4. For an excellent introduction to trans conversations across a variety of disciplines, see Paul Rhodes Eddy and James K. Beilby, "Understanding Transgender Experiences and Identities: An Introduction," in *Understanding Transgender Identities: Four Views* (Baker Academic, 2019). For a helpful overview of terminology as it has developed, see Susan Stryker, *Transgender History: The Roots of Today's Revolution*, 2nd ed. (Seal, 2017), chap. 1.

5. Quoted in Kate Bornstein, *Gender Outlaw: On Men, Women, and the Rest of Us*, rev. ed. (Vintage, 2016), xiii. Eddy and Beilby state the complexity well: "The transgender community now includes such a wide array of gender-variant people. This means that to ask the question of what lies behind the 'transgender experience' is actually to ask the question of what lies behind cross-dressing, drag expression, genderfluidity, transsexuality and a host of other gender-variant expressions" ("Understanding Transgender Experiences and Identities," 22).

debate has been misguided, and I will conclude this chapter with the claim that thinking well about trans identities will happen when we think well about gender identities as such—that is, when we have a good grasp of how to engage marketing and families and food, we will also know how to think about trans questions.

One thread that will run throughout this chapter is that trans identities should not be seen as sui generis or exceptional. This is an outcome of placing normative trans questions in the realm of navigating social goods just as much as it is an extension of ongoing medical developments that no longer pathologize trans identities.[6] Whereas trans identifications were once seen as diagnosable medical conditions that needed medical intervention, I argue that they are expressions—"common to all of us," in the words of Bessel van der Kolk[7]—of the ways we negotiate friendship with the body in the midst of death for the sake of a gender identity. They are not necessarily medical deviations from an otherwise identifiable norm; part of my argument is that there are *no* such norms during death's reign. Since we all find ourselves plagued by death in our bodies, we all lack friendship with our bodies. Because our true selves are revealed only in resurrection, at death's defeat, what we must do now is engage the world of gendered goods faithfully, lovingly, and hopefully, all of which can be expressions of compassion.

Death and the Loss of Friendship with Our Bodies

According to the Christian tradition, death includes, but is much more than, the cessation of biological life. For instance, Alexander Schmemann asserts, "'Biological' or physical death is not the *whole* death, not even its ultimate essence. . . . Death is above all a *spiritual reality*, of which one can partake while being alive, from which one can be free while lying in the grave."[8] This claim is clear from Jesus's assertion that those who believe in him "will never die" (John 11:26), and it receives its warrant from the very first moment death is introduced into the biblical story. In the garden, God warns Adam that if he eats from the tree of the knowledge of good and evil, "in the day that you eat

6. For a survey of these developments, see Amets Suess et al., "Depathologization," *Transgender Studies Quarterly* 1, nos. 1–2 (2014): 73–77.

7. Van der Kolk, *The Body Keeps the Score*, 278.

8. Alexander Schmemann, *Of Water and the Spirit: A Liturgical Study of Baptism* (St. Vladimir's Seminary Press, 1974), 62–63.

of it you shall die" (Gen. 2:17). The serpent, deceitfully, provides an insidious counternarrative: "You will not die; for God knows that when you eat of it, your eyes will be opened, and you will be like God, knowing good and evil" (3:4). Of course, both Adam and Eve eat from the tree; but something curious happens: Their biological lives do not end. A surfeit of curses are placed upon them, making creaturely life tragic, burdensome, and abusive; but the very fact that they can bring forth children (3:16) or sweat from their faces (3:19) indicates that they are very much alive, at least biologically speaking. In fact, Eve is named "the mother of all *living*" immediately after the curses are placed (3:20, emphasis added). So, which is it? Are Adam and Eve dead or alive?

Of course, the answer depends on what we mean by death. Thomas McCall brings attention to a common distinction between *spiritual* death and *physical* or *biological* death.[9] Spiritual death refers to death as an experience of something lost when humanity's relationship with God is damaged, whereas physical death refers to the end of biological life. In light of Genesis's associations of death with knowing good and evil and the introduction of broken relationships between humans and the earth, one another, and God, another form of death certainly seems to be included in the narrative: spiritual death. Death, theologically, appears to be much more than the end of biological life, and many authors have argued that spiritual death colors the entirety of biological life. Thus Katherine Sonderegger explains, "These are the ways of the world of becoming: all good is seared by loss. We do not simply fear and grieve our deaths, and the deaths of those dear to us; rather, our very structure as creatures—limited, bounded, fragile—are haunted by death, the disorganization, failure and corruption of finite life."[10] When making dogmatic claims about death, therefore, we must make *qualitative* as well as *quantitative* claims: It affects the *quality* of creaturely life, and it affects *all* creatures after the advent of sin.[11] Creaturely life, even *redeemed* creaturely life, is characterized by a persistent struggle with death.

---

9. Thomas H. McCall, *Against God and Nature: The Doctrine of Sin* (Crossway, 2019), 314.

10. Katherine Sonderegger, "Finitude and Death," in *T&T Clark Companion to the Doctrine of Sin*, ed. Keith L. Johnson and David Lauber (Bloomsbury T&T Clark, 2016), 385.

11. I am here echoing Philip Ziegler's claim that "eternal life concerns not merely the *quantity* of human existence but more fundamentally its comprehensive eschatological *quality*" ("The Enmity of Death and Judgment unto Life," in *Eternal God, Eternal Life: Theological Investigations into the Concept of Immortality*, ed. Philip G. Ziegler [T&T Clark, 2016], 133). For Ziegler, if eternal life is this way, death must be too.

Though we can witness these dynamics in various places in Scripture, it is especially clear in Romans 5–8. In these chapters, death operates across a variety of levels—individual, social, and cosmic—lending it the impression of an agent with an ability to wreak havoc on humanity.[12] In 5:12, we see death as consequent upon the introduction of sin into the world. Sin and death, therefore, are now universal: "Death spread to all because all have sinned." Paul then attributes to death the ability to "exercise dominion" or "reign" (5:14, 17), serving as sin's particular instrument for domination (5:21). Croasmun observes, "Death so characterizes Sin's dominion that Paul can talk instead about Sin's dominion as the dominion of death itself."[13] Like Genesis, Romans links acts of sin with acts of death.

Paul emphasizes this connection as he proceeds. Sin is the sort of thing to which one is enslaved, and if one continues in one's enslavement to sin, it "leads to death" (Rom. 6:16). Even more, Paul notes that the "goal" (*telos*; my trans.) of acts done in bondage to sin is "death" (Rom. 6:21–22). Thus, a theologically accurate descriptor of sinful acts shows how they are in line with the reign of death. We can see this vivid portrayal of death in David Kelsey's concept of a "living death," a form of spiritual death. For Kelsey, living deaths are relationships where members diminish one another through the exploitation of power: "In a broad sense every diminishment of our partners' lives in relationships in which they are in some respect dependent on us is in one way or another an act of violence against them and, by the same token, against our own life. We oppress both them and ourselves, and we generate a vicious cycle of violence and oppression. The cycle spirals endlessly into new forms of reciprocal exclusion, diminishment, violation, and oppression. When life is lived as an endless cycle of mutual exclusion, diminishment, and oppression, it is a living death. The pattern is familiar enough."[14] Kelsey's notion of a living death expands death to include all acts, structures, and relationships that spring from sin and have sin as their end. All of us, therefore, live in a world mired in living death; such is the reign of sin. Both qualitatively and quantitatively, a life of sin is a living death.

Such descriptions need to be considered alongside the life, death, and resurrection of Jesus Christ. Paul, in Romans 6, makes clear that the death of

12. For death's multiple levels, see Matthew Croasmun, *The Emergence of Sin: The Cosmic Tyrant in Romans* (Oxford University Press, 2017), 19–22. Croasmun summarizes the first seven chapters of Romans as "a story of enslavement to s/Sin through law that results in death" (104).

13. Croasmun, *Emergence of Sin*, 125; see also 121.

14. David H. Kelsey, *Imagining Redemption* (Westminster John Knox, 2005), 76.

Christ subverts the reign of sin: "We know that our old self was crucified with him so that the body of sin might be destroyed, and we might no longer be enslaved to sin" (6:6). "Death no longer has dominion over" Christ because he was resurrected (6:9), and because we are united to Christ in his death, we also have "died to sin" (6:2). So, while it *was* the case that "sinful passions were at work in our members to bear fruit for death" (7:5), Paul can call this "sin, working death in me" (7:13). In Christ, therefore, the death to which we were captive no longer possesses any sting (1 Cor. 15:55–56). And yet, we still die, sin, and are sinned against. The living death described by Kelsey still affects those in Christ. So, while we are no longer enslaved to sin, we still feel its downward force, witness its destruction, and participate in its defeated rule.

This is where Paul's emphasis on the hope of resurrection is crucial to remember. Romans promises that "hope does not disappoint us" (5:5) and that we "*will* . . . be saved through him from the wrath of God" (5:9, emphasis added). This future-oriented thread runs through Romans 5–8, with future-tense verbs serving as gentle reminders that while we have died with Christ, the fullness of the promise remains in the future. This is clearest in Romans 6:5: "For if we have been united with him in a death like his, we *will* certainly be united with him in a resurrection like his" (emphasis added). The two sides of the conditional are as distant as our true selves are from our current selves: Currently, we are united in his death, but we *will* share in his life when we are resurrected. Paul seems to be saying in Romans 6:5–9 that *only resurrection* defeats death in its entirety. While we are still on pilgrimage in this life, we can experience only the beginnings of what resurrection will be like, the scent of the meal wafting out of the kitchen before it is fully enjoyed. This is obviously better than having no meal at all—we cannot say that we are *only* or *merely* slaves to sin—but we cannot comprehensively claim for the already what is reserved for the not yet. Only when we enjoy a resurrection *like his* will we be free of death completely, even as we enjoy the current benefits of his death and life now. Though biologically alive, Adam and Eve could also be pronounced spiritually dead.

Although we cannot say that the "wretched man" of 7:24 can be applied to those in Christ *without qualification*, we also cannot say that we are completely free of the "body of death."[15] Just as we *will be* united with him in

---

15. Though scholars like Dale Allison and Michelle Lee have argued that *body* in Paul broadly describes a collective capable of action, it is clear here that *sōma* refers to a literal human body in light of Paul's reference to his "inmost self" and his "members" (Rom. 7:22–23). Croasmun notes how Paul usually means *body* collectively, "save for in Rom 7:23–24, in which

a resurrection that is to come, so we also *will be* rescued from the body of death. But just as resurrection is a promise we can only anticipate now, our freedom from the body of death is complete only when the last enemy is taken away. Therefore, we still groan "while we wait for adoption, the redemption of our bodies" (8:23). Only bodies that groan from death hope for a coming deliverance. This is why Paul began with hope in 5:5 and now ends with hope in 8:25: "But if we hope for what we do not see, we wait for it with patience." This is the experience of bodies now in his terms: They groan, they are weak, and they require deep prayer as they await transformation (8:26).[16]

How can we draw together these Pauline claims about sin, death, and the body? As we have already noted, our relationship with our bodies is in tension and requires eschatological patience. Bodies now are not what they should be, even if they can experience a taste of the redemption to come. Because the gap between bodies now and bodies as they will be still exists, life before the resurrection is one where friendship with the body, as Augustine, van der Kolk, and Kenyon helpfully put it, has been lost and is being recovered. The last enemy has not been fully removed, even if it has been defeated, and so friendship is imperfect and will remain that way until we are resurrected. If the problem with our bodies is death, the only possible solution is its opposite: resurrection. Christ has been raised, and we will be raised with him; but until then, these bodies will remain difficult. This is true of all human bodies under the conditions of sin. This may be more or less apparent depending on the particular difficulties one's body presents. Though it may be quite obvious to someone, say, suffering from chronic pain or advanced arthritis, it is no less true of those who can, for the moment, push death's effects out of mind. My intent here is to claim that this is true of every human being during the saeculum. While the specific loss of friendship will differ from person to person, all loss of friendship with the body shares a root cause: death. In the next section we will see how this theological picture can clarify questions

---

the macrocosm of the Body of Sin has become a microcosm within the constituent's individual body" (*Emergence of Sin*, 118).

16. Elsewhere, Paul makes his hope for the resurrection of the dead just as clear. After claiming that he wants to "know Christ and the power of his resurrection and the sharing of his sufferings by becoming like him in his death," he says that we expect Christ to come in the future, when he "will transform the body of our humiliation that it may be conformed to the body of his glory" (Phil. 3:10, 21). The dynamics are exactly the same: We are united to Christ in his death, and we will have bodies conformed to his resurrected body when we ourselves are resurrected.

regarding trans identities in order to conclude that the hope of resurrection beckons us to cultivate compassion until the last enemy is defeated.

Contemporary Approaches to Trans Identities and Their Deficit

Trans identities have become increasingly visible in recent years,[17] and this greater visibility has generated a debate about how best to understand such identities. Contemporary approaches have developed the following bifurcated line. In the presence of conflict between one's body and one's gender identity, those on one side of the line argue that *bodies* must be preferred over psychological identities, while those on the other side argue that *psychological identities* must take priority. This is largely because the discussion has been framed around whether or not trans identities should be understood as psychological pathologies.[18] This division naturally forces a choice between the alternatives. However, I will argue in this section that this debate, with its assumed terms, is neither the best way to think about trans identities broadly nor a theologically adequate one. In particular, the assumed terms of the debate do not adequately represent the experiences of trans individuals or the commonalities between trans experiences and those of cis individuals as we all navigate the gendered world of social goods; furthermore, the assumed terms of the debate theologically mischaracterize the nature of the conflict.

Two groups recommend the prioritization of sexed bodies over gender identities in the face of conflict: gender-critical feminists and Christian theologians in some evangelical and some Roman Catholic traditions. The former rose to prominence with the publication of Janice Raymond's book *The Transsexual Empire*, which she wrote when she was a PhD student under

17. For helpful histories of trans persons before the contemporary emergence we know today, see Joanne Meyerowitz, *How Sex Changed: A History of Transsexuality in the United States* (Harvard University Press, 2002); Stryker, *Transgender History*, chap. 2; Rachel Mesch, *Before Trans: Three Gender Stories from Nineteenth-Century France* (Stanford University Press, 2020); Leah DeVun, *The Shape of Sex: Nonbinary Gender from Genesis to the Renaissance* (Columbia University Press, 2021); Kit Heyan, *Before We Were Trans: A New History of Gender* (Seal, 2022).

18. Originally, gender variance was seen as a psychological condition to be fixed from a medical perspective. Today, it remains designated as a psychological condition, yet not one that necessarily needs correction but something more like alleviation. This is easily traced in the different editions of the *Diagnostic and Statistical Manual of Mental Disorders*, which in its fourth edition considered "gender identity disorder" to be a pathology but changed the term to "gender dysphoria" in its fifth edition, preferring approaches to relieve distress. See Suess et al., "Depathologization."

Mary Daly.[19] It finds its mature expression in works by theorists like Sheila Jeffreys, Kathleen Stock, and Holly Lawford-Smith.[20] For example, in asking whether gender-critical feminism is trans-exclusionary, Lawford-Smith makes clear the priority this view places on biologically sexed bodies: "Gender-critical feminism is feminism for females, not feminism for feminine 'gender identities' or feminism for feminine 'gender performances.' Because of this, it includes transmen, and excludes transwomen. It does not exclude trans people in general: on the contrary, it is very concerned to include transmen and female nonbinary people, because it is concerned with the harms done on the basis of female sex and as a result of the (attempted) imposition of norms of femininity."[21] Gender-critical feminists, then, prioritize biological sex over against mental gender identity precisely because they seek to address harms against female bodies.

While they do not share these feminist political concerns, some contemporary theologians have produced similar arguments. We have already seen an example of the former in the work of Abigail Favale, and another can be found in the work of Andrew Walker, who understands God's creation of humanity as male and female to mean that *male sexed bodies* and *female sexed bodies* are part of God's design (Gen. 1:26–29, 31).[22] Put another way, what Genesis 1 refers to is the goodness of *sexed bodies*, and presumably not something like gender identity. This is clear in Walker's definitions of masculinity and femininity: "Genesis tells us that a man is a human whose physical design is organized for reproduction with his sexual counterpart, a woman, or wife, with whom he can physically become 'one flesh' (2:24). Similarly, Genesis reveals that a woman is a human whose physical design is organized for reproduction with her counterpart, a man, or husband."[23] Walker is clear that such organization occurs "at the level of their genetic make-up," making

19. Janice G. Raymond, *The Transsexual Empire: The Making of the She-Male* (Beacon, 1979). Daly preempted some of Raymond's arguments in her book *Gyn/Ecology*, where she calls "transsexualism . . . an example of male surgical siring which invades the female world with substitutes" (Mary Daly, *Gyn/Ecology: The Metaethics of Radical Feminism*, 2nd ed. [Beacon, 1990], 71).

20. Sheila Jeffreys, *Gender Hurts: A Feminist Analysis of the Politics of Transgenderism* (Routledge, 2014); Kathleen Stock, *Material Girls: Why Reality Matters for Feminism* (Fleet, 2021).

21. Lawford-Smith, *Gender-Critical Feminism*, 115–16.

22. Andrew T. Walker, *God and the Transgender Debate: What Does the Bible Actually Say About Gender Identity?*, 2nd ed. (Good Book, 2022), 53.

23. Walker, *God and the Transgender Debate*, 56.

it a feature of the body.[24] What is one to do when one has a sense that one does not belong to one's body? Walker is careful to say that this experience *on its own* is not sinful (provided it is not acted upon), but he ultimately holds that anything less than the arduous affirmation of the body over the mind is a transgression against God's intention. Thus, trans identities are

> not compatible with following Christ. . . . As we have seen, God has created human beings in his own image as male and female. Our identity, therefore, is defined by God in his purposes for his creation and in his new creation in Christ. The design of humanity is purposeful and good, and part of our design is that we are men and women. To deny or overturn that distinction is to nullify God's revelation both in nature and in Scripture. . . . Let me underline that experiencing gender dysphoria does not mean you are not a Christian. But it does mean that a settled rejection of God's purposes for us as male or female cannot be reconciled with following Christ. Someone can embrace a transgender identity or find their identity in Christ, but not both.[25]

Walker, in the end, takes a forceful position: In the presence of conflict between gender identity and bodies, we must prioritize bodies. Experiencing the conflict is to be expected, but failing to land on one side of that divide is failing to be a Christian.

This emphasis on the preference of sexed bodies over gendered minds is evident in other theological work.[26] Of these authors, Preston Sprinkle is representative in his clarity. He says that there is a "foundational question" underlying trans debates: "*If someone experiences incongruence between their biological sex and their internal sense of self, which one determines who they are—and why?*"[27] His answer, after careful and charitable discussion, is clear: "I would say that the Bible and science offer much more evidence to support the view that our biological sex determines who we are. Our sexed bodies determine whether we are male, female, or both; and our embodiment

24. Walker, *God and the Transgender Debate*, 57.

25. Walker, *God and the Transgender Debate*, 154.

26. See Katie McCoy, *To Be a Woman: The Confusion over Female Identity and How Christians Can Respond* (B&H, 2023), 101–2, who argues that our "embodied selves" need "to define or direct our gender identity."

27. Preston M. Sprinkle, *Embodied: Transgender Identities, the Church, and What the Bible Has to Say* (David C Cook, 2021), 24. Sprinkle repeats a version of the question on page 147: "*Is the soul or the body more ontologically significant for a person's status as male or female when there is incongruence?*"

is an essential part of how we image God in the world. I don't think the Bible or science offers enough evidence to suggest that our gender (identity or role) overrules sexed identity, even if we experience incongruence."[28] In a moment, I will argue that the problem lies precisely in the way Sprinkle and others have formulated the question; but it is clear that these authors believe the best framing of the question is one about conflict and preference for the body over the mind.

As mirror images to the authors just discussed, other theologians and theorists affirm that gender identities should take precedence over bodies. For instance, Susannah Cornwall argues that we should prefer an "inner sense of self" over against bodies.[29] In previous work, Cornwall adopts the view that bodies are constructed through the discursive practices of human beings,[30] and she now applies it to discussions regarding trans identities, noting that bodies are "in flux and development over time."[31] Because of this, prioritizing the body as an immutable entity does not make sense, and attempts to change it in order for it "to become more like the body an individual senses they should always have had" are extensions of a perfectly natural fluidity.[32] Cornwall makes her conclusion clear:

> We need not cling to our bodies and need not relate to God in Christ in these bodies as we used to understand them. *We might be called to let go of, especially, the notion that our ontology is grounded in our biology: our outer nature (our biology?) is, after all, wasting away, even as our inner nature (our sense of self—even, anachronistically, our identity?) is being renewed*, "because we look not at what can be seen but at what cannot be seen; for what can be seen is temporary, but what cannot be seen is eternal" (2 Cor. 4:16–18).[33]

---

28. Sprinkle, *Embodied*, 152.

29. Susannah Cornwall, *Constructive Theology and Gender Variance: Transformative Creatures* (Cambridge University Press, 2023), 13.

30. For a broader discussion of Cornwall's metaphysics of the body, see Fellipe do Vale, *Gender as Love: A Theological Account of Human Identity, Embodied Desire, and Our Social Worlds* (Baker Academic, 2023), 194–96.

31. Cornwall, *Constructive Theology and Gender Variance*, 189. Cornwall grounds this in a theological picture that affirms humanity's creative agency alongside God's: "God as creator does not create alone but in, through, and with God's creatures. God's creatures are transformative" (351).

32. Cornwall, *Constructive Theology and Gender Variance*, 226.

33. Cornwall, *Constructive Theology and Gender Variance*, 247 (emphasis added). In other places (e.g., 186), Cornwall clarifies that human beings are bodies and souls in unity. The presence of unity, however, does not seem to preclude the prioritization of identities over bodies in the presence of conflict.

The body is transforming, wasting away, and our inner identity possesses a clarity, stability, and autonomy that the body does not possess. Therefore, for Cornwall, should conflict arise, we must prioritize our inner selves over our bodies.

Trans author Jamison Green makes his perception of the necessary decision between bodies and minds especially emphatic in his narration of his transition. Thus Green: "If you're a girl in a male body, those feelings don't change just because you're in a male body. *It's your gender identity that's in the driver's seat.* . . . Trans people are greatly benefited by hormone replacement therapy (HRT) because our bodies have the internal, cellular receptors to process hormones *so that our minds and bodies connect, extending the brain into the body so we feel the connection resolving the conflict between the body and mind.*"[34] Green, like Cornwall, alludes to the malleability of the body, but his emphasis lies in the precise way the conflict between bodies and minds ought to be resolved: "extending the brain into the body," or having the body conform to that which was already inside "in the driver's seat." So if there is a conflict between bodies and minds, bodies must give way to minds.

Much of the conversation at present seems to revolve around affirmations that (1) trans identities originate from a *conflict* between bodies and minds, and (2) the way to resolve this conflict is to *prefer* or *prioritize* either the body over mind or the mind over the body.[35] It seems to me, however, that this is an inadequate way to frame matters for descriptive reasons and for normative theological reasons. More specifically, I want to argue that we have misdescribed trans experiences and misunderstood the (theological) nature of the conflict at stake.

First, these approaches to the question all betray a reductive simplification of what actually goes on in trans lives.[36] The simple forcing of a choice

---

34. Jamison Green, *Becoming a Visible Man*, 2nd ed. (Vanderbilt University Press, 2020), 8, 91 (emphases added).

35. Thus far, I have followed the authors just cited by assuming that bodies and minds are divisible entities and that minds are interchangeable with "gender identities" and "souls." All these assumptions need interrogation, especially in light of questions of personal ontology. For instance, many think that minds are features of bodies; can a division still occur on this understanding of human nature? I have not performed these interrogations, first, because the theological issues strike me as more immediately pressing, and, second, the authors in question do not seem to have metaphysical precision in their articulations of the issue, leading me to refrain from drawing metaphysical claims from texts where there may be none.

36. This should not be an option for theologians. As Scott Bader-Saye reminds us, "For theologians embedded in a tradition who wish to wrestle honestly with the experience of transgender people, the work cannot be anything but complex" ("The Transgender Body's

between bodies and minds obscures what is actually a very complex discussion surrounding the precise traits of trans identities. Talia Mae Bettcher has brought attention to the limited range of stories and theories available to trans people for understanding their genders, especially given the wide range of what it means to be trans:

> Many of the trans people I know identify as men or women or as trans men or women. Many of us have not undergone genital reconstruction surgery, and many of us do not want to; however, some of us have, and some of us do. Some of us have surgically altered our bodies in different ways (and some have not), some of us take hormones (and some do not), and some of us have had silicone injections (and some have not). For the most part, we believe our genital configurations don't undermine facts about who we are. For example, some of us trans women are very clear that we're unequivocally and entirely women (even female) while firmly disavowing any interest in genital reconstruction surgery. By contrast, some of us do not identify as men or women at all, and some of us take "trans woman" to mean someone who is indeed beyond the binary. Our self-identifications are generally complex and hard to pin down.[37]

Just as there is no one trans experience, there is also no singular response to those experiences. The complexity powerfully summarized by Bettcher is not, in actual practice, resolved by prioritizing minds or bodies, which returns us to the issue of impracticability from the introduction. In some cases, gender identities are prioritized, but in others, it seems as though no priority is obviously present. Bettcher herself notes how she has only been offered two simplistic theories for her experience,[38] and both models require making the choice between the body and the mind. But Bettcher found neither story appealing; she simply "found friendship and love" in particular communities and cultures that shared certain goods in common.[39] For Bettcher, the oversimplification of the theories on offer did not account for how she actually made sense of her experience.

In an eminently nuanced description of trans identities, sociologist Rogers Brubaker has suggested a set of heuristic categories that aim to honor

---

Grace," *Journal of the Society of Christian Ethics* 39, no. 1 [2019]: 76). Bader-Saye notes that the forced decision between bodies and identities is precisely where complexity is ignored (81).

37. Talia Mae Bettcher, "Trapped in the Wrong Theory: Rethinking Trans Oppression and Resistance," *Signs* 39, no. 2 (2014): 388–89.

38. Bettcher, "Trapped in the Wrong Theory," 383–84.

39. Bettcher, "Trapped in the Wrong Theory," 383–84.

the diversity mentioned by Bettcher. He distinguishes between three different varieties of trans experience: the "trans of migration," the "trans of between," and the "trans of beyond."[40] The trans of migration is the expression most obvious to the public eye, exemplified by figures like Caitlyn Jenner and Elliott Page. It "involves movement from one established sex/gender category to another," with the new category usually serving as "a permanent home."[41] This may take the form of a narrative according to which one is "born in the wrong body" or possesses an innate gender identity different from the one associated with one's sexed body. So, a transition in the form of migration occurs.[42] Within this category are those who see an internal gender identity as fixed, testifying to something that "is not chosen but given," and those who see that identity as fluid or more culturally determined.[43] Some perceive migration as facilitated through extensive surgery and hormone treatment; others feel no need for medical intervention, seeing an outward gender presentation as sufficient.[44] Finally, some who see themselves in terms recognizable to the trans of migration will want to identify themselves publicly as people who have transitioned, perhaps preferring to be called a "trans man" or a "trans woman," while others do not disclose their transition, making it easier to be recognized simply as a man or a woman.[45]

The "trans of between," as the name suggests, "involves a positioning of oneself with reference to the two established categories, without belonging entirely or unambiguously to either one and without moving definitively from one to the other."[46] It differs from the trans of migration in at least two ways: It receives much less public attention because of the difficulty individuals

40. Rogers Brubaker, *Trans: Gender and Race in an Age of Unsettled Identities* (Princeton University Press, 2016), 72.

41. Brubaker, *Trans*, 72, 75.

42. For examples, see Aaron Devor, *FTM: Female-to-Male Transsexuals in Society* (Indiana University Press, 2016); Jo Ivester, *Never a Girl, Always a Boy: A Family Memoir of a Transgender Journey* (She Writes, 2020).

43. Brubaker, *Trans*, 64, 76.

44. Thus Brubaker: "Since the early 1990s, however, the weakening of the binary model and of medical control has created space for new forms of transgender embodiment that do not involve genital surgery, or any surgery at all. This holds even for those who see themselves as transitioning from male to female or female to male; indeed it holds even for self-identified transsexuals, who may choose not to have genital surgery" (*Trans*, 98). Similarly, Bettcher observes how some trans individuals argue that surgical intervention, paired with a vision of trans as migration, only reinforces the "dominant understanding of what a man or a woman is" ("Trapped in the Wrong Theory," 390).

45. Brubaker, *Trans*, 78.

46. Brubaker, *Trans*, 72.

face in expressing the experience in a narrative form recognizable to others, and it sees the in-between space between a gender binary not as temporary but as a place to reside. "While the trans of migration embraces the logic of exclusive identification with a single sex/gender, . . . the trans of between refuses that exclusivity."[47] Here we might find nonbinary individuals (though they also identify themselves as beyond the gender binary).[48] Brubaker observes how occupying this in-between space can take "an oscillating form, involving movement back and forth between male and female identities or personae; a recombinatory form, defined by the selective mixing of elements from conventionally understood masculine and feminine repertoires; or a gradational form, defined by an intermediate position on a spectrum anchored and defined by the categories male and female."[49] For each of these expressions, of course, some practices and approaches might fit better than others, whether they are drag, cross-dressing, or some other form of presentation that enables the trans of between. It may even be as simple as a practice that serves as a point of connection to the gender from which the individual has departed but with which they still, on some levels, identify. As a trans man interviewed about his workplace experience says, "I have a lot of female socialization things that I'm not really willing to compromise because they're part of who I am."[50] Here, too, attitudes about surgery are complex and not formulated by one position.

Finally, Brubaker classifies the "trans of beyond," which "seeks to escape from the social and cultural force fields defined by [gender] categories."[51] This might involve finding a new gender category (*neo-categorical*), resisting gender categories (*anti-categorical*), or working for a world in which gender categories no longer exist (*post-categorical*). Recognizable neo-categorical forms are ones like ambigender, bigender, genderqueer, pangender, agender, or simply trans man or trans woman, where these last two are not identical to *man* or *woman*. One clear proponent of an anti-categorical trans identity is Christie Elan-Cane, who identifies as *un*gendered, received a mastectomy and a hysterectomy, and goes by the pronoun *per*, a shortened form of

47. Brubaker, *Trans*, 93–94.

48. See Peter Hegarty et al., "Nonbinary Gender Identities," in *Gender, Sex, and Sexualities: Psychological Perspectives*, ed. Nancy K. Dess et al. (Oxford University Press, 2018).

49. Brubaker, *Trans*, 94.

50. Catherine Connell, "Doing, Undoing, or Redoing Gender? Learning from the Workplace Experiences of Transpeople," *Gender & Society* 24, no. 1 (2010): 43.

51. Brubaker, *Trans*, 113.

person.[52] Finally, post-categorical trans individuals may take the convictions of anti-categorical theorists and partner them with a social vision and concrete prescriptions for political organization. For instance, Kate Bornstein, who was originally persuaded of the migratory model, now talks about "the need to do away with gender" and the "need to unlearn gender."[53] Bornstein says, "I've come to see gender as a divisive social construct, and the gendered body as a somewhat dubious accomplishment. . . . See, I'm told I must be a man or a woman. One or the other. Oh, it's ok to be a transsexual, say some—just don't talk about it. Don't question your gender any more, just be a woman now—you went to so much trouble—just be satisfied. I am so not satisfied."[54] Bornstein's description shows how a motivation to be post-categorically trans might take the form of a continued effort to challenge and overcome gender expressions deemed problematic or hegemonic. Continuing to challenge and question one's gender, even *after* surgery and hormone treatment, is one perceived way of doing that.

So, when we say "trans," we can mean *of migration*, *of between*, *of beyond*, or any of the subcategories within them. Or we might mean a blend of these, or not any of them at all. The point is that without conceptual clarification, talk about trans people, surgery, and—murkiest of all—transgender*ism* remains vague and unreflective. This is precisely how framing the question as a preference for either the body or the mind also remains: It may describe the situation of someone whose experience resembles a trans of migration and favors medical intervention, but it would not describe Kate Bornstein's post-categorical trans of beyond or Christie Elan-Caine's anti-categorical trans of beyond. Are these approaches systematically consistent? Probably not. Someone who finds a permanent home in another gender category will have different views than someone who is post-categorically trans. What these approaches are, in the end, is *different*. There is no one solution that can apply to all cases, and the present debate's proposal of such unilateral solutions indicates that it does not describe well enough. To that extent, claims of bodily or identity preference remain impracticable.

52. Brubaker, *Trans*, 116–17, summarizing several interviews Elan-Cane has done online. In this category, the explicit influence of Judith Butler is acknowledged, with trans writers like Riki Wilchins attributing their identities directly to Butler's work. Wilchins similarly rejects all gender categories.

53. Bornstein, *Gender Outlaw*, 46, 160.

54. Bornstein, *Gender Outlaw*, 185.

To describe well, we must return to the beginning and ask what accounts for this great diversity and complexity among trans persons. Is there something unique about trans identity that makes it so diverse, or is diversity a feature of gender identity as such? I want to argue for the latter conclusion. Trans identities are complex and variegated *precisely because the gendered goods that trans persons appropriate to form their identities are diverse and vary with context*. Many trans individuals have told their stories, and through those stories we find that navigating the gendered goods that populate our world is usually of much greater importance to trans people than a simple choice of mind over body or of body over mind. For instance, Jackson Bird, in his memoir, mentions how his having been born female "defined the name I was given, the clothes I dressed in, the way I was spoken to, the roles I was supposed to have in life, the amount I would get paid when I grew up, and so much more."[55] Clothing often plays an important role in identifying as trans and navigating the decision to transition in particular. For Bird, an eventual wardrobe transition proved to be a key part of his gender transition.[56] Of course, clothing is just one example; we might ask about hairstyles, music tastes, whether one wishes to join the Boy Scouts, the role the Harry Potter novels played in one's childhood, or other forms of social and cultural participation. The point is this: The variety of trans identities stems from the great variety of gendered goods before us. This conclusion places us right back where we began in the introduction to this book: Gender is about the organization of social goods, those goods vary widely, and our descriptive work must reflect that. Trans identities might be more than mere gender identities, but they are certainly not less.

If trans identities, like all gender identities, are about the organization of social goods to form identities, then our normative work must be focused on those social goods. The normative accounts surveyed above pay virtually no attention to gendered goods like clothing; their normative solution is detached and abstract. If someone is told to privilege body or mind, how are they supposed to think through what name suits them best or what hairstyles reflect them? Like Bettcher highlights, trans identities seem to orbit around a sense of shared social goods; our normative accounts must remain accountable to that. So, in many ways, trans questions are questions

---

55. Jackson Bird, *Sorted: Growing Up, Coming Out, and Finding My Place; A Transgender Memoir* (Tiller, 2019), xxiv.

56. Bird, *Sorted*, 227.

about how to think about gendered clothing well, or gendered food well, or gender dynamics in dating well—the very things we will discuss in later chapters of this book. The moral question pertinent to trans (and cis) persons is this: How do we navigate a world of gendered goods amid the turmoil of death?

The usual way we have come to understand trans identities is that they are a special case of complexity; if not a pathology, they are at least deviations from a norm, departures from a standard that other gender expressions meet. I believe this is misguided. Trans persons are not departures from "normal" gender experiences because, under the reign of death, the only "normal" gender experiences are the ones characterized by death's disintegration. All of us, cast into this world of gendered goods, are striving to appropriate them to our lives well. One's difficulty with fitting well into this world is not a unique failure of the individual; it is simply a result of the way the world has been mired in death. Cornwall is right, therefore, when she presses us to question this state of affairs: "I do not think that trans people are any *more* likely to be wrong about their self-narration than anyone else is, nor that trans people's self-narration should be subjected to any *more* scrutiny than anyone else's is. . . . Are trans people, by definition, more deluded about themselves, more limited in their self-understanding, than anyone else is? Individual trans people may, of course, experience self-deceit and a failure of psychic integrity, just as any cis person may do."[57] It seems to me more theologically accurate to reject the construal of the conflict as a departure from a norm because *there is, under death, no attainable or practicable norm.* Recall that under the reign of death, all of us await the redemption of our bodies. None of us, as long as death remains, is "normal." All of us experience this world and its various goods as burdensome, confusing, and challenging. To structure this world so that trans persons experience a unique sense of harm or shame because of this is to adopt a position of strength and imperviousness one cannot possess before the resurrection.

One way to see this is by inquiring what we mean by *conflict* when we describe the issue as a "conflict between gender identities and bodies." Various theories have been offered in the effort to explain why the dissonance characteristic of trans experiences might arise, including psychological theories (the conflict is a disorder of one's mental health) and biological theories (the

57. Cornwall, *Constructive Theology and Gender Variance*, 20, 150.

conflict is brought about by a variation of the brain's structure).[58] None of them has been particularly persuasive; as our understanding of trans experiences grows more and more complex, the less certain we have become about what causes the conflict under investigation.[59] Once again, we should expect this. The nature of the conflict will be as diverse as the social goods we use to understand our gender identities. Theologically, however, we have seen that there *is* an account that possesses sufficient flexibility to explain why it is that our bodies are hard to love: the reign of death and the resulting lack of friendship we have with our bodies. Trans identities are *one attempt to navigate* this lack of friendship, one way that our genders still await their redemption. Another, equally (if not more) demonstrative way that our genders require redemption are cis identities.

Recall the Pauline and Augustinian claim that what stands in the way of friendship with our bodies is death. Death, we have seen, is more than the biological cessation of life; it is the shadow that is cast over creaturely existence in the time before the eschaton. When we are raised, we will be friends with our bodies; but until then, the enduring presence of death makes that friendship tenuous. This lack of friendship caused by death, I want to claim, is the broad category under which trans experiences and all other experiences of difficulty with our bodies belong. If that is the case, we can universalize the judgment that all bodies now are liable to experience many forms of disarray. The conflict between sexed bodies and gender identities, merely one experience of this disarray, can be seen as a breakdown of friendship between us and our bodies. Viewing it this way helps us both to see what is theologically problematic about the accounts surveyed above and what a way forward requires.

Consider two friends, Jo and Amy, who have just entered into the worst argument of their long friendship. It seems genuinely intractable. On this issue, these two friends are stuck, and neither can take the other's side. It would be selfish for Jo to require Amy to abandon her convictions completely in order to resolve the argument, leaving Amy bereft of her point of view (or

58. For a helpful overview, see Eddy and Beilby, "Understanding Transgender Experiences and Identities," 21–33.

59. See Eddy and Beilby, "Understanding Transgender Experiences and Identities," 33: "In conclusion, when all of the research and the differing perspectives are taken into account, it seems that many scholars today are concluding that the specific causal mechanisms of transgender experience are exceedingly complex, are probably multidimensional, and, at this point in time, are simply something we cannot be certain about."

vice versa). Major conflicts in friendships are not usually resolved *unilaterally*; ideally, an avenue of love would be found *through* the conflict, not around it. It is a time to be creative and patient, seeking to affirm in the other what may have once seemed repellant. Jo and Amy will have resolved their argument *and* retained their friendship if both feel heard, valued, and understood and both can claim to have a stake in the solution that has been found. Just as compassion is needed in order for two friends to flourish in their relationship, so compassion is needed in order for bodies and gender identities to flourish in relation to each other. If there is a conflict between the two—and death is, theologically speaking, the most devastating of conflicts—it does not preserve the friendship to prioritize one over the other. That is a solution that goes around the conflict and sacrifices the friendship. If my mind and my body are at odds and I favor my mind over my body, or my body over my mind (as the authors cited above recommend), I have given up pursuing the friendship that will one day obtain at the resurrection of the dead.

We have good reason to think, moreover, that *both* bodies and minds are subject to the ongoing effects of death and contribute to the deathly conflict. Consider, for instance, how the Constitution of the World Health Organization defines health: "Health is a state of complete physical, mental and social well-being and not merely the absence of disease or infirmity."[60] The standard here is quite high, leading us to conclude that no one possesses the fullness of health now. This is precisely what much of the Christian tradition has said about bodies and minds in the here and now. Regarding bodies, Augustine says that "the health I now have in my flesh is not yet true health, nor does it deserve to be called so in comparison with the health I shall enjoy in everlasting rest, when this corruptible nature has been clothed in incorruption, this mortal nature in immortality."[61] Bodily health now does not compare to the bodily health we will one day possess. A simple appeal to the goodness of bodies in Genesis forgets that sin has exercised its reign through death, even for Christians.

The same goes for a unilateral preference for minds, identities, or even souls. Our minds are in deep need of redemption, just as much as our bodies

60. Constitution of the World Health Organization, April 7, 1948, https://www.who.int/about/governance/constitution.

61. Augustine, *Expositions on the Psalms, 33–50*, trans. Maria Boulding, The Works of Saint Augustine: A Translation for the 21st Century 3/16 (New City, 2000), 150. For an insightful discussion of Augustine's exegesis in relation to bodily health, see Simeon Zahl, "Sin and Bodily Illness in the Psalms," *Horizons in Biblical Theology* 42 (2020): 186–207.

(Rom. 12:2). Attention to the persistent and devastating challenges faced by, for instance, those with lifelong depression evidences this.[62] Our minds can quickly become hostile enemies. I am not saying, to be clear, that trans identities are just another form of mental illness; that would return us to the pathologizing tendencies common to previous discussions that I am rejecting. Rather, I am trying to show that gender identities are *not* in the "driver's seat" if that is taken to mean that they possess a stability or permanence that we should prefer over our bodies. As the definition of health just cited reminds us, *no one* is healthy of mind and of body. In the conclusion, I will discuss compassion in fuller detail, explaining that solidarity is one of its key features. My aim here is to specify one avenue of theologically oriented solidarity that fosters compassion. Apart from the solidarity of recognizing our common plight, in other words, compassion is not possible, let alone friendship with our bodies.

That is our state: redeemed bodies and minds that await the fullness of redemption. Death has been defeated, but not by us; as a result, our experience of liberation from death remains at a distance. Sonderegger puts these Augustinian insights poignantly: Augustine's world is a

> world ringed about and hemmed in by guilt and poverty and need. Everywhere in Augustine's polemics, Christians are shown as "crying out" to the Lord for mercy, for deliverance from intolerable burden and shame, for liberty from the prison of guilt. The clean divisions that sit down so squarely in the Pelagian landscape, so pleasing to the eye and mind, have broken down radically under Augustine's hand. The world has now become an enormous hospital ward, the whole creation groaning under the weight of suffering and death. We human beings are patients, to be sure—the patients in greatest calamity, huddled into a "mass of perdition." But the whole creation lies under the curse of Adam: cursed be the ground because of you. . . . From this condition, creatures call out for salvation.[63]

This is a pessimistic conclusion, and it is intended to be so. Every one of us suffers from this debilitating constraint of death. Until we are raised again, friendship with the body is not attainable in its entirety. As a result, for all of us—trans persons and (dubiously named "normal") cis persons alike—gender

62. See Tasia Scrutton, *Christianity and Depression* (SCM Press, 2020).
63. Sonderegger, "Finitude and Death," 390.

awaits redemption. We must regularly make clear the solidarity that we share in the effort to cultivate compassionate care.

In the meantime, is there anything we can do? I have already noted how trans identities are tasked with the same burden as any gender identity: navigating this social world, with its gendered goods dripping in death, in a way that expresses the love of God. While this is a pessimistic place to conclude, I believe it is a *hopeful* pessimism, and its hopefulness lies precisely in its ability to facilitate compassionate relationships here and now. We are all struggling with the complexity and difficulty of loving our gendered world and its deathliness, and we can recognize one another's struggle with compassion. Couenhoven points out how this appreciation of death and its eschatological deliverance "frees us to 'err' on the side of mercy. . . . This state of bondage points to a diminished freedom, which should give us compassion for sinners, who are typically not only agents of sin but sufferers of the same."[64] Zahl articulates it as follows: "Properly articulated, the doctrine of the Fall and its corollary, the doctrine of original sin, allow us to have universal compassion on ourselves and on one another in our sickness and our suffering, without evacuating sufferings of moral seriousness."[65] If it is true that sin and death have really done this much damage to us and to the creation as a whole, we can see one another as objects of compassion, recognizing one another through our common wounds as we heal in God's hospital. I am going to struggle to think about my clothing well, and I will engage in gendered clothing practices that produce death. Knowing that, I can be merciful to my neighbor, trans or cis, who is also struggling to navigate adornment practices in a manner that testifies to the life of Jesus Christ. Though our clothing struggles will differ, they will differ not in kind but in particularities. We are all struggling in a shared world of gendered goods. And for that, we can look at one another compassionately, encouraging a faithful and hopeful engagement that shows forth glimmers of death's end. Only through compassion can we see that "love is strong as death" (Song 8:6).

This is especially needed from the churches. Sociologically, sexual identity and gender identity serve as some of the strongest indicators of whether or

---

64. Jesse Couenhoven, "The Justice in Mercy: A Hopeful Pessimist's Account," *Journal of Religious Ethics* 48, no. 3 (2020): 412, 409. Couenhoven goes on to say that erring on the side of mercy can look like limiting how much blame we place on others, reshaping our punitive responses, or generally seeking to promote hope (409).

65. Zahl, "Sin and Bodily Illness in the Psalms," 203.

not someone attends a church regularly.[66] Though there are various ways to interpret this data, it would not be a stretch to claim that gender identity has become such an indicative issue because trans persons have not experienced compassion in churches. Sometimes this is because of explicitly abusive behavior; the absence of such behavior does not, however, indicate the presence of compassion. Very often, mercilessness is felt in the unspoken rules of a community: how to dress, how to speak, what a normal income amounts to, whether you are a member of the most represented type of family. Church communities committed to Christ's compassion must be willing to examine their unspoken rules. Such standards have communicated to trans persons that they possess no social capital in churches. This is not compassion. The merciful embrace of the vulnerable and "the least of these" (Matt. 25:40) ought to characterize the church. Churches do this when they actively communicate that they value the presence of trans persons in their midst. This is not a matter of being affirming or not, though valuable conversations about what it means to affirm or not affirm must be had; ostensibly, an affirming church can be quite merciless, while a nonaffirming one can communicate welcome and grace. It is more a matter of being aware of the unacknowledged social stratifications that occur around gendered goods. How does the church speak about trans identities? Are they aware of some of the distinctions made above? Would a trans person be invited to a meal, experience hospitality, be embraced? To far too many of these questions, the answer is a resounding no.

Compassion in the face of death is lost if we simply opt for the solutions promoted by the authors discussed above. According to this hopefully pessimistic picture, there are no quick fixes, perhaps no solutions at all, until our bodies are raised. We cannot remove the tumor of death ourselves. We cannot even stop its spread. What we can do is be compassionate to one another. Too often cis persons have called trans persons out of a hole dug for them by those who have cast them as victims of pathological psychological anomalies or as insouciant individualists who do not care for any sort of moral order. By contrast, in this section, I have attempted to encourage those who experience their gender identities as relatively unproblematic to

---

66. In their study of individuals who have left church in the United States, Jim Davis, Michael Graham, and Ryan Burge claim that "sexual orientation is a strong indicator of church attendance" and that their parents' "intolerant attitudes about gender" was a leading reason listed by young people who said they left the church because of their relationship with their parents. See *The Great Dechurching: Who's Leaving, Why Are They Going, and What Will It Take to Bring Them Back?* (Zondervan, 2023), 23, 92.

see that they are in a hole together with trans people, for we have all fallen in. This hole is defined by sin and death. Thankfully, we know that we will one day rise again. Until then, all we can do is respond with compassion to one another as fellow patients in God's hospital. Importantly, this means that there is no such thing as, in Abigail Shrier's unfortunate words, "irreversible damage."[67] Death is the worst possible kind of damage, and even it is not irreversible. The beauty of the Christian story about bodies is not that some of us are not damaged and some are. The truth is that we are all damaged, yet Christ's resurrection promises a resurrection for the rest of us, one in which all damage is restored and healed.

This is particularly important for trans persons. Though I have talked about death as *more* than the biological cessation of life, for many trans folks, the end of biological life is a persistent threat, whether through violence from others or through suicide, often brought about by the devastating isolation, bullying, harm, harassment, bias, income disparity, assault, or other forms of domination directed at trans persons.[68] I have argued that our common experience of death in our minds and bodies should summon a response of compassion, but compassion must be specific. An awareness of the way trans neighbors might experience death as a much more proximate reality should call forth compassion as a first response. I have sought to argue that, rather than simply claiming we should prefer bodies over minds, we ought to reevaluate how we understand the nature of the conflict between bodies and minds: It is a conflict caused by death, and our response should mirror the response of the one who came to rescue humanity from sin and death. That response is compassion.

Conclusion

In this chapter I have taken our bodies as the focus. I have sought to show that bodies are hard to love now because they await a coming redemption,

67. Abigail Shrier, *Irreversible Damage: The Transgender Craze Seducing Our Daughters* (Regnery, 2020).

68. For discussion, see Cody J. Sanders, *Christianity, LGBTQ Suicide, and the Souls of Queer Folk* (Lexington Books, 2020); Justin Tanis, "The Power of 41%: A Glimpse into the Life of a Statistic," *American Journal of Orthopsychiatry* 86, no. 4 (2016): 373–77. The title of Tanis's article is a reference to results from a study conducted by National Transgender Discrimination Survey showing that 41 percent of trans respondents claimed to have attempted suicide at some point in their lives, which is staggeringly higher than the 1.6 percent of the general population who say they have at some point attempted suicide.

summoning us to greater patience and compassion. The current state of affairs for humans is that we lack friendship with our bodies on account of death, which is more than the end of biological life. Death reigns in this "present evil age" (Gal. 1:4), and though we have been set free from death's rule, the benefits of that freedom come only at the introduction of death's antithesis: resurrection. As a result, we should expect conflict with our bodies and our minds; friendship has been lost and is being recovered. Human effort cannot eliminate death; rather, human effort is to be directed toward compassion for those who continue to feel death's oppressive hand. This is our conflict; but in trans discussions, many argue that this conflict should be resolved by favoring either the body or one's gender identity. I have sought to show that this is neither adequate to the complexity of experiences described by trans persons nor theologically responsible to the true condition of sin and death. Our bodies and minds will be friends, but they are not now. What we have now is compassion shown to us by Christ and to one another in Christ. Compassion is the truest response to the depths of death.

Readers looking for an argument that can be summed up as either "trans affirming" or "trans nonaffirming" (let alone one that either denounces "cultural confusion" or aims to promote the "right side of history") will hopefully not have found what they were looking for. My intent has been to not represent either, especially since such a reduction of options does not respect the moral complexity of this topic. No moral question of sufficient complexity admits of only two options. Yet, too many participants in these debates present questions of importance to gender as having only "yes" or "no" as viable answers, and in doing so, they reveal themselves to be more interested in public positioning than in helping those looking for God's mercy. In "conservative" claims to defend the body, priority will be given to sin and death in relation to trans identities, all while omitting compassion. In "liberal" claims to defend gender identities, compassion will be at the forefront, but no mention is made of the conditions that necessitate compassion in the first place—namely, sin and death. I hope to have shown that these are theologically inadequate responses. Love and eschatology require us to testify against the weight of death in compassionate love. Holding the conversation in the usual simplistic terms (to affirm or not to affirm) obscures the true task of gendered individuals: to engage the world of social goods they encounter with a love aimed at the world to come. Merely adopting a position, especially at the level of culture wars, can give the impression that the work is done. I am suggesting that it may not have even begun.

In the end, trans identities are gender identities. They might be more than that, but they are certainly not less. Like other gender identities, they navigate a world of social goods and organize them into an identity. Like other gender identities, they are fundamentally tasked with understanding the goods already present in this world—that is, they do not *decide* which social goods are on offer. Very often, trans folks need to navigate a world where the clothes, music, makeup, hairstyles, social-media trends, and so on are not chosen by them but set on display by marketers who aim to make a profit. How does that fact complicate all of our navigation of gendered goods? For that we need a discussion of gender and marketing.

3

The World Around Us Is Not of Our Own Making

Gender, Marketing, and Love

When I first suggested that Love was the way to transform business, grown CEOs blushed and slid down behind their annual accounts. But I kept at them. I knew it was Love that was missing. I knew that Love was the only way to ante up the emotional temperature and create the new kinds of relationships brands needed. I knew that Love was the only way businesses could respond to the rapid shift in control to consumers. Once we got comfortable with saying the "L" word, we delved more deeply into understanding its breadth and relevance to business. We wondered about a way to rank brands or anything else according to the intensity of Love people felt for them. The really great things would be placed near the top with lesser ones towards the bottom.[1]

—Kevin Roberts, former CEO of advertising agency Saatchi & Saatchi

In 2004, Kevin Roberts published his ideas about "lovemarks," a marketing method that centered its attention on the loves of the consumer. Marketing goods according to the objects of our loves, proposed Roberts, is how brands attract the loyalty of their buyers in a way that extends beyond a cold and calculated formula of exchange. In doing this, Roberts effectively

1. Kevin Roberts, *Lovemarks: The Future Beyond Brands* (PowerHouse Books, 2004), 57.

articulates an *ordo amoris* for marketers, telling them to be attentive to the intensity of love buyers felt for what was sold. Why just sell a cup of coffee, a hamburger, or a chicken sandwich when Starbucks can sell the well-being of its employees, Burger King the celebration of sexual freedom, or Chick-fil-A Christian authenticity? These ideas landed Roberts a 430-million-dollar deal with JCPenney, and they broadened the anthropology of marketers to include the loves of consumers.

At first glance, and for many of those in the industry, this is a positive shift. After all, who doesn't want sandwiches with a conscience, especially if they greatly increase brand loyalty? Upon closer inspection, however, this attention to the loves of a buyer tells a more insidious tale. Rather than giving the consumer greater choice by attending to the deepest aspects of who they are, the attempt to purchase the loves of a person reduces their freedom through the attempt to shape and convert their love to wrongly ordered ends. "All the clients and the bosses care about," writes Joseph Turow, "is whether they reach their targets with an appropriate return on investment."[2] A bit more polemically, Jean Kilbourne asserts that the job of marketers is "very specific: They are to use all of their powers of persuasion, explicit and implicit, to sell a particular product. That's all! No moral, no obligation to any other set of values."[3] Although marketing *claims* to be about providing persuasive goods and services to a segment of the market, their tactics for identifying their targeted segment really serve to limit and commodify the loves of human beings. The result is a reduction of available goods for identity formation, leading us to become the people marketers design us to be.

The focus of this chapter is gender and marketing, and we are going to see that marketing is hardly passive: It makes use of a highly intelligent set of strategies for capturing our loves and limiting our freedom. The worlds we encounter run the risk of being carefully cultivated by directors of marketing, and if our identities are shaped by the organization of social goods by means of our loves, then uncritical inhabitation of this world runs the risk of handing over our identities to those who stand to profit from them. The order of my loves will have been conformed to an order most favorable to those controlling the goods I see on my Instagram feed or in aisles of the

2. Joseph Turow, *The Daily You: How the New Advertising Industry Is Defining Your Identity and Your Worth* (Yale University Press, 2011), 9.

3. Jean Kilbourne, *Deadly Persuasion: Why Women and Girls Must Fight the Addictive Power of Advertising* (Free Press, 1999), 27–28.

grocery store. Unpacking this picture and making an argument for what I will call the strong theory of marketing will be the focus of the first section of this chapter. In the second section, I will show how it applies to gendered goods. The goods available for our organization into a gender identity have been placed there strategically, and that strategy is not designed to help us become better women and men; it is designed to bring in profits. Though I buy products whose brand identities align with my political beliefs, and those with opposing political beliefs buy products whose brand identities align with theirs, we are both doing essentially the same thing—namely, lining the pockets of the wealthy. That is what marketing strategy is designed to do.

What does virtuous gendered living look like in such a world? The third section of this chapter will argue for a constructive approach to navigating a marketed gendered world. Perhaps counterintuitively, it will argue neither for a revolution nor for Christian sectarianism. The world, even if infiltrated by marketers, is still God's. Theological warnings about contemporary economic practices must be tempered by an affirmation that creaturely goods are not intrinsically evil.[4] All the same, given the bleak picture of marketing I will paint, we should still hope for change. The response to the ubiquity of sin is compassion, which itself can bring change. This raises the question about what Christian hope can mean for systemic change. With authors like Cornel West and Luke Bretherton, I will argue that it looks like *conversion*. In the face of the restricted freedoms gendered advertising presents, Christians must work to expand our options for gendered living.

Focusing on gendered marketing will, I hope, offer a bird's-eye view that leads us to question the kinds of debates we have. Often debates orbit around whether one gender should wear the clothing of another gender without investigating who decided what clothes get placed on the racks in the first place. Or again, churches hold men's events oriented around red meat without thinking of how the association between men and meat was produced historically by those who sell the meat. Examples proliferate here, but it seems to me that often we are stuck in the *what* questions of gender without asking

4. Thus William Cavanaugh warns, "There is nothing inherently idolatrous about material culture as such, and we need to avoid simplistic denunciations of materialism, as opposed to a supposedly more salutary spirituality or religion or transcendence. . . . Not just material things but the desire for them become gods, because they take the place of the worship of the true God" (*The Uses of Idolatry* [Oxford University Press, 2024], 286, 281).

about their *why* and their *how*. As I have argued,[5] however, the Christian task, when it comes to gender, is not so much about judging *what* gendered goods ought to be loved (though that will always have some role to play) as it is about questioning *why* we love them and *how*. Focusing on gender and marketing is one way to do that.

The Nature of Marketing and the Enchanting Limitation of Our Loves

The argument of this chapter must begin with a clarification of what marketing is. Thankfully, theologian and former researcher in marketing Emily Beth Hill has provided a magisterial engagement with this topic in her book *Marketing and Christian Proclamation in Theological Perspective*. She notes how marketing has developed out of a historical shift from focusing on the product being sold to focusing on the consumer,[6] evidenced in the move from ads that had paragraphs of information about the products to ads that promise something bigger for the buyer. But marketing involves more than advertisements. Hill notes how there are four main components to marketing: (1) the target market, (2) customer needs, (3) integrated marketing, and (4) profitability.[7]

First, when identifying their target market, marketers generally want to know *who* is buying, *how* they are buying, *what criteria* they use to make their choice, and *where and when* they choose to buy.[8] Second, marketers account for customer needs. These involve both the needs the consumer already possesses when engaging a product *and* the needs that the product can generate from stimulation.[9] "I didn't know I needed that" is the optimal consumer response sought by marketers focusing on this component of the job. Taken together, identifying target markets and needs generates an important element of marketing often referred to as "market segmentation." Hill describes it as follows: "The goal is to create many segments within the population, each of

5. See Fellipe do Vale, *Gender as Love: A Theological Account of Human Identity, Embodied Desire, and Our Social Worlds* (Baker Academic, 2023), 167.

6. For a detailed account of this historical development that divides the historical moments with more precision, see William Leiss et al., *Social Communication in Advertising*, 4th ed. (Routledge, 2018), part 1.

7. Emily Beth Hill, *Marketing and Christian Proclamation in Theological Perspective* (Lexington Books / Fortress Academic, 2021), 73.

8. Hill, *Marketing and Christian Proclamation*, 78.

9. Hill, *Marketing and Christian Proclamation*, 79.

which has similar needs and desires, but are also large enough groups to be targeted efficiently and effectively."[10] Through focus groups, neuromarketing, the placement of cookies on web browsers, the tracking of clicks on web pages, the recording of search-engine terms, the cataloging of website registration forms, the monitoring of social media activity, the gathering of locations through phones, and an ever-evolving arsenal of approaches, marketers are able to cultivate a fairly sophisticated profile of consumers and their interests. From these metrics—provided by firms whose main service is to collect and sell such information—companies are able to determine who is a desirable target and who is not.[11] Ads are then delivered to a specific *type* of person at a specific place and at a specific time. You might receive ads for expensive gym equipment before your YouTube video, while your fellow church member might get fast-food ads, but both will be based on inferences and assumptions made on your respective profiles.

This leads into Hill's third component of marketing, integrated marketing: Once marketers have decided "which consumers to target and how to position their products and services within that market," they "move on to plan and implement specific strategies to reach that target, aiming to satisfy both the needs of the market segment and their own organizational goals such as sales growth, loyalty, or profit."[12] The goal is to "apply detailed knowledge of the consumer in order to communicate and interact with the consumer in the most relevant, engaging way," measured by making sales, generating relationships, or other forms of value.[13] It is in integrated marketing that one encounters the "four *p*'s"—product, price, promotion, and place—and it is also where advertising figures into the equation. So far, the entire mechanism of marketing has operated behind the scenes, often without the notice of actual consumers. When it comes time to surface, a company ideally presents a brand that communicates publicly exactly what they intend. Hill notes that there are two major theories about the effectiveness of advertising, a strong theory and a weak theory: "According to the strong theory, advertising is persuasive enough to actually convince people to buy a product they have not purchased before. . . . On the other hand, the weak theory claims that advertising does not have a direct, immediate effect on sales but primarily increases brand

10. Hill, *Marketing and Christian Proclamation*, 80–81.
11. Turow, *Daily You*, 96.
12. Hill, *Marketing and Christian Proclamation*, 97.
13. Hill, *Marketing and Christian Proclamation*, 100.

awareness."[14] In other words, those who hold to the strong theory maintain that marketing somehow *causes* individuals to purchase a good through its communicative actions, while the weak theory maintains that this attributes too much power to ads, which only inform the people who already wish to be informed. This is a debate about the amount of human agency involved in purchasing: Do ads persuade an individual, maybe even *coerce* them? Or do they merely *inform* that individual about the goods available for purchase?[15] Both strong and weak theories ultimately agree on Hill's fourth component of marketing—namely, that the end goal of marketing is profitability.[16]

For the purposes of this chapter, I will focus on two elements of this complicated process: the strong theory of advertising (the view that ads do not merely provide information but are sufficiently strong to cause customers to do certain things, even if ads are not the *sole* causes) and market segmentation (the creation of categories of people that indicate their purchasing potential). By creating these segments and employing strategies aimed at invoking our loves, it seems to me that the strong theory is likely correct. Advertisers are not just informing; in Hill's words, marketing "wants to exploit individuals by telling them who they are."[17] Ads teach us to find our identities in our consumption, and then they limit the range of possible objects for consumption, thereby limiting our identities. While we play a substantial part in the purchase, ads have already exercised an influence on our perception of who we are and thus make a sizable causal contribution. As Kevin Roberts admits, advertisers know that we are what we love, and they have chosen to commodify this basic human reality to reshape our identities as consumers.

One way to argue for the strong theory is to notice *how* market segmentation occurs. Noticing how marketing firms gather their information on consumers and the criteria by which they sort them to determine who is a desirable target reveals "a fundamental lack of audience respect on the part of the media-buying system even as its practitioners use rhetorics of consumer power to hide it."[18] This is the central argument of media-systems professor Joseph Turow's book *The Daily You: How the New Advertising Industry*

14. Hill, *Marketing and Christian Proclamation*, 107.
15. For a history of this debate, see Turow, *Daily You*, 15–17.
16. Hill, *Marketing and Christian Proclamation*, 105.
17. Hill, *Marketing and Christian Proclamation*, 179.
18. Turow, *Daily You*, 18.

Is Defining Your Identity and Your Worth, along with his later books.[19] If we understand the processes of market segmentation and targeting, we will see that marketing is no passive process. Rather, through highly advanced techniques like biometric voice recognition and tracking shopping patterns, marketers are able to discern the fundamental pattern of our desires, predict where and when a successful purchase or promising relationship will occur, and place products and ads in the places of greatest success. The result is a world where the goods we encounter have been diligently and carefully coordinated to attract the segment to which we belong. Only people like us will see this ad, because only people like us will buy what is communicated or get hooked by this message. In the end, argues Turow, we are only as free as marketers allow us to be.[20]

Another angle to take, and one that connects with the theological interests of this book very closely, is to notice how marketing aims to tap into affective states in the consumer to shape their identities.[21] This is not something kept hidden by marketing firms; as the Nielsen measurement firm declares, "We're ruled by our emotions, and so are the ads we watch."[22] They go on to show how their company has developed sophisticated measurement techniques for emotional responses to ads, promising greater sales when these are taken into account. The aim, says Hill, is to cultivate an "emotional

---

19. See Joseph Turow, *The Aisles Have Eyes: How Retailers Track Your Shopping, Strip Your Privacy, and Define Your Power* (Yale University Press, 2017); Joseph Turow, *The Voice Catchers: How Marketers Listen in to Exploit Your Feelings, Your Privacy, and Your Wallet* (Yale University Press, 2021).

20. See Turow, *Daily You*, 18: "It becomes clear . . . that these spaces are constrained and channeled by industry logics shaped by new media-buying mindsets that speak directly to whether, when, and how items are presented to particular audiences for attention. Increasingly, it is the media-buying system that is the prime mover in the emerging digital world." For another angle to this kind of argument, see the work of Sut Jhally, especially *The Spectacle of Accumulation: Essays in Culture, Media, and Politics* (Peter Lang, 2006); and Sut Jhally, *The Codes of Advertising: Fetishism and the Political Economy of Meaning in the Consumer Society* (Routledge, 2014). Finally, for a broader argument with the same conclusions, see George A. Akerlof and Robert J. Shiller, *Phishing for Phools: The Economics of Manipulation and Deception* (Princeton University Press, 2016).

21. For a particularly strong constructionist account of this, see Roberta Sassatelli, *Consumer Culture: History, Theory and Politics* (SAGE, 2007), 109: "Through consumption then, social actors not only contribute to the fixing of a series of cultural classifications, not only express themselves through symbols or communicate their social positions, but also constitute themselves and their social identities."

22. "We're Ruled by Our Emotions, and So Are the Ads We Watch," Nielsen, January 2016, https://www.nielsen.com/insights/2016/were-ruled-by-our-emotions-and-so-are-the-ads-we-watch/.

connection" in order to shape the consumer's identity: "In a very real way, then, brands have captured human love and worship and turned them into capital."[23] Because the acquisition of our loves is a stated part of market segmentation and advertising, it seems that the claims to mere information made by the weak theory are unsustainable.[24] "When you see what you want, it possesses you," states an ad for a Capezio handbag.[25] If a handbag is looking to possess me by seizing my loves, I should not mistake it for a passive entity.

One of the first feminist critiques of advertising was provided by Jean Kilbourne, and she flags the emotionally formative nature of ads by focusing specifically on how they exploit addiction, which she sees as a species of distorted love. For Kilbourne, advertising "turns lovers into things and things into lovers" by exploiting "our very real and human desires."[26] Kilbourne is aware that what brings someone to the point of purchase is a complex set of affective pulls, and one of the strongest forms of these affective pulls is addiction. She argues, "The basic message of advertising . . . is that an individual has a need or a problem that a product can meet or fix," and if that need is addictive, then the product will be purchased with high frequency.[27] This is emphatically true of products *designed* to be addictive, like cigarettes and alcohol, and Kilbourne does not mince her words about the true aim of the billions of dollars spent each year for ads in these industries: "Every time an addict recovers, someone loses money, whether it's the pusher on the corner or the pushers in the boardrooms. This is the bottom line."[28] Profitability remains the telos of marketing, and Kilbourne draws relentless attention to the fact that marketers are aiming to profit from dangerous and addictive products. She wrote before the cultural takeover of iPhones, but it is not hard to see how such considerations can apply just as easily to them. Emotional pull is involved in marketing, but in the worst ways.

---

23. Hill, *Marketing and Christian Proclamation*, 102, 105.

24. Thus Hill: "This reveals that marketing is not neutral but a vast network of activities that intercede in daily life to guide individuals toward the ends of business and economic growth in a way that feels like freedom and self-expression" (*Marketing and Christian Proclamation*, 76).

25. Pictured in Kilbourne, *Deadly Persuasion*, 87. Though dated, Kilbourne's book is filled with examples of ads that stretch the credulity of passive advertising beyond a breaking point.

26. Kilbourne, *Deadly Persuasion*, 27, 77. Later printings of Kilbourne's book change its title, tellingly, to *Can't Buy My Love*.

27. Kilbourne, *Deadly Persuasion*, 294.

28. Kilbourne, *Deadly Persuasion*, 229.

Kilbourne is aware that misusing emotional pull is not a conscious endeavor, either on the part of marketers or on the part of consumers. Marketers are not deviously scheming in their boardrooms to foster addiction in children, and we are not consciously deciding the intensity with which we will attach ourselves to our phones. These dynamics operate at the subterranean affective level, which is why marketers can say that they are not responsible for choices made by consumers to develop a dependency on addictive products. "Above all," writes Kilbourne, "addiction is a romance, a love affair—a relationship that goes terribly wrong. . . . We end up looking for love in all the wrong places—which could be the very definition of addiction."[29] Ads seek to reach us through our loves (by playing emotional music, by showing an estranged family coming together over a meal, by depicting inspiring moments of human generosity). Since this is so, we cannot conclude that they are merely informing us of their products. The attempt to generate an emotional response is not merely an informative exercise. Rather, with an appropriate theological anthropology, we can see that they are operating on a more fundamentally exploitative level.

In this section, I have sought to argue for a fairly strong theory of marketing because I am persuaded of a fairly strong theology of human love in identity formation.[30] By tapping into our loves and segmenting them into categories into which we fit, marketing actively shapes our identities in the effort to make us the kind of people who bolster profit. If they are interested in virtue or the promotion of our common lives, it is only accidentally the case. There is nothing intrinsic to marketing that requires the formation of virtuous buyers or a proper orientation to a holy telos. What *is* intrinsic to marketing is an attempt to gather information to generate highly specific market segments on the basis of their loves. The result is that our identities are commodified, our freedom is restricted, and the world of goods that surrounds us is not our own. It has been put there to make us into the kinds of people desired by those who stand to benefit by those categories. Gender categories, as the next section will uncover, are no exception.

---

29. Kilbourne, *Deadly Persuasion*, 233. Here Kilbourne is speaking of her own experience with alcoholism and addiction to cigarettes. For helpful accounts of addiction along these lines, see Kent Dunnington, *Addiction and Virtue: Beyond the Models of Disease and Choice* (IVP Academic, 2011); and Cynthia Geppert, *Addiction and the Captive Will: A Colloquy Between Neuroscience and Augustine of Hippo* (T&T Clark, 2024).

30. For those details, see do Vale, *Gender as Love*, chap. 5.

Gender and Marketing: Disney Princesses, Barbies, and . . . Feminism?

Many people probably do not remember a world without the hegemony of Disney princesses. But such a world *did* exist, at least until December 1999.[31] It was then that Andy Mooney, the recently appointed Scottish chairman of Disney Consumer Products, attended a Disney On Ice event where he witnessed masses of little girls wearing homemade princess dresses. To a marketer like Mooney, this was a massive missed opportunity for profit. The next day, he began work on the Princess Project, which was the beginning of Disney's efforts to market their characters separately from a movie's release. Before long, the ubiquity of Disney princesses, with which we are so familiar, emerged (including their notorious inability to make eye contact with one another, ostensibly to protect brand cohesion). It is an understatement to say that Mooney's strategy was financially successful. By 2009, his Princess Project had made Disney four billion dollars. Simultaneously, he altered the range of possible exemplars for little girls worldwide.

Peggy Orenstein, who has dedicated much of her writing to the cultural world of girls in the United States, became aware of the way Mooney's advertising strategy fixes rigid gender norms during a conversation with her then three-year-old daughter at the supermarket. After responding with suspicion to her daughter's admiration of aisles and aisles of Disney princess merchandise, Orenstein wondered, "What was it about my answers that confounded her? What if, instead of realizing: Aha! Cinderella is a symbol of the patriarchal oppression of all women, another example of corporate mind control and power-to-the-people!, my three-year-old was thinking, *Mommy doesn't want me to be a girl*?"[32] To her daughter, what it meant to be a girl was a matter of responding to and appropriating the social goods *meant* for girls in the aisles of the grocery store, goods placed there by the likes of Andy Mooney. Orenstein goes on to wonder,

> From the time she is born—in truth, well before—parents are bombarded with zillions of little decisions, made consciously or not, that will shape their daughter's ideas and understanding of her femininity, her sexuality, her self. How do

31. This story is recounted in Peggy Orenstein, *Cinderella Ate My Daughter: Dispatches from the Front Lines of the New Girlie-Girl Culture* (Harper, 2011), 13–14.

32. Peggy Orenstein, "What's Wrong with Cinderella?," in *Don't Call Me Princess: Essays on Girls, Women, Sex, and Life* (Harper, 2018), 326 (emphasis added).

> you instill pride and resilience in her? Do you shower her with pink heart-strewn onesies? Reject the Disney Princess Pull-Ups for Lightning McQueen? Should you let your three-year-old wear child-friendly nail polish to pre-school? What's your policy on the latest Disney Channel "it" girl? Old Dora versus New Dora? Does a pink soccer ball celebrate girlhood? Do pink TinkerToys expand or contract its definition? And even if you think the message telegraphed by a pink Scrabble set with titles on the box top that spell "F-A-S-H-I-O-N" is a tad retrograde, what are you supposed to do about it? Lock your daughter in a tower?[33]

Orenstein is identifying the way advertising reinforces the social categories that make up our gendered expectations. We cannot help but absorb some sense of what it means to be women and men from the ubiquitously marketed goods around us. In the terms developed in the previous section, the market segmentation that identifies the loves by which sellers seek to lure consumers often takes on distinctly gendered categorization.[34] We are segmented, in other words, by our genders according to the variations of masculinity and femininity marketers believe sell the best.

In her history of advertising, Juliann Sivulka states that though marketers have employed a variety of variables to distinguish desirable targets, "segmenting by gender was the most pervasive."[35] There are several reasons for this, some of them pragmatic and others socially formative. Pragmatically, profits increase significantly when goods are split by gender.[36] If a toy cannot be passed down from an older sibling to a younger one because of its gender markers, there is a good chance that parents will buy two toys instead of only one. Orenstein cites a marketing executive at LeapFrog who told her of their identification of the "pink factor": "If you make a pink baseball bat, parents will buy one for their daughter. . . . Then, if they subsequently have a son, they'll have to buy a second bat in a different color. Or, if they have a boy first and then a daughter, they'll want to buy a pink one for their precious little girl.

33. Orenstein, *Cinderella Ate My Daughter*, 7.

34. For an early argument with this conclusion, see Erving Goffman, *Gender Advertisements* (Harper & Row, 1979).

35. Juliann Sivulka, *Soap, Sex, and Cigarettes: A Cultural History of American Advertising*, 2nd ed. (Cengage, 2012), 219.

36. See Orenstein, *Cinderella Ate My Daughter*, 37: "Splitting kids, or adults, or for that matter penguins, into ever-tinier categories has proved a surefire way to boost profits. So, where there was once a big group that was simply called 'kids,' we now have toddlers, preschoolers, tweens, young adolescents, and older adolescents, each with their own developmental/marketing profile."

Either way, you double your sales."[37] Market segmentation by gender, sheerly on account of the math involved, makes a company more profit.

There are also elements of gender marketing that are more obviously aimed at the formation of our identities. Through pointedly persuasive communicative acts, marketers use idealized portrayals of women and men to trigger the expressions of love that are most likely to compel us to act. Our loves can appear in different manifestations—as fear, shame, guilt, embarrassment, aspiration, inferiority, or any other emotional yearning for some good—and gendered ads are designed to activate these loves in the effort to rectify them with their product. Sociologist Anthony Cortese argues as much: "To be successful, an ad must be persuasive on two levels. First, it should raise your anxiety level. It should persuade you that you need something; it should make you feel guilty, inferior, or somehow 'less than.' Second, an ad must provide the solution. If an ad captures you on both of these levels you are generally hooked."[38] To raise anxiety and insecurity, ads present "culturally sanctioned ideal types of masculinity and femininity" that "subscribe to very limited notions of what constitutes femininity."[39] Connecting these loves with one's product has been shown to increase sales dramatically. Nobody actually looks like a Disney princess—it is anatomically impossible, apart from the removal of several vital organs—but that does not prevent many from aspiring to through the products they buy.

In the last section, we saw authors like Emily Beth Hill, Joseph Turow, and Jean Kilbourne argue that marketing restricts our freedom. William Cavanaugh summarizes their conclusions well: "Marketing is not robotic control but rather sets the parameters in which individual choices are made."[40] We are only as free as they allow us to be because the goods available for purchase are restricted by market forces. This is also the case for gender. Through these persuasive communicative gestures, the gendered goods available for our organization into an identity are a limited set. The idealized women and men we persistently see in ads "reinforce the facile, and yet insidious, gender stereotypes, as usual taking blithely for granted not just the difference but the inequality between men and women. . . . Any deviance from the norms

37. Orenstein, *Cinderella Ate My Daughter*, 43.

38. Anthony J. Cortese, *Provocateur: Images of Women and Minorities in Advertising*, 4th ed. (Rowman & Littlefield, 2015), 76.

39. Cortese, *Provocateur*, 65, 66.

40. Cavanaugh, *Uses of Idolatry*, 321.

regulating acceptable visibility of gender and of other intersecting axes of identification would receive strong reaction, and sometimes advertising plays precisely on this."[41] It is a familiar feminist apothegm that we can be only what we can see; advertising restricts our freedom so that we can see only what marketers want us to see, with the result that we can be only what makes them profit.

Consider an example. In her history of women and cars, Nancy Nichols notes how, in the early twentieth century, women were generally discouraged from driving gasoline-powered vehicles on account of the vehicles' unsafe construction. Specifically, many saw women as unfit for driving cars because they "believed that the vibrations from the motor would cause sexual arousal, a concern first raised as an argument against the bicycle and one that carried over powerfully to the remarkably shaky car."[42] If a woman chose to drive a gasoline-powered car, it would be within reason that she would feel self-conscious and out of place behind the wheel, so electric vehicles were developed for them. Marketers quickly latched on to this potential anxiety by advertising clothing for women that matched their cars. Nichols notes how, in the first decade of the twentieth century, an ad from Saks Fifth Avenue emerged in which "page after page describes garments ranging from pragmatic to luxurious—those that went well beyond the requirements needed to travel safely."[43] If a woman felt insecure behind the wheel on account of the cultural pressures that surrounded her, the solution was not, say, challenging the sordid sexualization of feminine stereotypes. What she needed was a matching outfit from Saks Fifth Avenue. Only then would she be safe. (Coincidentally, notes Nichols, it was from this impulse that terms like *bonnet* and *skirt* were associated with the part of a vehicle that covered the engine and lined the sides.)[44] The ads tapped into a woman's loves and restricted the available expressions of her femininity for the sake of profit.

In their books on gendered marketing directed to children, Lyn Mikel Brown, Sharon Lamb, and Mark Tappan draw together a fitting conclusion from these developments: "Marketers, illustrators, authors, songwriters, TV products, movie scriptwriters, buyers for mall stores, and more are currently

41. Roberta Sassatelli and Rossella Ghigi, *Body and Gender: Sociological Perspectives* (Polity, 2024), 164.

42. Nancy A. Nichols, *Women Behind the Wheel: An Unexpected and Personal History of the Car* (Pegasus, 2024), 48–49.

43. Nichols, *Women Behind the Wheel*, 28.

44. Nichols, *Women Behind the Wheel*, 27.

competing with you for the right to teach your little girl what it means to be a girl," and what they offer is "much too limited a version of what a girl can be."[45] Through market segmentation and persuasion, restrictive portrayals of women and men become the fodder for a version of gender identity oriented not toward the love of God and neighbor but toward the bottom line. There is a latent objection to be made here, though: This may have been the case in the twentieth century, but isn't it true that we are living in a new era of advertising, one much more friendly to *feminist* interests? Haven't we gone from the 1992 Teen Talk Barbies, whose first words were "Math class is tough!," to a *Barbie* movie in which Barbie considers her death, wears Birkenstocks, and is sensitive to the cultural contradictions of being a woman?[46] Witness Dove's highly successful Campaign for Real Beauty, featuring genuinely diverse women, the stated intent of which is to broaden conceptions of beauty for women. Surely the era of excessively thin women and impossibly muscular men is over.

This criticism is only superficially correct. Advertisements like the *Barbie* movie and Dove's Campaign for Real Beauty are part of what Andi Zeisler has called "marketplace feminism." Having noticed that, as of about 2014, "feminism got *cool*," Zeisler develops this concept to describe an application of the term *feminism*, used primarily by marketers, that lacks consideration for systemic injustices and political change.[47] She highlights how it is "decontextualized" and "depoliticized" and focused only on "whatever elevated girls as consumers."[48] Her book catalogs the rise of "celebrity feminism." Well-known women like Emma Watson, Taylor Swift, Natalie Portman, and Beyoncé embraced the feminist label, while Lady Gaga, Kelly Clarkson, Katy Perry, and Shailene Woodley resisted it. Undergarments with the word *feminist* printed on them were sold. And meetings emerged such as the Thrive conference, hosted by Arianna Huffington and Mika Brzezinski, ostensibly organized to help women thrive in business, but conference goers were presented with ads

45. Sharon Lamb and Lyn Mikel Brown, *Packaging Girlhood: Rescuing Our Daughters from Marketers' Schemes* (St. Martin's Press, 2006), 1, 30. See their companion volume in which the same argument is made for boys: Sharon Lamb et al., *Packaging Boyhood: Saving Our Sons from Superheroes, Slackers, and Other Media Stereotypes* (St. Martin's Press, 2009).

46. For a critical history of Barbie and the debates surrounding her feminist qualifications, see M. G. Lord, *Forever Barbie: The Unauthorized Biography of a Real Doll* (Liveright, 2024).

47. Andi Zeisler, *We Were Feminists Once: From Riot Grrrl to CoverGirl®, the Buying and Selling of a Political Movement* (PublicAffairs, 2017), x; see also 117: "Starting in 2014, headlines that used to invoke feminist refusal began glowing with admiration for those who nodded to its importance."

48. Zeisler, *We Were Feminists Once*, x, 177.

by sponsors like Kenneth Cole, JP Morgan Chase, and Westin. Rather than promoting political change, Zeisler concludes, marketplace feminism "has transmogrified from a collective goal to a consumer brand."[49]

Zeisler's criticism of marketplace feminism is that it commodifies the words of feminist engagement (words like *empowerment* and *choice*) but does not alter the final end of marketing. Simply saying that a product will empower women—or literally printing the word *feminist* on it—"doesn't change the goal: to make you buy things."[50] She expands: "The purpose of a brand is . . . deeply at odds with the necessary evolution of movements to address issues that are about more than what trickles down from the highest echelons. The diversity of voices, issues, approaches, and processes required to make feminism work as an inclusive social movement is precisely the kind of knotty, unruly insurrection that just can't be smoothed into a neat brand."[51] In the end, marketplace feminism is little more than marketing's attempt to co-opt a brand that they perceive would be persuasive to women in order to increase sales; it should not be mistaken for authentic political change.

Consider once again Dove's Campaign for Real Beauty. Zeisler points out an odd contradiction at its heart: While most women involved and surveyed concluded that beauty must be defined in much wider terms, the *product* Dove was advertising in those campaigns was lotion whose purpose it was to smooth out cellulite.[52] Their ultimate purpose—the end for which they promoted a putatively feminist goal—was to point out women's physical flaws in order to generate negative loves whose resolution is found in their product.[53] This was, by marketing standards, hugely successful. Sales doubled in three years, and after ten years, Dove's revenue went from 2.5 billion to 4 billion dollars.[54] Zeisler's conclusion is an important reminder of the way the cultural forces

49. Zeisler, *We Were Feminists Once*, xv.

50. Zeisler, *We Were Feminists Once*, 15.

51. Zeisler, *We Were Feminists Once*, 76–77. See her discussion of Spanx feminist marketing: "That would be great if changing the rules was actually what Spanx is about. But Spanx is a business, and its embrace of feminism isn't about women's equality. It's about a company boosting revenues that have fallen behind those of competitors offering less punishing undergarments and workout clothes" (79).

52. Zeisler's analysis of the campaign can be found in her *We Were Feminists Once*, 240–47.

53. A particularly ham-fisted example of this was Dove's deodorant ad that promised women their "armpits" could be turned into "underarms."

54. Zeisler, *We Were Feminists Once*, 241. She is careful to point out that some of that money went to Dove's charitable efforts in supporting women, but this is a qualified positive: Most companies have some charitable arm whose aims and purposes are difficult to quantify.

of death are always willing to distort and commodify creaturely goodness for sinful ends:

> Dove's stated goals might be sincere, but the company is still part of a system whose bottom line depends on perpetuating female insecurity—and subtly encouraging women to blame themselves for it. And yet, simply because few other companies have dared to engage with the subject of mediated beauty standards, Dove continues to be seen as the company that cares. The fact that it cares just enough not to put revenues in jeopardy (and not enough to cease inventing new insecurities and products to address them) isn't important in a marketplace where simply flirting with body acceptance still seems radical.[55]

Dove's Campaign for Real Beauty, along with marketplace feminism, forms just another part of the marketing machinery. Simply because it employs feminist words and concepts does not mean that its *ends* are feminist; rather, it accepts the means without the ends. Its end is the same as the automobile advertisements of the early twentieth century that appear so sexist today, namely, to make a great sum of money.

By segmenting consumers along gendered categories and luring our loves with communicative acts designed to appeal, marketing exercises a massive influence on gender. It is too strong to say that we are entirely passive in this affair—after all, our loves must be *lured*. It is more accurate to say that through its causal influence, marketing restricts the possibilities of gender expression to those that are productive for their bottom line. If gender is about the organization of social goods to manifest an identity by means of our loves,[56] marketers have seized many of the occasions wherein we encounter those goods and have restricted them to those that they design. If gender involves clothing, marketers have decided what clothes line the racks and crop up on Amazon. If gender involves food, marketers have decided what food is found at the grocery store. If gender involves family, marketers have crafted the images of family we encounter in our movies, novels, and social media. And the list goes on. It is important always to remember that marketing's end goal is not virtue, godliness, or flourishing. If those things happen, they are proximate goals to a more fundamental, ordering end: profit.

---

55. Zeisler, *We Were Feminists Once*, 244.
56. For the detailed lines of this view, see do Vale, *Gender as Love*, chap. 5.

The Urge to Revolution, the Temptation of the Sect, and the Call to Conversion

This is a bleak picture, and it is but one section of a larger portrait painted by theologians who have been concerned with finance-dominated capitalism (of which marketing is an aspect) and its incompatibility with the central affirmations of the Christian life and confession.[57] So far, I have attempted to add my voice to this chorus. Marketing, through its seemingly ubiquitous reach and influence that aims at capturing our loves, has so limited the available goods for the formation of gender identity that our understandings of femininity and masculinity are now difficult to separate from the ones construed by marketers for their profit. The waters of gender formation are polluted, so it is only with great difficulty that we can organize the social goods around us to form an identity that reflects the redemptive intentions of Jesus Christ.

Theologically, the way to articulate this problem is with attention to the ways marketing distorts the right order of our loves. Recall that marketing has its own end for the sake of which all of its operations are organized: profit.[58] The way it organizes its operations, at least in part, is through establishing an order of love, with profit as its summum bonum and consumer goods as its facilitating means. This is a parody of the way God has made all things to be gifts whose reception must point to the Giver and that must be loved according to the Giver's specifications.[59] Through its appeals to our loves, marketing substitutes devotion to God and thankful reception of creation

57. One of the clearest examples of this line of argument can be found in the work of Kathryn Tanner, whose goal is "a way of telling the Christian story and its vision of economy that will bring out its great contrast with the economic principles that rule the world of our experience" (*Economy of Grace* [Fortress, 2005], x). See also her *Christianity and the New Spirit of Capitalism*, where she argues that "the work ethic of finance-dominated capitalism is incompatible with fundamental Christian commitments" through its attempts to co-opt the entirety of a worker's life and reduce it to financial terms (*Christianity and the New Spirit of Capitalism* [Yale University Press, 2019], 198). For a nuanced summary and account of Christian theology's relationship to economics, see D. Stephen Long, *Divine Economy: Theology and the Market* (Routledge, 2000). There are, of course, some insightful dissenting theological voices, such as Brent Waters, *Just Capitalism: A Christian Ethic of Economic Globalization* (Westminster John Knox, 2016); and D. Glenn Butner, *Work Out Your Salvation: A Theology of Markets and Moral Formation* (Fortress, 2024). As we will see, I think these views can be harmonized with attention to the saeculum.

58. This is not to say that marketing does not accomplish other goals, some of which are beneficial. My claim is that these are *accidental* to the marketing machinery, whereas profit is essential to it.

59. For details on the gifting of all creation, see do Vale, *Gender as Love*, chap. 4.

with buying and selling. According to theologian Harvey Cox, the market has embedded within it "an entire theology, which is comparable in scope if not in profundity to that of Thomas Aquinas or Karl Barth," making it an "*ersatz religion.*" Modern advertising plays its part as an analogue to missionary and evangelistic efforts by churches.[60] Tanner, similarly, observes how finance-dominated capitalism creates a culture where workers must be totally committed to work, whereas Christian identity requires recognizing that "God is the universal equivalent of all objects of value in that their ultimate, underlying value is to enable Godwardness."[61] Marketing is not designed to enable the relativizing orientation to goods necessary to Christian fidelity. Whereas we ought to have a "bounded desire" for goods, marketing summons us to an identity where our loves are built on these finite goods.[62] So, marketing looks to summon as much of our love as possible, but it does so with no other ultimate goal than buying: "Consumerism is marked by desire with no *telos* other than consumption itself."[63] Christian identity requires an orientation of life where God is our highest good, the source of our joy, and all creatures are beautiful gifts to be loved in God; marketing makes profit and consumption our highest good, that around which our identities are built and for which our loves are co-opted.

So, I intend to join those theologians objecting to the ways the market and its forces have polluted the common lives of God's creatures. We must exercise caution here, however. There is a temptation to take objections like these and think that their resolutions must take the form of a revolution or a sectarian separation from the forms of life dominated by the market. I wish to resist this temptation. Revolutions presume and promise more than they

60. Harvey Cox, *The Market as God* (Harvard University Press, 2016), 7–8; see also 83: "How, exactly, do companies hawk their hollow products? For the answer, look to the methods of The Market's equivalent of missionary and evangelistic outreach, . . . its advertising department." Cox further observes that the kind of evangelism undertaken by ads is "by generating desire" (238).

61. Tanner, *Christianity and the New Spirit of Capitalism*, 95.

62. Mary L. Hirschfeld, *Aquinas and the Market: Toward a Humane Economy* (Harvard University Press, 2018), 123. Hirschfeld, a former economist turned theologian, shows how economists operate with a fundamental anthropology that guides the way they think about the world. That anthropology comes with assumptions about how human preferences and practical reasoning work, which she concludes are at odds with a Thomistic understanding of human happiness (see *Aquinas and the Market*, xiii, 39–42).

63. William T. Cavanaugh, *Being Consumed: Economics and Christian Desire* (Eerdmans, 2008), 74. Cavanaugh explains that this is why ads "must be invested with mythologies, with spiritual aspirations; things come to represent freedom, status, and love" (48).

can deliver, requiring the revolutionary to adopt a stance "outside" the system and an ability to implement a state of affairs whose moral qualities are simply beyond any human's ability to bring about.[64] Sectarianism, while always attractive to Christians throughout history, also assumes a communal purity that it will not be able to deliver. Both of these alternatives are theologically inadequate. Recall from chapter 1 that we now live during the saeculum, that ambiguous time between Christ's first and second comings during which there necessarily remains a mix of wheat and tares, whose separation can come only at Christ's return (Matt. 13:24–30). Myths of progress and narratives of decline are equally poor renderings of how Christ has defined our time. Revolutions tend to be aligned with "a progressive view of history" so that we can "cross the threshold into an emancipated future,"[65] lending it the quality of a myth of progress. By contrast, sectarianism considers history to have sunk so far down into depravity that any hope for change and a common life are discarded, requiring a narrative of decline. In a theological register, revolution attempts to separate the wheat from the chaff before the eschaton, whereas sectarianism forgets the creation and providence of all things by God.

Bretherton offers a helpful reminder at this juncture: "What capitalism is not is all-determining. That claims too much on its behalf. When assessing systems of domination, it is important to recognize that there is always an interplay of structure and agency, and these structures are never stable, involving as they do complex and shifting configurations of multiple institutions and processes."[66] So, while I want to testify to marketing's pervasive corruption of the gendered goods we encounter, I also think that the saeculum summons us to engage it nonetheless. At no point can we claim to overthrow or escape the saeculum. There is no other way than to go through it. Thus, maintains Bretherton, "one can view Christianity and capitalism as ultimately

64. Relevant to our topic, Jack Goldstone notes how "without exception to date," it has only been men who "seize most of the major political, military, and economic leadership posts, while women are encouraged to return to their homes and families. Even where women are given opportunities to gain an education, work, and enter the professions, they remain underpaid yet still bear the main burden for raising children and maintaining homes" (*Revolutions: A Very Short Introduction*, 2nd ed. [Oxford University Press, 2014], 39). If there is going to be a gender-equitable revolution, it would be the first one.

65. Luke Bretherton, "Political Theology, Radical Democracy, and Virtue Ethics; or Alasdair MacIntyre and the Paradoxes of a Revolutionary Consciousness," *Political Theology* 22, no. 7 (2021): 643.

66. Luke Bretherton, *Christ and the Common Life: Political Theology and the Case for Democracy* (Eerdmans, 2019), 352.

antithetical to each other—capitalism being the latest iteration of Babylon—while still seeing scope for ad hoc cooperation in the here and now to achieve penultimate goods."[67] While the theologians who argue that marketing, capitalism, and the economy are riddled with the malaise of sin can be right, their conclusions are *normative*, whereas living during the saeculum requires describing one's conditions well in order to approximate justice in small steps of hope. In the end, while marketing's corruption is everywhere, something more theologically creative and nuanced than revolution or sectarianism is needed. Rather than forming a revolution or a sect against the forces of gendered marketing, therefore, I suggest that we engage in acts of *conversion*.

In *Gender as Love* and the introduction to this book, I argue that our task in relating to gendered goods is not to define them for every time and place but to describe our world well in order to love it rightly; it is not a question of *what* gendered goods to love but of *how* to love them. When it comes to structural change in domains like marketing, the kind of love we should demonstrate to marketed goods is a converting love. Conversion, whether applied literally to human beings or metaphorically to structures, processes, and goods, indicates the presence of transformative change while retaining personal continuity and the need for growth.[68] Theologically, argues Bretherton, conversion is a better analogue to how social change can occur than either previously considered alternative.[69] Conversion is a fitting posture of love shown to goods during the saeculum because it neither denies the past nor forecloses the future: It "can encompass the simultaneously retrospective and prospective nature of radical change through time" by taking the goods served by marketers and converting them to different ends.[70] Converting love is a way for Christians to participate—in small, hope-filled ways—in God's work as both creator *and* redeemer.

---

67. Bretherton, *Christ and the Common Life*, 351. Hirschfeld agrees: "What is needed is not a theological economics that simply rejects mainstream economics but rather a theological economics confident enough in its own voice, and knowledgeable enough about economics, to offer a more nuanced evaluation about what we can and cannot learn from economists" (*Aquinas and the Market*, 18).

68. For a philosophical exploration of major changes, see L. A. Paul, *Transformative Experience* (Oxford University Press, 2016). Biblically, these dynamics are represented in places like 1 Tim. 3:6, where the need for the growth of a new convert is implied.

69. "Theologically, a sober and simultaneously radical hope for change in this age is to seek the conversion of capitalism, that is, its reconfiguration from within and without by redirecting its discursive and structural apparatus to different, God-given ends" (Bretherton, *Christ and the Common Life*, 353).

70. Bretherton, "Political Theology, Radical Democracy, and Virtue Ethics," 643.

This was first proposed by theologian and political philosopher Cornel West in his attempts to find a way to live hopefully in the midst of corporate market institutions that try to institute "the market-inspired way of life over all others."[71] His proposal is a "politics of conversion" that has a "love ethic . . . at the center" and "proceeds principally on the local level."[72] In this sense, a politics of conversion conforms much more to the theological picture of a love-centered and local politics during the saeculum for which I have been arguing in this book. West draws on Malcolm X's notion of "psychic conversion," but he insists on a version of it where a common life is formed in love: We are summoned to "a mode of being in the world, an improvisational mode of protean, fluid, and flexible dispositions toward reality suspicious of 'either/or' viewpoints, dogmatic pronouncements, or supremacist ideologies, . . . to attempt to galvanize and energize world-weary people into forms of organization with accountable leadership that promote critical exchange and broad reflection."[73] Through communal and broad-based efforts, a politics of conversion takes the issues faced by women and men and redirects the goods and acts done in the name of domination toward attainable, hopeful goals. In this sense, rather than revolutionary or sectarian, a politics of conversion is *lovingly subversive*.

What kind of conversion should we seek as we navigate a massive world of marketed gendered goods? If marketing operates by restricting the operative freedom of persons and the goods that populate their lives, our converting love can seek to expand the freedom of gender expression by attaching ourselves to gendered goods differently. If advertising relies on the presentation of rigid and narrow ways of being women and men, the sort of converting love that must be demonstrated by Christians is one that looks to subvert that rigidity and narrowness. This was demonstrated by Paul when he recommended that all women in the church in Corinth wear a veil. The veil was a gendered good that at that time was usually reserved for the wealthy and socially "pure." In Christ, Paul subverted the practice of veiling by expanding the range of persons who would wear a veil.[74] It can similarly happen when someone watches a Dove Real Beauty commercial and, rather than purchasing anticellulite cream, cultivates a sense of worth and self-love that requires no purchases.

71. Cornel West, *Race Matters*, 25th anniversary ed. (Beacon Press, 2017), 17.
72. West, *Race Matters*, 18–19.
73. West, *Race Matters*, 104.
74. For more detailed discussion, see do Vale, *Gender as Love*, 104–9.

It can happen when someone watches the *Barbie* movie and is inspired to have insightful and compassionate conversations about gender theory and the expectations that characterize the social experiences of women and men. In general, it happens when something meant to foster a greater hunger for consumption in order to boost profit is converted to a different use, oriented to an end that genuinely adds a little justice and compassion to the world. While profit may still come in, it will come with other attached goods that undermine the assumption that profit is our greatest love. The options are wide open to the degree that one turns one's conversion to the promotion of justice and Christ-given worth.[75]

As Augustine points out, "Sin consists *not in the things themselves*, but in the unlawful *use* of them. Now the use of things is lawful when the soul remains within the bounds of God's law and subject to the one God in unqualified love and regulates other things that are subject to it without greed or lust."[76] Converting love is one particular kind of use whereby things are turned to the love of God, neighbor, enemy, and self rather than greed. In line with the balance of descriptive and normative tasks outlined in the introduction, I am proposing this vision of taking wrongly ordered goods and recalibrating them through creative and collective agency as a way of affirming the need to be aware of the world as it is while serving as an ambassador of the world to come.

Conclusion

My aim in this chapter has been to give a broad depiction and analysis of the ecosystem wherein we must love our gendered world well. In the introduction, I noted the need for both descriptive and normative tasks in a gender theology that attends to the real lives of concrete people. I then argued for a vision of political engagement that sees history for what it is—awaiting Christ's harvest—and engages primarily in community-organizing efforts, looking to generate political change from the bottom up. Chapter 2 reminded us of

75. Refer here to my fuller discussion of grace and justice in do Vale, *Gender as Love*, 216–28.

76. Augustine, *The Literal Meaning of Genesis*, in *On Genesis*, trans. Edmund Hill, The Works of Saint Augustine: A Translation for the 21st Century 1/13 (New City, 2002), 1.1.13. For an insightful application of Augustine's notion of *use* to economic concerns, see Charles Mathewes, "On Using the World," in *Having: Property and Possession in Religious and Social Life*, ed. William Schweiker and Charles Mathewes (Eerdmans, 2004).

the way death exercises considerable influence during the saeculum, with the result that loving self, neighbor, enemy, and God is a massively difficult experience. All these considerations are in the background of what I have argued here related to gender and marketing. Marketing is not a passive craft but a set of processes aimed at cultivating and harvesting our loves for the sake of profit. We need to describe this process well, and its implications for gender, before we can say what to do about it. I have tried to show that the way marketers segment consumers according to categories that meet them at the point of their most fervent desires is a major way the social forces of death misalign our identities, gendered or otherwise. If our gender identities are about organizing social goods to form an identity, then the social goods available for organization are both beyond our control and also strategically placed to maximize persuasion and reshape the order of our loves.

There is no escaping this. It is, in fact, a feature of the particular manifestations of the saeculum and its deathly tendencies. While it may be tempting to escape it through revolution or sectarianism, we will come to find that the saeculum endures. Our job, as converted people of God, is to extend this converting love to redirect the goods intended for evil for the sake of the good. This is the work of God, through God's people, in God's world. Once again, the Christian task is to love the world rightly by using it well.

As mentioned above, this chapter and, to some extent, the two that preceded it have sought to provide a bird's-eye view of gendered goods. Politics, bodies, and marketing tend to name systemic or generalized sets of goods with which we interact. In the next chapter and those that follow, we will turn to even more concrete aspects of gendered lives, going from the bird's-eye view to an on-the-ground perspective. We begin with clothing. By discussing it, we will witness in even greater detail the work of converting love in a world mired in death but awaiting redemption.

4

Communicative Garments and Wearing Christ

Gender and Clothes

> For thousands of years human beings have communicated with one another first in the language of dress. Long before I am near enough to talk to you on the street, in a meeting, or at a party, you announce your sex, age and class to me through what you are wearing—and very possibly give me important information (or misinformation) as to your occupation, origin, personality, opinion, tastes, sexual desires and current mood.[1]
>
> —Alison Lurie, Pulitzer Prize–winning author

Wearing clothes is a communicative act. Wearing a team's shirt to a sporting event, a musician's tour shirt to a concert, or elegant garments to a wedding all convey something of importance. As novelist Alison Lurie suggests, clothing has a language, and this language has the ability to convey a great deal about the wearer and the world in which it is worn.[2] This is true of the ways our clothes symbolize our participation in groups or our personal identity, but sometimes our appearance is also *literally* communicative. Consider, for instance, the legal controversies in

1. Alison Lurie, *The Language of Clothes* (Holt, 2000), 3.
2. See further Roland Barthes, *The Language of Fashion* (Bloomsbury Academic, 2013).

the 1960s and 1970s in the United States and Britain over policies policing the length of men's hair, in which such policies were categorized judicially as violations of free speech.[3] "Long hair was associated with delinquency and antisocial behavior" at that time.[4] Though at first this association was indirectly communicated, it quickly became explicit when school administrators began to impose strict dress codes regulating boys' hair. Some were detained in classrooms for the day, expelled from school, or even forced to undergo a haircut upon entering school grounds. This escalated into litigation processes, especially when the American Civil Liberties Union (ACLU) became involved. The ACLU argued that "one's appearance was protected speech" and that the "dress codes violated the First Amendment by limiting a students' freedom of expression."[5] In the end, there were eighty court cases related to men's hair between 1965 and 1978, with a case present in the majority of federal circuit courts. Eleven of these even applied to the U.S. Supreme Court. Though they were all denied, both the scope and the importance of the communicative function of clothing are clearly demonstrated by these court cases.[6]

The focus of this chapter is on the communicative function of clothing, though this is by no means the *only* function clothing performs. Clothing *protects*—a heavy jacket will protect from a harsh Chicago winter, and a hazmat suit will protect from hazardous materials. Clothing also *enhances* human bodies—I might be able to run farther while wearing the right shoes or complete a longer hike while wearing the right boots. But for the purposes of this book, the most interesting function of clothing is how it communicates. Clothes, writes Paul Griffiths, "badge their wearers: they identify their wearers as being of a kind, serving a function, or participating in a kind of activity. . . . They serve to communicate something about their wearers."[7] In this chapter, I will describe how clothing performs at least four communicative roles: First, clothing *communicates inward personal identity*. Second, clothing *performs outward personal communication*. Third, clothing *enforces group distinction*. And fourth, clothing *establishes group*

3. In this chapter, I will consider clothing alongside its peripheral associations, such as hairstyles, within the same broad category.

4. Jo B. Paoletti, *Sex and Unisex: Fashion, Feminism, and the Sexual Revolution* (Indiana University Press, 2015), 133.

5. Paoletti, *Sex and Unisex*, 130, 138.

6. Paoletti, *Sex and Unisex*, 129.

7. Paul Griffiths, *Christian Flesh* (Stanford University Press, 2018), 80.

solidarity.[8] Each of these communicative dimensions to clothing is relevant to gender, as I will show. Through these descriptions, I conclude that clothing plays an eminently important role within the network of social goods that make up gender. As costume historian Jo Paoletti states in her history of children's clothing, "Gender distinctions are among the oldest and most widespread functions of dress."[9] We can extrapolate that claim even further. Clothing, in most cultures, serves to mark out someone as more or less feminine or masculine, as aiming to belong to neither category, or as playfully performing the expectations of another gender.

But we cannot stop there in a theological analysis of clothing and gender; we must also ask whether this is the way things ought to be. My normative proposal will proceed by developing a new account of modesty. Modesty, since at least Tertullian's treatise *On the Apparel of Women* (ca. 202), has been limited both in the way it has focused only on particular traits of clothes (rather than on clothing's communicative value) and in the way it has primarily provided prohibitions and limitations for women. Through an engagement with Tertullian and with biblical texts about clothing, I shall argue that both of these limitations are misguided. Modesty is a virtue that should neither be focused merely on the exposure of skin nor be emphasized for women. Rather, it is a general virtue for both women and men whose primary emphasis has to do with communicating one's worth in Christ as one wears the clothing available to one in one's time and place. In short, a Christian's clothing choices are primarily about communicating that their worth is *not* in what they wear but in the one in whom they are clothed—namely, Christ.

The Communicative Functions of Clothes

As I write this paragraph, I am wearing a sweatshirt I purchased when I was an undergraduate, and it bears my former university's name. My wearing it connects me to a previous point in my life and reflects the importance of that time and place to the person I am now. This is a feature of the first communicative role of clothing: *Clothing communicates inward personal identity*.

8. These four roles are captured nicely by Paoletti: "We dress to express ourselves—age, gender, race, religion, as well as personality—and to place ourselves in context: place, time, occupation, kinship, and communities" (*Sex and Unisex*, 18).

9. Jo B. Paoletti, *Pink and Blue: Telling the Boys from the Girls in America* (Indiana University Press, 2012), 8.

In some way, who I am is reflected in the clothes I wear. In a well-known line from *Hamlet*, William Shakespeare has Polonius tell his son, Laertes, "Apparel oft proclaims the man." Mark Twain elaborates on this by saying, "Clothes make the man."[10] Observing these dynamics, Paoletti claims that "clothing is . . . bound up with the most serious business we do as humans: expressing ourselves as we understand ourselves."[11] Clothing is identity forming, and this formation of our inward selves happens in at least two discernible ways.

One is by helping us make coherent sense of our life narratives. My university sweatshirt helps me connect who I am now with who I was then; if I want to signify that this time was important to me, I will wear it again. Married couples will also sometimes wear the clothes in which they were married for portraits of a significant anniversary. Clothing often serves as an indicator for the important junctions of our lives that render them coherent: "Planning the right dress is a way to tell my story, to reveal who I am and who I aspire to be."[12] An important part of bearing an identity is the story that discloses that identity, and the coherence of that story will often depend on certain points of significance. Very often, those moments are remembered with reference to the clothing we wore.

Additionally, clothing communicates inward personal identity by relieving or exacerbating our insecurities and other elements of our emotional lives. Perhaps I am insecure about how much weight I have put on in recent months; my clothing may enable me to draw attention away from this fact, or it may highlight it uncomfortably. Going up a clothing size can often feel like an indictment. Theologian Michele Saracino emphasizes this inward element of clothing in her treatment of the topic. She notes how "it is important to reflect on our rituals and processes of dress," to see both how they "tell our stories" and how they "reveal our anxieties about being a creature in relation to God and others."[13] In chapter 2, we witnessed the theological and social difficulties that attend to cultivating friendship with the body. Clothing is

10. William Shakespeare, *Hamlet* (Macmillan, 2016), 23. The Twain quotation comes from page 6 of a privately published work from 1927 titled *More Maxims by Mark Twain*, compiled by Merle Johnson and displayed at the Rubenstein Library at Duke University.

11. Paoletti, *Sex and Unisex*, 13.

12. Michele Saracino, *Clothing*, Compass: Christian Explorations of Daily Living (Fortress, 2012), 33.

13. Saracino, *Clothing*, 5. Saracino's particular emphasis is on the ways clothing serves to aid the denial of our limits: "Dress has become an accomplice to humanity's denial of limits, fostering conceptions of human existence and resulting in destructive relationships" (24–25).

often one of the ways this cultivation occurs. We may ask, How does this shirt feel on my body? Does it adequately convey who I am? Or, if that is too strong of an expectation, Does it convey something about me that is not true to who I am? The connections to gender here are fairly clear. Gender is about identity, and clothing is a central tool for discovering, clarifying, emphasizing, and concealing identity. Lauren Winner calls our attention to the way "fashion" was a verb before it was a noun—you fashion a bowl out of wood, for instance—and reminds us of the way clothing "shapes us." She says, "This is why some of us enjoy clothes so much, we love changing our clothes and trying a different look—every time we change into a different kind of clothing, we can play at being a different kind of self."[14] For this to occur, clothing must communicate inward identity to some extent. If I am wearing the kit of Bristol City Football Club, one can infer that I am a supporter of Bristol City Football Club. This is one reason Halloween is so appealing: For one evening, we can highlight some eccentric aspect of ourselves and put it on display.

This first communicative role of clothes is closely associated with the second: *Clothing performs outward personal communication.* Clothing is not just inward facing; it also externally communicates those personal identities (or at least some version of them we feel comfortable with the world seeing). It is customary, for instance, to wear black to a funeral. It used to be the case that those mourning the death of a loved one would wear black for months; women would wear black dresses and men would wear black armbands. Years ago, if you were seen wearing the black of mourning, you would be treated with a bit more respect, served a little more quickly at the store, given a little more leeway if you were short with someone. It was assumed that life is quite difficult for you at the moment. Today, these practices have largely been abandoned, but their absence is felt. Author Meghan O'Rourke describes the following experience after riding the subway five days after her mother's death: "A man elbowed me aside, . . . and I felt bruised and angry; if I had been wearing mourning clothes, I furiously thought, he would have taken greater care. . . . In those moments, I wanted a way to show my grief rather than tell it."[15] Without the black clothing of mourning, O'Rourke lost a way to communicate.

14. Lauren F. Winner, *Wearing God: Clothing, Laughter, Fire, and Other Overlooked Ways of Meeting God* (HarperOne, 2016), 38.

15. Meghan O'Rourke, *The Long Goodbye: A Memoir* (Riverhead Trade, 2012), 157.

What happened to the practice of wearing mourning clothes? The story is more gradual than drastic, but factors like the overwhelming number of deaths experienced during World War I made the repetitive use of mourning clothes difficult, and the increase of women entering the workforce required a different kind of dress that reflected the challenges faced.[16] As a result of these historical developments, black clothing was altered in its communicative capacity. This alteration was catalyzed by a central figure in fashion history, Gabrielle "Coco" Chanel. Born in 1883, Chanel was launched into fame for inventing what is commonly known as the "little black dress" in 1926. She took a color that was associated with mourning, with religion (it was the color worn by the nuns in the convent where she was raised and taught to sew), and with destitution (economically poor women were known to wear black), and she made it a mark of elegance blended with utility. The little black dress became the uniform of postwar women, and Chanel intended it to be the counterpart to a man's suit.[17] One critic called the little black dress "poverty de luxe" and asked Chanel, "For whom, Mademoiselle, do you mourn?" Chanel is said to have responded, "For you."[18] The critic's question indicates the shifting act of communication that wearing black performed. Rather than communicating poverty, mourning, or religious devotion, it began to communicate a new-world elegance. The critic did miss one meaning formerly attached to black clothing: Chanel modeled her dresses after what she called "puritanism," with the simplicity of the little black dress imitating the austerity and asceticism of the nuns who raised her. Like so many of our social goods, the little black dress represents a secularization that remains haunted by its religious past. This is a particularly clear example of how clothing communicates inward identity outwardly. John Harvey observes,

> We . . . use clothes to bring out different "sides": our serious side, or our fun or sexy or reckless side, or our masculine or feminine side. We may do this deliberately, or quite unconsciously, but when we use our clothes in this way we are bringing something that is inside us outside, perhaps magnifying and enhancing it in the process, and changing the balance of just what we are. . . .

---

16. See Lucie Whitmore, "'A Matter of Individual Opinion and Feeling': The Changing Culture of Mourning Dress in the First World War," *Women's History Review* 27, no. 4 (2018): 579–84.

17. Kimberly Chrisman-Campbell, *Skirts: Fashioning Modern Femininity in the Twentieth Century* (St. Martin's Press, 2022), 67–71.

18. Quoted in Chrisman-Campbell, *Skirts*, 70.

> Clothes are like a lens: they bring us, or a part of us, into focus, and push the less wanted selves back towards the shadows.[19]

The clothing we wear is one way we navigate and organize our identities for public display, and it is adjustable: It can be used to make aspects of who we are more obvious or more hidden.

This outward communication has gendered overtones. If we want to communicate conformity (or nonconformity) to some set of gendered characteristics in our time and place, clothing is one of the most intuitive ways to do so. Consider the example of "sexiness" of clothing.[20] Paoletti describes the "peacock revolution" in men's fashion during the late '60s and early '70s (a short-lived time when business suits were traded for colorful and patterned jackets with no collar) and concludes, "The peacock's display has a purpose beyond vanity or self-expression: to attract admiring peahens. The new clothing was supposed to be sexy, in stark contrast to the business suit, which projected an image of a reliable breadwinner."[21] To communicate personal creativity and financial stability, men began to wear different varieties of formal wear in the effort to attract partners who would associate such traits with sexiness. There is a dark side to sexiness, however. Shahidha Bari reminds us that the experience of being perceived as sexy can be quite different for women: "The unsettling truth is that sometimes women dress to deter advances and avoid censure: they dress to keep the world at a distance, compelled by fear."[22] In a world where the public's first response to hearing about sexual assault might be "What was she wearing?," the perception of sexiness becomes dangerous and undesirable for women because of the expectations associated with dress and how they are paired with the common misassigning of blame for sexual assault to assaulted women themselves.

These first two communicative roles reflect individualized adornment functions, but clothing also has to do with groups. The third communicative function of clothing to consider, therefore, is how *clothing enforces group distinction*. Trivially, we can see this in the way a sports stadium will be

---

19. John Harvey, *Clothes: The Art of Living* (Routledge, 2008), 35–36. This was a central emphasis of psychologist J. C. Flugel's book *The Psychology of Clothes* (International Universities Press, 1971).

20. For broader reflection on this term, see Adrienne Evans and Sarah Riley, *Technologies of Sexiness: Sex, Identity, and Consumer Culture* (Oxford University Press, 2014).

21. Paoletti, *Sex and Unisex*, 73.

22. Shahidha Bari, *Dressed: A Philosophy of Clothes* (Basic Books, 2020), 66.

divided by the colors of the teams being supported. But we can also see group distinction providing occasion for violence, as in the case of the 2007 murder of a young woman and serious injuring of a young man simply because they were dressed as goths. Their clothing distinguished them from the group to which the five young men who assailed them belonged, and that distinction alone motivated horrific violence.[23] Lauren Winner highlights how "clothing underlines socioeconomic distinctions," with associations often made between clothing that makes one look elegant and clothing that makes one look shabby.[24] The clearest historical example of clothing's group distinction along socioeconomic lines had to do with sumptuary laws.[25] These were laws that regulated what clothing could be worn by persons belonging to certain groups divided by class, race, geographic origin, or other lines. They were largely operative in medieval Europe—such as when Jewish persons were required to wear yellow badges or pointed hats[26] or when Milanese middle-class workers were banned from wearing silk and gold above a certain price point[27]—but we can see vestiges of such group distinction in the example, mentioned above, of the litigious behavior surrounding men's haircuts in the 1970s. Sumptuary laws even made it into ecclesial documents: Canon 68 of the Fourth Lateran Council, for instance, required Christians and Muslims to dress differently. In sumptuary laws we see clothing distinguishing groups with as much force as statecraft could provide.

This function of clothing is perhaps the most salient for gender. Women and men are often distinguished from one another by the clothing associated with exemplary members of each group. Perhaps the most obvious example of this is the notorious color distinction according to which pink is associated with girls and blue with boys. This distinction, however, was not always in place, and how it came to have the established role it now has illustrates how clothing shapes gendered groups. As Paoletti writes in her history of gendered clothing for children, "For American babies and small children, white dresses were once

23. See Harvey, *Clothes*, 1–2.

24. Winner, *Wearing God*, 48. See also Robert Covolo, *Fashion Theology* (Baylor University Press, 2020), 54: "Fashion has undoubtedly been used for establishing class distinctions and expanding the subjective realm."

25. For more on sumptuary laws, see Ruthann Robson, *Dressing Constitutionally: Hierarchy, Sexuality, and Democracy from Our Hairstyles to Our Shoes* (Cambridge University Press, 2013).

26. Paoletti, *Sex and Unisex*, 123.

27. Tara Isabella Burton, *Self-Made: Creating Our Identities from Da Vinci to the Kardashians* (PublicAffairs, 2023), 30.

like T-Shirts are today: essentially neutral. . . . Before the eighteenth century, there were only three broad categories of clothing, which signified a mixture of age, gender, and occupation: infant clothes (diapers, swaddling, and long dresses), trousered styles (most men and boys over the age of about seven years), and skirted styles (women, male clergy, and children under seven)."[28] Until the early twentieth century (and arguably as late as the 1960s), pink and blue were not rigidly gendered colors. Instead, all children under seven wore long dresses until they reached an age appropriate to graduate to more mature clothing. The reasons for this are fascinating: "Gendered dress was considered inappropriate for young children, whose asexual innocence was so often cited as one their greatest charms. . . . Few parents in 1880 would be comfortable dressing their year-old son to express his masculinity or choosing clothing to accentuate their infant daughter's femininity."[29] Children's clothing was not seen as a training ground for gendered expression; because of its connotations with sexual attraction, gendered expression was best seen as something to be held off until a certain age. Until then, all children wore white dresses trimmed with ribbon, lace, and braids. The result is that it is difficult to discern boys from girls in the black-and-white portraits of the nineteenth century.

Underlying this practice is a theory of gender according to which its development did not arise until certain bodily maturation processes were in place; with the abandoning of that understanding in favor of a model where social forces play a much bigger role in gender formation, we see an increase in gendered children's clothing and a solidification of pink and blue as markers of gender.[30] Alongside this shift in perspective about gender's fundamental properties came developments in child psychology arguing that gendered training needed to occur earlier and earlier. Thus Paoletti: "Since very young children were capable of learning gender identity (including the 'wrong' one), sharp gender distinctions *should* be taught—and the earlier the better. . . . Clothing needed to take on a pedagogical or even therapeutic role."[31] One of the easiest and most effective ways of doing so was through color.

The association of femininity with pink and masculinity with blue was not smooth, however. There was not much agreement about which gender

28. Paoletti, *Pink and Blue*, 19–20.
29. Paoletti, *Pink and Blue*, 26–27.
30. See Paoletti, *Pink and Blue*, 61.
31. Paoletti, *Pink and Blue*, 77, 80.

should go with which color until the 1960s. Paoletti cites a parenting advice magazine from 1918 that gives the following advice: “Pink or Blue? Which is intended for boys and which for girls? . . . The generally accepted rule is pink for the boy and blue for the girl. The reason is that pink, being a more decided and stronger color, is more suitable for the boy, while blue, which is more delicate and dainty, is prettier for the girl.”[32] As recently as 1918 pink was gendered as masculine because it was a “more decided and stronger color,” whereas blue was seen to be more “delicate,” “dainty,” and “pretty.” Blue’s feminine credentials went further. Blue was also the color associated with the Virgin Mary, and baby girls dedicated to a virginal life would wear blue, sometimes even exclusively (as Napoleon III and Empress Eugenie’s daughter did for the first seven years of her life).[33] Pink and blue were used inconsistently when it came to distinguishing gender categories. Not until market forces in the 1960s solidified the connection did we have the patterns we still see today.[34]

The history of pink and blue, therefore, is a history of clothing being used either to distinguish gendered groups (as now) or to resist doing so (as in the nineteenth century). The groups were confused and mottled, but various forces were invested in their clarification. This is by no means an isolated episode for gender, of course. In *Gender as Love*, I considered the example of head veils in the ancient world and their use to distinguish women who were seen as respectable and pure from those who were not.[35] This was another case of group distinction through gendered clothing. When Paul noticed that this practice established a system of worth opposed to the grace of Christ, he sought to make the church a space where all women had the worth associated with veiling. One way to read 1 Corinthians 11:4–16 is to understand Paul as eroding the category distinctions established by clothing.

Clothing distinguishes groups, but it also *establishes group solidarity*, the fourth communicative function under consideration. “On Wednesdays we wear pink,” informs Regina George in the film *Mean Girls*, establishing a

32. Paoletti, *Pink and Blue*, 85.

33. Paoletti, *Pink and Blue*, 87.

34. This corroborates the point made in the previous chapter about Disney’s marketing. Disney princesses of this era (notably Snow White and Cinderella) wore blue. It also goes some way to explain the point made in chapter 2 about the 1960s being a pivotal era for those issuing jeremiads.

35. Fellipe do Vale, *Gender as Love: A Theological Account of Human Identity, Embodied Desire, and Our Social Worlds* (Baker Academic, 2023), 104–9.

group by means of its clothing.[36] Just as clothing distinguishes groups, it also solidifies and coheres the resulting categories. Paul Harvey observes, "When we wear clothes, we are no longer alone: we have put on *membership*. . . . It may be an ethnic force, a race; a social class, or an income-bracket; or a religious faith."[37] In Christian history, the most obvious example of group solidity through clothing (and its lack) was the early Christian practice of nude baptism. For much of the church's earliest practices, men and women were separated for baptism, where they removed their clothing to indicate that their approach to God did not take into account any prior worth they possessed.[38] Once they emerged from the water, they were given a white robe: "Candidates for baptism stripped off their garments, were immersed, and donned white robes, which were variously interpreted as signifying purity, incorruptibility, the protection of the Holy Spirit, a return to prelapsarian sinlessness, a mystical marriage to Christ, or a sharing in the glory of his resurrection."[39] Those baptized would no longer be able to see differences among themselves, at least not with respect to their clothing. When gathered in their white robes, all that mattered was the new gift of Christ they had received and the promises they now inherit. This will be important for the normative claims made in the next section.

Though there are gendered dynamics in these baptismal practices, we can see clothing's ability to establish group solidarity with respect to gender in the unisex fashion movement of the 1960s and '70s. In resistance to the growing world of rigidly defined gendered clothing, the unisex movement sought forms of resistance by providing styles that either combined elements of masculinity and femininity, displayed themselves more neutrally (like turtlenecks or jogging suits), or borrowed clothing usually expected of another gender and incorporated it into one's own fashion.[40] The most obvious example of the

36. *Mean Girls*, directed by Mark Waters (Paramount Pictures, 2004). Thank you to Dustyn Keepers for reminding me of this quote.

37. Harvey, *Clothes*, 72. See also Bari, *Dressed*, 3: "Dress is, at its heart, really about memory, meaning, and intimacy: the ties, if you like, that bind. In clothes, we are connected to other people and places in complicated and unyielding ways."

38. For discussion of the historical details, see Thomas M. Finn, *Early Christian Baptism and the Catechumenate: Italy, North Africa, and Egypt* (Wipf & Stock, 2020); Everett Ferguson, *Baptism in the Early Church: History, Theology, and Liturgy in the First Five Centuries* (Eerdmans, 2013).

39. Adam Serfass, "Unraveling the *Pallium* Dispute Between Gregory the Great and John of Ravenna," in *Dressing Judeans and Christians in Antiquity*, ed. Kristi Upson-Saia et al. (Ashgate, 2014), 79.

40. Paoletti, *Sex and Unisex*, 30.

unisex trend that survives today is the prevalence of women wearing trousers, especially jeans. Before 1965, women wore trousers largely for informal occasions, but this changed after the mid-sixties. Trousers were perceived to be equally appropriate for women in formal settings as well as everyday wear. When denim grew in popularity in the '60s, "just about everyone wore jeans, regardless of age, sex, class, or race."[41] For a very brief period of time, denim trousers brought about a sartorial equality that few articles of clothing have ever managed. You wore the same jeans—cut, color, and length—no matter who you were. There was one group, bound together by their jeans.

As with most equalizing social goods, this did not last. Perceiving a market gap, brands began to notice that there was money to be made in providing specifically *feminine* jeans. They began to show up in the 1970s, and their distinguishing feature was that they hugged hips more closely.[42] Other women's trousers also underwent modifications, most notably zippers being placed at the side of the waist or at the back on account of the sexual overtones implied by a front zipper.[43] The history of women and trousers involves a negotiation of what kinds of group solidarity were appropriate. Could women and men be grouped together when it came to denim trousers? For a while they were, but that did not last. So instead, the group that crystallized was the one whose participants were deemed fitting to wear *women's* trousers. This had an interesting result when it came to the unisex movement of those decades, a span of years during which parents attempted to raise their children without gendered goods.[44] Rather than establishing greater equality between women and men, it had the result of making women's fashion all the more pronounced: "The final effect was not that women's clothing became more masculine, it was that most of the elements they borrowed became either feminized (like jeans did) or were no longer considered masculine."[45] Counterintuitively, the more unisex fashions sought group solidity, the more gendered clothing became. All the same, it became this way because of its ability to solidify groups.

So far, I have argued that clothing performs a variety of functions, but most important to gender is clothing's *communicative* function. Clothing is

41. Paoletti, *Sex and Unisex*, 49.

42. Paoletti, *Sex and Unisex*, 50.

43. Paoletti, *Sex and Unisex*, 28.

44. See the short story by Lois Gould called *X: A Fabulous Child's Story* (Daughters Publishing, 1978). In it, "X" is a child raised neither as a girl nor as a boy. Needless to say, *X: A Fabulous Child's Story* was deeply controversial after its publication.

45. Paoletti, *Sex and Unisex*, 51.

communicative in at least four ways: It communicates inward personal identity, performs outward personal communication, enforces group distinction, and establishes group solidarity. The examples above show that these four functions are intertwined; we communicate inwardly by trying out adornments that communicate outwardly, and groups are solidified as they are distinguished. These divisions are conceptual and heuristic, for in ordinary life they often occur all at once and not in easily divisible patterns. They also all play a role in informing gender. Clothing is one of the primary goods we organize, by means of our loves, into a gender identity—precisely because of its communicative function—leading us into a deeper understanding of ourselves and of the groups to which we belong (or do not belong). This, it seems to me, is descriptively true. It is hard to live in the world and not communicate through clothing in some capacity or another. What can Christian theology and ethics say here? What sorts of communicative acts are most fitting for Christians? And what difference does it make for our choice of threads that we have been clothed in Christ?

A New Modesty: Love and Resurrection in the Theology of Clothing

One of the remarkable elements of the Christian faith is its ability to be translated into any number of cultures while retaining its essential features. This religious flexibility also commits it to a certain kind of moral flexibility: There is no Christian uniform or mode of dress that would mark out all Christians in all places and all times.[46] The clothing we wear now would scandalize a Christian from one thousand years ago, and the clothing worn by Christians in 1025 would be, in many respects, scandalous to modern sensibilities (recall the nude baptisms of the early church). And yet, all these practices can be Christian, even for Christians who think theologically about their clothes. The Christian gospel admits of both surprising freedom *and* an added responsibility when it comes to cultural goods like clothing.

A central theme of this book is that the moral evaluation of gendered goods depends on the context in which those goods are used, where use is a feature of our loves, and this carries over into the communicative contexts of

46. See Griffiths, *Christian Flesh*, 100: "There is no distinctive Christian dress, and no distinctive Christian attitude to clothes or nakedness."

clothes. It is not enough for Christian discipleship that an individual shops in the clothing section of their gender. Harvey summarizes the application of this insight to clothing nicely: Clothes "are not bad in themselves, and they have at best a supporting role in assisting bad acts and deceptions. . . . If we ask what clothes *do* for us, the perspective changes, from the view that we get if we look at clothes from the outside."[47] When Harvey draws attention to what clothing *does*, he is emphasizing clothing's *function*, and the central function we have been considering in this chapter is communication. The trouble, however, is that Christian attention to clothing has often misunderstood its communicative use, restricting it to something less than what we find in everyday practice. Nowhere is this more evident than in Christian understandings of modesty.

The central biblical texts that motivate theological articulations of modesty are 1 Peter 3:3–4 and 1 Timothy 2:9–10:

> Do not adorn yourselves outwardly by braiding your hair, and by wearing gold ornaments or fine clothing; rather, let your adornment be the inner self with the lasting beauty of a gentle and quiet spirit, which is very precious in God's sight.

> Women should dress themselves modestly and decently in suitable clothing, not with their hair braided, or with gold, pearls, or expensive clothes, but with good works, as is proper for women who profess reverence for God.

Both texts are addressed to wives/women, which has led interpreters to construals of modesty that focus only on women. Both also include women's clothing, jewelry, and hair, associating them with aspects of a woman's character: a "gentle and quiet spirit" in 1 Peter, and "good works" and "reverence for God" in 1 Timothy.[48] Of the two, only 1 Timothy 2:9–10 employs terms for modesty of dress: "Women should dress themselves modestly and decently."[49] Though it is often tempting to assume particular understandings of these terms that resonate with contemporary patterns of dress, they rather paint the picture of someone who has a clear head about how she dresses and remains attentive to the sensibleness of the communicative acts

47. Harvey, *Clothes*, 21–22.

48. For an argument that the latter text results in a sexist set of instructions, see Adela Yarbro Collins, "The Female Body as Social Space in 1 Timothy," *New Testament Studies* 57 (2011): 155–75.

49. "Modestly and decently" is the NRSV's translation of "*aidous kai sōphrosynēs*."

she performs through her clothing.[50] The modesty in question, additionally, is less about hem lengths and more about the character of the wearer, the worth she possesses, and whether that worth is anchored in character or in wealth.[51] The modesty being commended, when considered in context, concerns how wealth and class are displayed in the communities in which women's agency and communicative acts are received. Women, because they had different avenues than men in antiquity for expressing honor, often employed clothing to communicate their status, as was the case with head veils in 1 Corinthians 11.[52] The biblical focus of modesty, therefore, is on clothing's communicative power and how it conveys status and honor: "Jewellery and adornment could be important ways for a woman to communicate her own and her family's status. . . . An important dimension of a woman's economic power was her jewellery box."[53] When 1 Peter 3:3 and 1 Timothy 2:9 commend women to be modest, therefore, it is primarily a summons to be wise and deliberate about the kinds of communicative acts regarding wealth and honor that their clothes perform.

This is not, however, how these texts have been received in historical and contemporary understandings, and we can take Tertullian's treatments of modesty as representative of this tendency. Tertullian dedicated more attention than most to the question of Christianity and clothing, and his engagement is thoroughly theological. For Tertullian, the doctrine of creation, a theological ethic of sexuality, and Christ's redemption should all figure into how one thinks about modesty. Additionally, he recognizes that modesty is a virtue for men as well as women (even though he devotes considerably less

---

50. See James Reiher, "Is There Anything More That Can Be Said About 1 Timothy 2:8–15? 'Propriety,' a Surprisingly Significant Word," *Priscilla Papers* 37, no. 3 (2023): 24: "This word's first and foremost meaning is being 'clear-headed,' or a 'rational thinker,' or 'not muddled in thought.' . . . The key theme of this famous paragraph is that all the members of the church should be clear-thinking, mature Christians, whose sound thinking leads to mature Christian life seen in the appropriate virtues and behaviours."

51. Thus Alicia J. Batten, "Neither Gold nor Braided Hair (1 Timothy 2:9; 1 Peter 3:3): Adornment, Gender and Honour in Antiquity," *New Testament Studies* 55 (2009): 492: "Adornment was one of the sources of a woman's economic power as well as a means of signaling her status to the community," and it "could and did earn her criticism."

52. Batten, "Neither Gold nor Braided Hair," 486: "The details of costume and public presentation had significance far beyond the taste of the individual person; they were signs of status (not only of a man or woman or slave, of course, but of the household) and reflected moral and political meanings. Dress and grooming mattered for how a person was to be perceived by others."

53. Batten, "Neither Gold nor Braided Hair," 486, 491.

space to men and reserves his harshest critiques for women). Despite some strengths, Tertullian's understanding of modesty deeply misconstrues clothing's communicative function by focusing only on how women might tempt men and how he thinks they lie through their clothing.[54] As a result, he misses the claims of the New Testament texts and forgoes most of the communicative capacities of clothes.

For our purposes, Tertullian's most relevant treatise on the topic is *On the Apparel of Women*, written about 202 CE.[55] Tertullian claims that modesty is not merely a matter of abstaining from illicit sex; it includes "the arrangement of dress and ornament, the studied graces of form and brilliance."[56] In the treatise, we can discern two arguments for why women should avoid immodest clothing. First, immodest dress tempts one's neighbor to sin. Thus Tertullian: "Why are we a source of danger to our neighbor? Why do we import concupiscence into our neighbor?"[57] Note that Tertullian places the blame on the woman who dresses immodestly; she "imports" the concupiscence into her neighbor. He continues: "You have been made the sword which destroys him."[58] He considers the act to be morally equivalent to robbery; just as a robber is to blame when an estate is plundered, the estate owner is nevertheless ladened with the infamy of having been robbed, even though only the robber is at fault.[59] Tertullian is clear that no blame should be assigned to the man who casts a concupiscent glance at an immodest woman. To support this, he makes the (empirically implausible) claim that "no wife is 'ugly' to her husband," so that he does not require her to dress in any way that accentuates beauty. So, if a woman is dressed in an immodest way, the only remaining reason for doing so is that she is attempting to arouse the desire of someone who is not her husband, because "a believing husband does not require" beauty.[60] If that is true, then a woman possesses no reason to dress immodestly other than a desire to sin since she does not have the desires of her husband in mind. She, therefore, bears the unilateral blame for any wrongful desire generated.

54. For more on Tertullian's notion of modesty, see Kate Wilkinson, *Women and Modesty in Late Antiquity* (Cambridge University Press, 2015), 33, 126.

55. Tertullian, *On the Apparel of Women*, in vol. 4 of *Ante-Nicene Fathers*, ed. Alexander Roberts et al. (Christian Literature, 1885), https://ccel.org/ccel/tertullian/women_apparel/anf04.

56. Tertullian, *On the Apparel of Women* 2.1.

57. Tertullian, *On the Apparel of Women* 2.2.

58. Tertullian, *On the Apparel of Women* 2.2.

59. Tertullian, *On the Apparel of Women* 2.2.

60. Tertullian, *On the Apparel of Women* 2.4.

Tertullian's second argument claims that immodest clothing is equivalent to lying. Women who wear makeup "add to [God's] work, taking these additions, of course, from the adversary artificer." These women "wear a fictitious face," "lie in [their] appearance," and "seek after what is another's."[61] God has made them with a specific body possessing a certain appearance, claims Tertullian, and according to nature, that is what these women were meant to look like. So when they cover up nature, they lie about their appearance. Instead of the goodness of their created nature, women who wear makeup put on "meretricious attractiveness."[62] In fact, their act of lying puts them in collusion with the father of lies, the devil. "They who rub their skin with medicaments, stain their cheeks with rouge, make their eyes prominent with antimony," claims Tertullian, "sin against Him." At this juncture we find the most familiar quotation of this treatise: "Whatever, then, is plastered on, that is the devil's work."[63] Tertullian, with an emphasis on the natural appearance of women, claims that if immodesty and lying are to be avoided, only natural appearance can be displayed.

We must be careful of the historical transposition that occurs any time questions of modesty are under consideration: Tertullian's context is not my context, and he did not face the market-driven and image-focused world that the church faces now. All the same, whatever else he is doing, Tertullian still intends to make normative, biblical arguments meant for Christian instruction, and there are numerous faults with those arguments. For our purposes, we can focus on how his instruction is misguided and restrictive with regard to its appreciation of clothing's communicative abilities. For Tertullian, clothes have exactly two communicative roles: salacious temptation and lying. Those are the two actions we can perform with our clothing, and avoiding them results in modesty. But this is shortsighted, at best, and misogynistic, at worst. It is an impoverished understanding of modesty. The paradigmatic cases of temptation and lying that Tertullian has in mind almost exclusively involve women: In his theological account of clothing, they bear all the blame for any sinful desires generated in men. Men are content with the natural appearances of their wives, says Tertullian, so it can only be that immodest women want to be seen as attractive by other men. But Tertullian makes claims here without any support; this is a false portrayal of how men

61. Tertullian, *On the Apparel of Women* 2.5.
62. Tertullian, *On the Apparel of Women* 2.12.
63. Tertullian, *On the Apparel of Women* 2.5.

desire and of women's purposes for dressing. As we have discussed at length above, there are many more morally appropriate reasons to wear something luxurious or eye-catching. Additionally, Tertullian mischaracterizes the nature of sinful desire. If a man finds himself with sinful desires after observing a woman's appearance, the blame for the sinful desire is his and only his. A woman cannot control a man's desire by means of her adornment, especially in light of the shifting and culturally contingent forms of adornment that are considered "sexy." This trajectory of reflection on Christian modesty is experienced today when women are both compelled to wear the best clothing and makeup available to work and are also derided and shamed by men for doing so. Saracino observes that Tertullian's work "is really an excuse for one individual or group to control and dominate another," such as when "women are encouraged to look a certain way through articles of clothing, makeup, and jewelry yet are ridiculed if they go too far."[64] If this is where one's account of modesty concludes, it is theologically unviable.

While Tertullian rightly draws our attention to modesty, it seems to me that he fails to discern the direction of the biblical materials in their testimony to communicative agency. We simply have no reason to think that these are the only two communicative acts performed by dress, nor that Tertullian's account of temptation and lying is adequate. Though there are a variety of avenues to explore surrounding modesty and cultural expression,[65] my aim here is to offer an alternative theological account of modesty that looks to appreciate the variety of communicative gendered acts clothing plays and places a central emphasis on one governing communicative act: displaying union with Christ. In other words, Christians are free to communicate through adornment in all the various ways available to them, yet they must order their communicative acts so that they are calibrated for one chief act of communication: *communicating reconfigured worth through union with Christ in love until he returns*. This, I argue, is what the biblical material actually points us to and what more closely aligns with a practicable and nonsexist vision for modesty.

Recall that the chief verses that inform theological articulations of modesty, 1 Peter 3:3 and 1 Timothy 2:9, are primarily about communicating wealth,

64. Saracino, *Clothing*, 69.

65. See, e.g., Saba Mahmood's fascinating discussion of modesty, veils, and the Islamic revival in her *Politics of Piety: The Islamic Revival and the Feminist Subject*, rev. ed. (Princeton University Press, 2011).

honor, and status. In *Gender as Love*, I referred to this cluster of concepts as one's *worth*.[66] So, when Christians think about clothing's communicative forces, they must think about their own worth and about how that worth is transformed by union with Christ. This is precisely how Scripture discusses clothing: It unites our literal clothing with the spiritual clothing we have in Christ, a clothing that comes with reconfigured worth and moral responsibilities. Consider one of the most well-known passages where Paul employs the language commonly associated with getting dressed, Colossians 3:8–10.[67] There Paul is instructing the church to take some vices off and put some virtues on. We put off anger, rage, malice, slander, and filthy language from our lips; like a garment that has been covered in mud, these things must be taken off. Paul reminds us, "You have *taken off* your old self with its practices and have *put on* the new self, which is being renewed in knowledge in the image of its Creator" (vv. 9–10 NIV, emphasis added), using words typically applied to clothing. Our sanctification, says Paul, is the kind of act that resembles removing filthy garments and putting on clean ones. But like a new outfit, these clothes require some getting used to. Sometimes parents purchase clothes for children that are slightly too large, claiming that they will "grow into them." In the same way, Paul claims, we must grow into the new clothes we have been given in Christ.

But what parts of us must grow? In Colossians 3, the notion of growth assumes an eschatological direction, and Colossians 3:4 sets these moral claims against such a background: We grow into our clothes only when Christ who is our life appears. Just as there is an eschatological direction, there is also a motivation of love. The way we grow into this life in Christ is through our love. After listing all the virtues needed for growth, Paul instructs, "And over all these virtues put on love, which binds them all together in perfect unity" (v. 14 NIV). For Paul, all virtue is an expression of the right kind of love, because if we love correctly, we conduct ourselves in all the ways appropriate to our new dress in Christ. Julian of Norwich articulates it rather beautifully: "For us [God] is everything that is good and comforting and helpful. He is our clothing, wrapping and enveloping us for love, embracing us and guiding us in all things, hanging about us in tender love, so that [God] can never leave

66. Do Vale, *Gender as Love*, 216–28.

67. See further Rosemary Canavan, "Letter to the Colossians 3:1–17," chap. 6 in *Clothing the Body of Christ at Colossae: A Visual Construction of Identity* (Mohr Siebeck, 2012).

us."[68] The process of growing in the love of God is like growing into the most comfortable article of clothing you have.

Romans 13 is one of the clearest places in Scripture where clothing, worth in Christ, and moral action in love are found. Using the same word as Colossians 3:10, Paul similarly urges us to clothe ourselves with Christ Jesus: "Clothe yourselves with the Lord Jesus Christ" (Rom. 13:14, my trans.). As in Colossians, we have to grow into this clothing by awaiting a resurrected body that is yet to come. Verses 11–12 summon us "now" to awake from sleep because the night is gone and the day is "near." Christians, claims Paul, are like those who get up before dawn and get dressed for the day, even though the day has not quite dawned yet. Because the dawn has been promised, such an act makes sense, but for those who have only known the nighttime, getting dressed for a new day seems strange. But an eschatological anticipation ushers Christians to be dressed in anticipation of the coming dawn before it arrives by clothing themselves with a *person*—namely, Jesus Christ.

Paul is also clear that eschatological anticipation takes the form of rightly ordered love shown forth in moral action. In Romans 13:9–10 Paul makes just the same point as he did in Colossians. The commands of God "are summed up in this one command: 'Love your neighbor as yourself.' Love does no harm to a neighbor. Therefore love is the fulfillment of the law" (NIV). Those who have been clothed in Christ are those who love rightly. *What it means to await our resurrected true selves is to love rightly*, to have a love that is genuine (12:9) and plays itself out in acts of common regard (12:15). Already we see emerging the two major themes I have argued constitute the normative task: eschatological attention and the flexible and creative disposition of love that jointly bring us to our true selves, selves that are clothed in Christ.

How may these threads be drawn together to bring us to a new theology of modesty? As Christians, our clothing practices must be informed by how we have been clothed in Christ. As Brent Waters asserts, "The promise of appearance is that it can be a faithful and truthful witness to Christ, to the Word made flesh. . . . We should take care for how we appear to one another if we are at all concerned about embodying a faithful and truthful witness to Christ."[69] In Christ, we have been given a gift on the basis of no prior worth

68. Julian of Norwich, *Revelations of Divine Love*, trans. Elizabeth Spearing (Penguin Books, 1999), 7 (Short Text 4).

69. Brent Waters, *Common Callings and Ordinary Virtues: Christian Ethics for Everyday Life* (Baker Academic, 2022), 210.

of our own, as our worth is established through union with him. Through union, worth is generated where no prior worth existed.[70] Now, we should no longer regard persons "from a human point of view" (2 Cor. 5:16), for their worth is attributable to only one thing: having been clothed in Christ. Recall, moreover, that clothing is communicative, and one of the ways it structures acts of communication is through status. Inwardly, we believe ourselves to be of a certain worth by wearing certain clothes; outwardly, we might project a greater or lesser worth through our clothes; and we group and separate individuals on the basis of a human structure of worth by their clothes. But this is precisely what Scripture, and the theology of modesty, pushes against. Modesty, in short, amounts to this: Because Christ has reconfigured all human structures of worth for those united to him, our social practices must be measured by this new standard. Clothing can no longer be used to communicate human standards of worth. All communicative acts of adornment must now be governed by this communicative act, one made by motions of love in eschatological anticipation and imagination. In this sense, we are not unlike the newly baptized members of the earthly church who could not distinguish among themselves because they all wore white robes. Though we are not literally wearing the same garments, we are summoned to the same communicative goal—namely, conveying that our worth is bound to Christ, who is our life.

There is one biblical passage that articulates this particularly well—namely, Galatians 3:27–28. Here Paul connects our clothing in Christ with the past event of our baptism, a fact that ought to change the quality of our relationships. Because "you who were baptized into Christ have clothed yourselves with Christ," it follows that "there is neither Jew nor Gentile, neither slave nor free, nor is there male and female" (NIV). As I have argued, this assertion is not about the eschatological removal of gender.[71] Rather than eschatologically *erasing* those features that feel like burdens to us now, Paul is telling us that grace reconfigures the worth we attach to such attributes. No longer can clothing serve as a basis for exclusion, ranking, or value for Christians,

70. This is a view defended at length by John M. G. Barclay, *Paul and the Gift* (Eerdmans, 2015); see also John M. G. Barclay, *Paul and the Power of Grace* (Eerdmans, 2020). See the discussion in do Vale, *Gender as Love*, 216–25.

71. See do Vale, *Gender as Love*, 228–35; and Fellipe do Vale, "Gender Identity: To Infinity and Beyond," *Pro Ecclesia* 32, no. 1 (2023): 24–46. See also Bruce Hansen, *"All of You Are One": The Social Vision of Gal 3.28, 1 Cor 12.13 and Col 3.11*, Library of New Testament Studies (T&T Clark, 2010).

"for you are all one in Christ Jesus" (Gal. 3:28 NIV). Or, as Lauren Winner articulates the point, "On Paul's terms, Jesus is not the kind of clothing that creates social divisions but the kind of clothing that undoes them. Jesus is not a Vineyard Vines dress or a Barbour jacket; He is the school uniform that erases boundaries between people. Or at least that is the kind of clothing Jesus wants to be. . . . When we put up walls in the name of Jesus, we are turning the Lord into an expensive designer dress."[72] Modesty, understood in this sense, is less about how much skin is shown than about how much worth is recognized. Clothing in Christ should no longer be a source of division and separation but a signal of mutually recognized worth that generates acts of love providing a foretaste of eschatological glory.[73]

So what *can* we wear? This book is no style guide, and I think the question is framed incorrectly. It's not about *what* we wear but about *how* we wear it. No clothing is out-of-bounds considered apart from its communicative action, and all clothing can be used to communicate misdirected worth. Only in this way can we retain the translatability of the Christian gospel in all times and places. So *how should* we wear our clothing? There is a good example of rightly aligned adornment in the book of James. In 2:8, James repeats the affirmation we have seen in Paul that loving one's neighbor fulfills the law. This motivates his well-known claim that "faith by itself, if it has no works, is dead" (2:17). The case that he uses to *introduce* the life of faith working itself out through love involves favoritism displayed through clothing. In 2:1–7, we see all four functions of clothing being employed to measure the reaction of a church gathering to someone clad in wealth and someone clad in poverty. Suppose, says James, "a person with gold rings and in fine clothes comes into your assembly" and "a poor person in dirty clothes also comes in" (2:2). These two people outwardly signify wealth and poverty through their

72. Winner, *Wearing God*, 50.

73. There is an objection to be made here, however. Paul Griffiths speculates that "Christian resurrected flesh, heavenly flesh, will necessarily be naked" on account of the fact that clothing has lost its value in baptism (*Christian Flesh*, 88). This is situated in Griffiths's broader eschatological picture according to which artifacts—objects made through creaturely agency—do not endure in the resurrection (Paul J. Griffiths, *Decreation: The Last Things of All Creatures* [Baylor University Press, 2014], 305). Griffiths operates with criteria for endurance that seem to me unnecessarily strict, and he introduces a disjunction between that which is created and that which is resurrected. Resurrection, it seems to me, is a validation and perfection of creation, whereas Griffiths seems to sustain only that which is necessary for a repetitively static worship of God. Here I cannot engage his criteria in depth, so I allow the reader to measure our respective eschatological pictures for their merits.

clothing; they are communicating the moment they walk into church (notice that the wealth of the first person is unmistakable even without a word like *rich* or *wealthy* being used in the description, an indication that conclusions about inward identity are made from what is displayed outwardly). They are noticed (2:3) by the church members, who make "distinctions" (2:4) among themselves. Those with clothes that communicate wealth sit in a position of prominence (solidifying their group), and they are distinguished from those who sit at the feet of others, those wearing the clothing of poverty. Inward, outward, and group communication are all on display here.

But James is emphatically clear that such behavior is a violation of the faith that culminates in works of love toward God and neighbor, and this is because that faith has structured a new system of worth. Acting to generate such distinctions introduces a form of worth that is alien to the kingdom promised to them by the one they love (2:5). Though clothing is often used to make such distinctions, they are distinctions judged by the law (2:8–11). Elsa Tamez summarizes James's condemnation of favoritism helpfully: "James calls their attention to this favoritism and reminds them that the poor are precisely the ones who shall inherit the reign promised to those who love God."[74] This is because "favoritism always favors the rich, never the poor," and such favoritism makes the material circumstances of a person a condition of their salvation and belonging—something the gospel does not tolerate.[75]

It is not difficult to see how many Christians still operate with this external system of measuring worth. The evils that caused the most harm in this world drew their energy from stratifications of worth according to human standards, and very often, the tool for solidifying these standards was the communicative power of clothing. The poor come into the church and still are oppressed, just as the church is oppressed by the rich (James 2:6). James tells us that this is not how faith that loves its neighbor acts. Rather, "those members of the body that we think less honorable we *clothe* with greater honor" (1 Cor. 12:23, emphasis added). This, in the end, is how we communicate with our clothing in a truly modest manner. Observe that James does not mention skin exposure; the elements of clothing he focuses on are the ones used to introduce fleshly standards of worth. True modesty is different;

74. Elsa Tamez, *The Scandalous Message of James: Faith Without Works Is Dead* (Crossroad, 1990), 25.

75. Tamez, *Scandalous Message of James*, 44.

it is seen when we witness to the adornment of others and see the honor and worth they possess in Christ.

So the goal is to dress for love. In practical terms, this means expanded freedoms *and* greater strictures. Freedom is expanded: There is nothing about observing the worth of another in Christ that prohibits women's exposed clavicles, men's painted nails, the wearing of makeup, or having a nice outfit reserved for special occasions to look especially luxurious. Its evaluation needs to take into account the character of the one who is adorned. At the same time, *every item of clothing* can become a tool for oppression when used wrongly. This is why Tertullian's analysis of clothing erred; he failed to see how clothing enacts harm. When clothing is used to communicate that some humans are worth more than others (and any article of clothing can be used in this way), it is immodest. It no longer communicates that one is clothed in Christ.

Conclusion

It is interesting that whenever early Christians sought to make their use of clothing reflect their faith, the erasure of human distinction was always the result. This was true in baptism, when all were dignified to wear white robes; in veiling, when all women were given the privilege of veiling; and in the garb of monasteries, where all dressed in the same way to indicate similarity of devotion.[76] The point is not that clothes do not matter; it's that they matter so much that their communicative function should witness to one's worth in Christ, and the early Christians thought sameness accomplished this very neatly. Clothes can perform a variety of communicative functions, such as signaling inward personal identity, performing outward personal communication, enforcing group distinction, and establishing group solidarity. All these functions are evaluable under the new worth we have received in being clothed with Christ. This is how the descriptive and normative unite for our purposes. Descriptively, we need to focus on the way clothing communicates, and then we ought to attend to communicating Christ normatively through reconfigured worth. Then we have questions to ask ourselves: How do our clothing practices reflect the new creation in Christ? How do I dress to show that my identity has been shaped by a gift I did not deserve and now have a

76. This is a helpful point made in Griffiths, *Christian Flesh*, 91.

responsibility to reciprocate? How do I keep myself from clustering groups of people according to their modes of dress and thereby obscuring their true worth? What kinds of systems do I operate within that solidify the grouping of the poor in their oppression by means of outward signals like clothing? Living with such wisdom is what modesty is about and should always have been about.

5

Steaks and Salads, Diets and Desserts

Gender and Food

The uncompromising truth is that obesity is a result of gluttony.

—*Life Magazine*, 1954[1]

Whenever you see a fat Christian, you're looking at a man who is not walking with the Lord.

—C. S. Lovett[2]

The truth of the matter is that when our bodies are overweight, we are carrying around more than the excess pounds: we are carrying excess weight in our hearts.

—Carole Lewis[3]

Of all the gendered goods considered in this book, food is the only one that we actually take *inside* of ourselves as we make it a component of our identities.[4] Our practices of consumption are often directed

1. Quoted in Mary Louise Bringle, *The God of Thinness: Gluttony and Other Weighty Matters* (Abingdon, 1992), 103.

2. C. S. Lovett, *Help, Lord—the Devil Wants Me Fat!* (El Camino, 1977), 19.

3. Carole Lewis, *Back on Track: A 16-Week Challenge to Help You Reach Your Weight-Loss Goals* (Regal Books, 2003), 63.

4. Thus Norman Wirzba, *Food and Faith: A Theology of Eating*, 2nd ed. (Cambridge University Press, 2019), 6: "When you eat another creature, you do not simply make contact with

at shaping our bodies in a more desirable direction. We eat in the aspiration to achieve a certain body, and those aspirations are often given gendered, moral, and spiritual overtones. There are strong connections between eating practices and gendered ideals, just as there are similarly strong connections between eating practices and the perceived moral qualities of an individual. Being a good woman or man, it is often supposed, can be measured by how one eats. Where do such connections come from? Why think that restricting our eating—usually synonymous with dieting—can give us a certain kind of body? And why think that the pursuit of a certain kind of body through the manipulation of eating is a duty only for women?

This chapter will explore the relationship between food, dieting, and gender. Through a description of diet culture, I will argue that a problematic moral vision for food has come about, which I will call, following Mary Louise Bringle, *caloric Pelagianism*. According to caloric Pelagianism, food possesses an *intrinsic* moral value, not a moral value indexed to its contextual use. "Good" food is seen as healthy and spiritually beneficial, and this health and spirituality is measured by one's thinness. By contrast, "bad" food is sinful—specifically *gluttonous*—where sinfulness is measured by how fat[5] one is. Individuals within diet culture are seen to possess unbound wills: They can choose whether they will be sinful or righteous, and nothing internal is stopping them from doing so. The net result, within diet culture, is that being fat is identified with being sinful whereas being thin is next to godliness, and whatever category one lands in is one's own fault. Diet culture, moreover, predominantly impacts women. As philosopher Kate Manne states, "As we grow older, many of us continue to punish ourselves: eating only 'virtuous' foods, or not eating at all, or eating to the point of discomfort—sometimes, before purging. . . . In all of these ways and more, fat bodies are depicted as a moral problem, and people as a moral failure."[6] To this we may add, with theologian Mary Louise Bringle, a *spiritual* failure: "The person who abstains

it. You take it 'inside' of yourself, digest it, and incorporate it within. With an intimacy that rivals sexual union, the other's flesh and your flesh 'become one flesh.'" Or again, Emily J. H. Contois, *Diners, Dudes, and Diets: How Gender and Power Collide in Food Media and Culture* (University of North Carolina Press, 2020), 2: "Because food is consumed—literally taken into our bodies—and experienced on multiple levels of taste, emotion, and memory, its power is distinct when compared to other consumer objects and habits."

5. Throughout this chapter, I use the word *fat* in accordance with its contemporary academic usage in disciplines like fat studies. In this usage, *fat* is a word being reclaimed in the effort to remove the negative connotations associated with it.

6. Kate Manne, *Unshrinking: How to Face Fatphobia* (Crown, 2024), 81–82.

from eating takes on heroic qualities in our thinking; the modern day-to-day dieter replaces the early Christian ascetic as one who is revered for great will power in resisting temptation."[7] This is the core of the descriptive task.

After this descriptive exercise, I will raise several objections. One objection will have to do with the embodied matters: There are good biological and psychological reasons to think that diets do not work. They do not work because each of us humans, on account of our creatureliness, has a "set point" for our weight that is remarkably difficult to live outside of. Strikingly, as they promote harmful dieting practices, many of the same Christians who argue that sex is relatively fixed fail to see that weight is also relatively fixed. Another objection has to do with theological matters: Gluttony, in the Christian tradition, simply is not the opposite of dieting. It is failing to regard food as God's gift. Thus, this second objection has to do with the nature of sin, connecting with my description of caloric Pelagianism. Drawing on the theological claims made in the first chapter, I will argue that diet culture has made two mistakes: It has regarded sin as an intrinsic feature of creatures, and it has wrongly portrayed gluttony as dieting's opposite. In response, I will offer an alternative normative proposal that understands sin through the lens of love and eschatology with which this book operates. Put simply, being fat is not a sin. This is true because of the ineffectiveness of diets and our biology; it is also true because the doctrine of sin should be an occasion for compassion, not for the punishment of bodies. The result is an analysis of just how much gendered food practices have fallen short of the joyous purposes of eating that God has intended and the way eating relates to the cultivation of friendship with our bodies.

Diet Culture, Thinness, and Gluttony: The Impact on Women

Though women are not the only ones impacted, diet culture—the systems built around the idea that merely controlling how and what we eat will yield the bodies of our choosing—impacts women the most. A woman who fails to have her ideal body, therefore, is said to have a failure of self-control and moral capability.[8] Thus Manne: "Misogyny . . . finds in fatphobia a powerful

7. Bringle, *God of Thinness*, 54.

8. For a historical account of this, see Joan Jacobs Brumberg, *Fasting Girls: The History of Anorexia Nervosa* (Vintage, 1988); Joan Jacobs Brumberg, *The Body Project: An Intimate*

and convenient ally: it constructs a ready-to-hand hierarchy among girls and women based on the infinitely gradable metric of body mass, usefully complicated by body shape, breast size, waist-to-hip ratio, and various markers of privilege. . . . Femininity and fatness are an especially dire combination. Fat women are often suspected of being weak-willed."[9] The numbers testify to a staggering number of women who are impacted: 91 percent of women who are college-aged, 80 percent of thirteen-year-olds, and 50 percent of girls between eleven and thirteen see themselves as overweight and state that they are trying to lose weight.[10] When asked if they would like to weigh less, 71 percent of women said they would, leading Gina Kolata to conclude that "nearly every woman in America thinks she's too fat."[11] Cole Kazdin observes how women are twice as likely as men to suffer from eating disorders, which is why the weight-loss industry—reported to be worth 192.2 billion dollars in 2019 and projected to reach 300 billion dollars by 2027—is predominantly populated by women.[12] In the group she studied, theologian Hannah Bacon observed how there was only one man in attendance, and he was automatically disqualified for the "Woman of the Year" award given by the weight-loss group.[13] Or again, in Lynne Gerber's study of the Christian weight-loss church group First Place, she observes how the "overwhelming majority" of members were women, leading her to conclude that "Christian weight loss has long been the domain of women, as has weight loss culture more generally."[14] What I will refer to as diet culture—the systems of weight-loss groups, diets, and strategies upheld by the assumption that we can achieve the bodies we desire through the exercise of our wills in restricting our food—is a concern primarily for women, making it a gendered good that requires our

History of American Girls (Vintage, 1997). For contemporary studies, see Manne, *Unshrinking*, chap. 2.

9. Manne, *Unshrinking*, 117, 133.

10. Hannah Bacon, *Feminist Theology and Contemporary Dieting Culture: Sin, Salvation and Women's Weight Loss Narratives* (T&T Clark, 2019), 34.

11. Gina Kolata, *Rethinking Thin: The New Science of Weight Loss—and the Myths and Realities of Dieting* (Farrar, Straus & Giroux, 2007), 65.

12. Cole Kazdin, *What's Eating Us: Women, Food, and the Epidemic of Body Anxiety* (St. Martin's Press, 2023), 5, 15. It is poignant to note, however, that the gender category suffering the most from disordered eating is trans persons. See Elizabeth McNaught et al., *Eating Disorders: The Basics* (Routledge, 2024), 25.

13. Bacon, *Feminist Theology and Contemporary Dieting*, 31.

14. Lynne Gerber, *Seeking the Straight and Narrow: Weight Loss and Sexual Reorientation in Evangelical America* (University of Chicago Press, 2012), 13.

attention.[15] As Bringle summarizes, "Food is a human issue, to be sure; but it is preeminently—at least in contemporary culture—a women's issue."[16]

A large part of the reason for this has to do with the evolution of beauty standards; women (and especially white women) have been expected to be thin in order to be beautiful.[17] Though in the space of this chapter I cannot rehearse the history of how this has come to be,[18] there are some poignant examples that establish the point. Historian Sabrina Strings has noted how the figure of the Roman goddess Venus gradually developed as an artistic "standard by which true beauty could be measured."[19] Various women were depicted as Venus to illustrate their superior beauty, and by the sixteenth century, this included women of African descent. As racial theories began to emerge, however, a need to distinguish white Venuses from nonwhite ones drove artists to depict black Venuses as fat.[20] To accomplish this, authors like François Bernier and others began using the derogatory term *hottentot* to designate black female appearance. *Hottentot* was a term of derision originally applied to the people of the Cape of Good Hope and Cape Town in South Africa by members of the Dutch East India Company in the seventeenth century,[21] but it evolved into a set of standards for depicting black women in art. In accordance with the assumptions of the racial science of the time, so-called hottentot women were depicted as fat.[22]

It was by these standards that Saartjie "Sara" Baartman, eventually known as the "Hottentot Venus," was measured. Born around Cape Town in the 1770s, Baartman was sold as a slave to a free man named Hendrik van Jong. In an effort to reduce his debt, van Jong began to display a nude Baartman to soldiers. When Scottish surgeon Alexander Dunlop saw her, he came to the conclusion that he could make a lot of money exploiting Baartman in London. So Dunlop deceived the illiterate van Jong to bring Baartman to London and marketed her as the "perfect specimen" of "that race of people" whose naked

15. For corroboration of this claim, see Kandi M. Stinson, *Women and Dieting Culture: Inside a Commercial Weight Loss Group* (Rutgers University Press, 2001).

16. Bringle, *God of Thinness*, 36.

17. The classic argument for this claim can be found in Susie Orbach, *Fat Is a Feminist Issue* (1978; repr., Penguin, 2016).

18. For that history, see Sabrina Strings, *Fearing the Black Body: The Racial Origins of Fatphobia* (New York University Press, 2019).

19. Strings, *Fearing the Black Body*, 137.

20. Strings, *Fearing the Black Body*, 41.

21. See Strings, *Fearing the Black Body*, 52, 72.

22. Strings, *Fearing the Black Body*, 86.

body could be ogled for the right price.[23] Dunlop toured Baartman widely throughout England, with spectators gawking at her proportions. This erotic display enabled Dunlop to pursue his dreams of wealth (of which Baartman did not see a cent), but its effect on perceptions of female beauty was far more long-lived. It confirmed to many, including anthropologist and racial theorist Georges Cuvier, that fatness and blackness were intrinsically linked and that beautiful white women were meant to be thin. Strings explains how Baartman, the "Hottentot Venus," became the antithesis of the Venuses of the past: She taught Europeans what it meant to be beautiful by demonstrating to them what *not* to be—namely, fat and black.[24] Female beauty became associated with white thinness through the exploitation and commodification of black women like Baartman.

We can also see how dieting and thinness became associated with women by observing how they are *not* associated with men. Emily Contois has recently argued that "the dude" is a paradigmatic figure in food advertising that teaches consumers to think that men are not dieters.[25] For a number of years, channels like the Food Network and diet brands wanted to grow their popularity with men, who consistently avoided them. In the effort to increase profit from this market segment, companies marketed the dude to them. Contois describes the dude: "The dude resists professional accomplishment and endorses slacking off, while maintaining masculine social power. Similarly, dude food plays around as it resists the typical standards of haute cuisine."[26] Dude food includes burgers, pizza, and hot dogs, and is characterized by spicy, hearty, and meaty flavors offered in large portions. It is represented by chefs like Guy Fieri, but it can be seen in the aisles of any grocery store. Rather than calling them *diet* soda or *diet* yogurt, low-calorie foods marketed for men emphasize how much they can pack in so little. For example, Dr. Pepper Ten labeled itself as the "manliest low-calorie soda in the history of mankind" and was promoted with commercials that claimed, "It's not for women."[27] Powerful Yogurt experimented with alternative yogurt flavors for men—like bourbon and scotch, which did not taste

23. Dunlop as quoted in Strings, *Fearing the Black Body*, 89–91.

24. Strings, *Fearing the Black Body*, 98.

25. For more detail, see Katherine J. Parkin, *Food Is Love: Advertising and Gender Roles in Modern America* (University of Pennsylvania Press, 2006); Kate Cairns and Josée Johnston, *Food and Femininity* (Bloomsbury, 2015).

26. Contois, *Diners, Dudes, and Diets*, 20.

27. Contois, *Diners, Dudes, and Diets*, 64, 65, 81–84.

good enough to succeed—and outfitted their low-calorie yogurt's container with a six-pack of abs.[28] There was even an industry for specifically men's cookbooks, with titles like *Bake It Like a Man*, *The Real Man's Cookbook*, and *DudeFood*, the last of which gives high-protein recipes intended to help men get their sexual interests in bed with them (and includes pictures).[29] The emergence of dude food, writes Contois, communicates "the assumption that men desire and demand real flavor and satisfying taste more than women do."[30] This can be seen by the paltry male participation in commercial weight-loss groups: Roughly only 10 percent of members of Weight Watchers, Nutrisystem, and Jenny Craig are men.[31] As a result, Weight Watchers devoted 10 million dollars to their "Lose Like a Man" campaign in 2011, while Jenny Craig launched "Jen Works for Men" in 2010.[32] These masculine diet systems endorse what Nutrisystem for men calls "man food—burgers, pizza, and chips."[33] Dudes, dude food, and dude diets all establish the point through their desperate appeal to a population they cannot seem to reach. Men, so it seems, do not diet and must eat the sorts of food that do not make them thin.[34]

When we take stock of the development of beauty standards for women and the way dieting is not seen as something "for dudes," we begin to see why it has been the case that if women are to be perceived as beautiful, they must be thin and white. In addition to these developments in aesthetics and marketing, we must also pay attention to the theological contributions that have nourished diet culture. Christian thought has a historically complex relationship to food, and parts of that history associate eating with sin. For some in the early church, for example, the original sin committed in the garden was not pride but *gluttony*. Basil of Caesarea claimed, "It was gluttony that betrayed Adam to death and brought wickedness upon the world, thanks to

28. Contois, *Diners, Dudes, and Diets*, 69, 85.
29. Contois, *Diners, Dudes, and Diets*, 29–36.
30. Contois, *Diners, Dudes, and Diets*, 67.
31. Contois, *Diners, Dudes, and Diets*, 89.
32. Contois, *Diners, Dudes, and Diets*, 90. Their marketing included sports figures like Charles Barkley to add to their masculine appeal. Barkley appeared in drag to show how this diet is in fact not for women.
33. Quoted in Contois, *Diners, Dudes, and Diets*, 99.
34. The famous example of this development is the association of men with steaks and women with salads. There is a history to these associations that reflects the marketing Contois analyzes. For that history, see Paul Freedman, *American Cuisine and How It Got This Way* (Liveright, 2019), 211–20; Paul Freedman, *Why Food Matters* (Yale University Press, 2021), chap. 6.

the lust of the belly."[35] Basil's younger brother Gregory of Nyssa concurs, calling "the pleasures of eating and drinking" the "mother as it were of all forbidden enjoyment."[36] Finally, in the fifteenth century, Nilus of Sora simply says, "It was the desire of food that spawned disobedience; it was the pleasure of taste that drove us from Paradise."[37] Even Geoffrey Chaucer, in the fourteenth century, testifies to this: "I speak the truth; gluttony was the vice that first flung Adam out of Paradise."[38] We shall have occasion to return to the topic of original sin below, but it is enough to notice here that there is a strand in Christian history that "identifies the paradigmatic disobedience with an image of *eating*."[39] In that strand lie the seeds that eventually blossomed into diet culture.

That blossoming occurred with the arrival of two common dry goods found in most American pantries: graham crackers and Kellogg's cereal. Sylvester Graham—inventor of the former—was an early nineteenth-century Presbyterian minister who advocated eating only plants, just as Adam and Eve putatively did. He claimed that the consumption of other foods leads to diseases associated with our fall into sin, and his ideas stimulated a variety of dietary movements in the United States.[40] The relationship between Christian obedience, dietary restriction, and good health was taken up in the late nineteenth century by Dr. John Harvey Kellogg, the inventor of Kellogg's Corn Flakes. In western Michigan earlier in the century, Kellogg's father had heard Sylvester Graham lecture on the sin of eating meat, and this set the Kellogg family on a lifelong quest to unite food and faith. Also influenced by Graham was Ellen White, the eventual founder of Seventh Day Adventism, of which Kellogg eventually became an influential member. Kellogg's father

35. From *Sermo de Renuntiatione Saeculi*, quoted in Kenneth Stone, *Practicing Safer Texts: Food, Sex and Bible in Queer Perspective* (T&T Clark, 2005), 27.

36. Gregory of Nyssa, *De virginitate*, in vol. 5 of *Nicene and Post-Nicene Fathers*, 2nd series (Eerdmans, 1986), chap. 21.

37. Nilus of Sora, *Tractatus de octo spiritus malitiae* 1, quoted in Herbert Musurillo, "The Problem of Ascetical Fasting in the Greek Patristic Writers," *Traditio* 12 (1956): 16.

38. Geoffrey Chaucer, *The Canterbury Tales*, rev. ed., ed. Nevill Coghill (Penguin Classics, 2003), 310.

39. Bringle, *God of Thinness*, 53. For a fuller analysis of sin, food, and women in early Christian history, see Caroline Walker Bynum, *Holy Feast and Holy Fast: The Religious Significance of Food to Medieval Women* (University of California Press, 1987); and Rudolph M. Bell, *Holy Anorexia* (University of Chicago Press, 1985).

40. For more on Graham and the others involved in these early developments of diet culture, see Hillel Schwartz, *Never Satisfied: A Cultural History of Diets, Fantasies, and Fat* (Anchor Books, 1986), chap. 2.

raised him with a theologically motivated vegetarianism, shared by White, claiming that the sinful consumption of meat is the cause of disease. As the Adventist movement grew, Kellogg established the Battle Creek Sanitarium, where he famously invented granola, meat alternatives, soy milk, and his famous cereal. All of this was done to further the theological ambitions of the Adventist church, but there was also a gendered and racial side to this story. Kellogg believed that "hottentot blood" caused illness, just as consuming meat did, so he made white women a special focus of his dietary advice and marketing.[41] The conjunction of a strong association between dieting and faith; the perception that thin, white women represented the pinnacle of beauty; and the ensuing cultural influence of Kellogg's products were strong catalysts for diet culture as we now know it.

While it would be too strong to claim that this vein of Christian history *caused* contemporary diet culture, we can at least say that it had a sizable influence on it. Marie Griffith, whose book *Born Again Bodies* details the story fully, argues that Christian thought and practice was used to generate "a general conviction about the devotional logic of physical discipline. Fit bodies ostensibly signify fitter souls, whose prayers appear particularly, perhaps exclusively, suffused with wonder-working power."[42] As diet culture developed, the religious zeal associated with dieting did not vanish—it simply *migrated*. Dieting used to have direct attachment to concrete points in the Christian story and to Christian doctrines, but as the emphasis on that story and its doctrine waned, the religious commitment merely shifted to enchant the dietary practices themselves.[43] As the title of one book written by a trainer of celebrities states, "Fitness is religion. Keep the faith."[44] Gerber summarizes the subsequent deification of dieting well: "In effect, this spiritual change involves redefining weight loss as a godly project, one that is sacralized by shifting motivation from worldly concerns with appearance to godly concerns of health and service. . . . Once that shift is made, weight

---

41. See Strings, *Fearing the Black Body*, 179.

42. R. Marie Griffith, *Born Again Bodies: Flesh and Spirit in American Christianity* (University of California Press, 2004), 6.

43. On the religious resonances of diet culture, see the work of Michelle Mary Lelwica, *Starving for Salvation: The Spiritual Dimensions of Eating Problems Among American Girls and Women* (Oxford University Press, 1999); Michelle Mary Lelwica, *The Religion of Thinness: Satisfying the Spiritual Hungers Behind Women's Obsession with Food and Weight* (Gürze Books, 2013).

44. Ray Kybartas, *Fitness Is Religion: Keep the Faith* (Simon & Schuster, 1997).

loss becomes a legitimate spiritual pursuit, and the questions, obsessions, and practices that underlie it become spiritual as well."[45] The inherent spiritual value of dieting—producing a body that externally testifies to internal worth and moral uprightness—is why churches can host weight-loss ministries that are virtually indistinguishable in practice from the secular counterparts (apart, of course, from the accompanying memorization of Bible verses). This is what Bringle calls the "god of thinness": "Dieting has assumed the fervor and proportions of a leading new 'religion' (albeit a gnostic one), with its own bible, its own ritual observances, and its own high priestesses and priests. . . . For the modern woman, sadly, thinness becomes a god unto itself."[46] Diet culture, once theologically justified with inherently Christian resources, has now outgrown its origins and become a god unto itself, and one that harms women throughout the world.

For our purposes, I want to focus on one particular aspect of this new religious observance—namely, its construal of sin. Diet culture, I want to argue, requires seeing sin as an intrinsic feature of creatures, a view that is incompatible with Christian affirmations regarding creation and sin. Following Bringle, I call this *caloric Pelagianism*: "We categorize some foods (carrots and celery, low-fat cottage cheese) as intrinsically good, our allies against the law of our members; others (chocolate, cookies, ice cream, fried anything) are intrinsically wicked, our sworn foes."[47] For diet culture, food possesses an intrinsic moral value: there are intrinsically good foods, and there are intrinsically bad foods. The former testify to righteousness in one's character, while the latter testify to sin in one's soul. We are basically in control of our ability to choose either good foods or bad foods, and there is no corrupting influence of sin on our wills. Sin's influence is exclusively on the outside, for it is genuinely within our power to be thin. This results in a secular doctrine of sin absent of compassion and yielding only shame and guilt.

Consider two illustrations of diet culture's cruel doctrine of sin. Theologian Hannah Bacon studied a secular weight-loss group in England who "recycled theological ideas in ways that aid the culture war on fat."[48] According to this diet program, prohibited foods are labeled "Syns." Members must

---

45. Gerber, *Seeking the Straight and Narrow*, 171.

46. Bringle, *God of Thinness*, 26, 84.

47. Mary Louise Bringle, "Confessions of a Glutton," *Christian Century*, October 25, 1989. See further Bringle, *God of Thinness*, 147.

48. Bacon, *Feminist Theology and Contemporary Dieting*, 4.

calculate the number of Syns they commit per day in order to stay within the parameters of the program. These Syns are counted and tabulated by the group, and there is an explicit connection made between how many Syns one commits and how much weight one fails to lose. Bacon observes: "Participants assume that the result of (wilful) disobedience is weight gain (fat) and a body that becomes other than what it should be."[49] However, the migration of the doctrine of sin into Syn removes any notion of the bondage of the will; dieters are completely in control of the number of Syns they go on to commit. "Unlike Augustine," writes Bacon, "they conceive of themselves as being utterly able to follow their own rational inclinations. Women believe that they should be able to transcend their passions and control their bodies, and this is ultimately demonstrated in the way losing weight is reduced to a simple matter of will power."[50] Because of this self-conception of control, failure is interpreted as a source of guilt and shame. Those who have gained weight at the weekly weigh-in face direct condemnation for their wrongdoing: "Guilt and shame are worn on the body as excess weight without members having to say a word."[51] Here Syn is not forgiven. Because of the complete control we have over the weight we gain, caloric Pelagianism returns only guilt for those who commit Syn.

We may also look to Lynne Gerber's study of the Christian weight-loss group First Place for evidence of caloric Pelagianism. She highlights how individual free choice is "the centerpiece of the ministries' accounts of how change occurs."[52] Just as Christians must choose every day to submit themselves to Jesus Christ, so also must they see their weight loss as an aspect of that choice. When it comes to dieting, however, the morally laden choice is focused on how many calories one consumes. In a fairly mechanistic fashion, if one chooses to consume more calories than one expends, then one has sinned.[53] Though the members of the group resist such an unambiguous

49. Bacon, *Feminist Theology and Contemporary Dieting*, 65.

50. Bacon, *Feminist Theology and Contemporary Dieting*, 66. In a secular context, the case remains the same. Kolata cites a member of a weight-loss group she studied: "He speaks about his struggles with the low-calorie diet and how frustrating it is to still be fat eight months after the study began. But the discussion that night is, in a sense, about free will. Does he have it or not? Is his eating a matter of choice? . . . It must be that free will, when it comes to eating, is an illusion. 'We believe we have it, we believe we control it, but then life gets in the way'" (*Rethinking Thin*, 153, 155).

51. Bacon, *Feminist Theology and Contemporary Dieting*, 84.

52. Gerber, *Seeking the Straight and Narrow*, 96.

53. See Gerber, *Seeking the Straight and Narrow*, 89, 87.

categorization of such an activity as sin, they nevertheless opt for language that is theologically associated with sin. Thus, overeating is considered "disobedience to God," "rebellion against God," as "weakness," as a "Scarlet Letter," as a lack of self-control, or as a "fleshly problem with a spiritual solution."[54] Most frequently, failing in one's diet program constitutes an act of *gluttony*. As one member stated, "Obedience is God's love language, and so we are not being obedient when we are gluttonous. You know gluttony is one of the things that God hates. He doesn't want us to overindulge in alcohol or food or sex or anything else."[55] As one medical doctor who spoke at First Place's national conference summarily stated, "If you're not fit, you can't be the best Christian you possibly could."[56] Ostensibly, being the best Christian you can be is within the remit of any ordinary believer. They have morally unbound free choice available to them in order to follow God,[57] and part of right choosing is avoiding sins like gluttony (where gluttony is understood exclusively as overindulgence). So, if one gains weight, one has only oneself to blame for failing to exercise one's will rightly: "Lack of success is due not to the disciplines themselves but to the failure to adequately give oneself over to them. . . . [People fail the diet] because God has given the gift of free will, a gift only rarely used to choose conformity to his will. . . . People who do not achieve results are depicted as not wanting change badly enough or unwilling to do the hard work change requires."[58] In short, according to diet culture, being fat is a sin, and especially for women.

This section has been an attempt to describe diet culture. I have sought to show that it operates by a fundamental premise: Merely controlling how and what we eat will yield the bodies of our choosing. This fundamental premise has acquired the status of a gendered good. It is predominantly women who feel diet culture's forces, whether due to evolving beauty standards or to how food is marketed to dudes. There is also a theological history to the emergence

54. For these descriptors, see Gerber, *Seeking the Straight and Narrow*, 27 and 91.

55. Gerber, *Seeking the Straight and Narrow*, 46. Importantly, gluttony is the same as overindulgence in the mind of this dieter. This is an association to which we shall return.

56. Gerber, *Seeking the Straight and Narrow*, 61.

57. For Gerber's description of the everyday theology of free will by which these Christians operated, see *Seeking the Straight and Narrow*: "God . . . gives people free will because it is the only solid foundation on which his love could be founded. Free will is present in every opportunity for choice encountered every day; not only is it not complete when one initially decides to follow God, but that decision itself invites the ongoing exercise of free will in order to conform to godly ideals." It is fundamentally a vision of sanctification that operates by choice alone.

58. Gerber, *Seeking the Straight and Narrow*, 184, 185, 182.

of diet culture that brings it close to the Christian doctrine of sin, from which it eventually detached as it morphed into a secular simulacrum. This secular sin is structured by caloric Pelagianism, the view that foods have intrinsic moral values and that our choices about what food we eat—and, by extension, about the kind of body we will have—are entirely within our control. Failing to exercise that control is sin in diet culture, sin that cannot be forgiven but must be repented of all the same. So, women, who are the principal targets of diet culture, face an uphill moral task that they cannot fulfill, one that results in a theologically and culturally enforced source of guilt and shame.

Diets Do Not Work and Weight Is (Mostly) Not Within Our Control: The First Objection

The main features of diet culture, including its fundamental premise, are misguided on several levels. Transitioning to a normative analysis of this picture, we can now consider two objections to diet culture, one having to do with the actual embodied effectiveness of dieting and the other having to do with the nature of sin. Put simply, diets do not work, and being fat is not a sin. First, diets do not work, and our weight is largely not within our control. As surprising as it may sound, this is not a contested claim within the weight-loss industry. In fact, the ineffectiveness of diets is a premise of the financial models by which these groups operate. When asked how he explains the fact that only 16 percent of users maintain their weight loss, Richard Samber, onetime financial chairman of Weight Watchers, responded, "It's successful because the other 84 percent have to come back and do it again. That's where your business comes from."[59] In other words, relapsing on one's diet and bouncing between one's desired weight and one's weight tendencies (referred to as *weight cycling*) is an assumption of Weight Watchers's methods. Its financial model could not work if diets *did* work.

There is, in point of fact, good reason to think that one's weight tendencies are more biologically fixed than is commonly believed. A great deal of evidence strongly suggests that human beings possess a biologically fixed weight range that they would need to exert almost constant effort to live outside of.[60]

59. Traci Mann, *Secrets from the Eating Lab: The Science of Weight Loss, the Myth of Willpower, and Why You Should Never Diet Again* (HarperCollins, 2015), 9.

60. Among the first to suggest this view were William Bennett and Joel Gurin, *The Dieter's Dilemma: Eating Less and Weighing More* (Basic Books, 1982).

Science reporter Gina Kolata summarizes the idea as follows: "The research shows that individuals have a range of weights, often spanning as much as 20 or 30 pounds, that they can achieve or sustain. Being at the bottom of your range usually means constant vigilance; being at the top can mean throwing all caution to the wind."[61] In other words, one's weight is less like one's character (which can be cultivated, trained, and habituated) and more like one's height (which is determined largely by biological factors). There are different ways scientists have sought to account for this reality, but the most common has to do with an appeal to genetics. A person's weight range is a function of their genetic inheritance more than it is attributable to their willpower. Two different studies lend substantial credibility to this claim: one on adopted children and another on twins.[62] A study of 540 adults who were adopted at a very young age (mostly within the first year of life) and raised apart from their biological parents showed that their weights resembled the weights of their biological parents rather than their adopted parents. The study on twins, drawing from the Swedish Twin Registry that includes 25,000 same-sex twins from 1886 to 1958, examined 311 twins who were raised apart and 362 twins who were raised together to see how much their body mass indexes (BMI) differed. Whether they were raised together or apart, researchers concluded that their BMIs were nearly identical, which is what should be expected if BMI is genetically derived. In fact, these researchers claimed that about 70 percent of a person's weight variation is attributable to genetics, which makes weight "more strongly inherited than nearly any other tendency, including . . . mental illness, breast cancer, or heart disease."[63] While these experiments reveal inductive, not deductive, reasons to think that weight is due chiefly to genetics (that is, they attempt to offer the best explanation for witnessed phenomena), those reasons seem more persuasive than the simple claim that our bodies are able to be shaped by our own willpower.

Two further studies strengthen the evidence for the claim that weight is set to a twenty- to thirty-pound range. These two studies are famous within the scientific community, and for good reason. The first of these, meant to show that eating fewer calories does not lead to weight loss, was conducted by Ancel Keys, who was responsible for giving the BMI the outsized influence

61. Kolata, *Rethinking Thin*, 188.

62. For summaries of these studies, see Kolata, *Rethinking Thin*, 121–22; Mann, *Secrets from the Eating Lab*, 19–20.

63. Kolata, *Rethinking Thin*, 123.

it currently enjoys.[64] Keys, a researcher at the University of Minnesota, conducted a study in 1958 with thirty-six healthy young men who were conscientiously objecting to military service. These men were restricted to roughly 1,600 calories a day and were required to exercise a great deal—roughly the same as what is recommended in modern diets. They lost 25 percent of their weight within six months, but they also had some horrifying psychological responses. They had previously lived fairly vibrant and cultured lives, but during their caloric restriction, the men were obsessed with food. Mann describes the effects well:

> The only thing they wanted to think about, or could think about, was food. They lost interest in their humanitarian mission [objecting to the war], stopped attending classes, and even lost interest in sex. Their conversations were about food, and their spare time was occupied with thoughts of wonderful meals they had in the past, or plans for what they would eat someday in the distant future. Several of the volunteers vowed they would take up careers in the food industry when the study ended—to open a grocery store or restaurant, become a chef, or work on a farm. Even those who had never cooked before started clipping recipes and reading cookbooks (including one volunteer who collected more than twenty-five cookbooks).[65]

In short, caloric restriction led to food obsession. One of the participants of the study, Samuel Legg, cut off the three middle fingers of his left hand with an axe. Though he could not say why he did it, he admitted that it could have been because he wanted the food he knew he would receive while hospitalized.[66] The Ancel Keys experiment has been held by many researchers in the psychology of eating to show that when the body is consuming the calories recommended by diets, it activates a starvation response that drives the body to retain the fat that remains and to eat more food.

A second experiment, conducted by Ethan Sims at the University of Vermont in 1967, sought to inquire about the opposite relationship between food and bodies: Does consumption of more food lead to a bigger body? After experimenting with students, Sims realized he needed a population that was not as physically active. So he turned (quite problematically, in retrospect) to

64. See further Todd Tucker, *The Great Starvation Experiment: Ancel Keys and the Men Who Starved for Science* (University of Minnesota Press, 2007).

65. Mann, *Secrets from the Eating Lab*, 25.

66. Tucker, *Great Starvation Experiment*, 169–72.

inmates in a state prison. Sims dramatically increased the number of calories they ate to see if their weight increased, with some eating as many as 10,000 calories a day.[67] Surprisingly, however, Sims discovered that the men did not gain weight at the expected rate. When he investigated the relative calorie intake of the participants, he found that their metabolism increased by 50 percent.[68] In other words, their bodies drastically increased their metabolism to keep up with the increased weight gain. In order to maintain their increased weight, the men would have to continue eating a calorie intake far greater than what they had been eating before the experiment began. Or, they had to make staying above their natural weight range their full-time occupation.

From these two experiments, and many others, it seems that diet culture's fundamental premise—that controlling how and what we eat will yield the bodies of our choosing—is thrown into considerable doubt. Kolata concludes, "There is a reason that fat people can't stay thin after they diet and that thin people can't stay fat when they force themselves to gain weight. The body's metabolism speeds up or slows down to keep weight within a narrow range. Gain weight and the metabolism can as much as double; lose weight and the metabolism can slow down to half its original speed."[69] Our bodies appear to have a weight range that it works rather diligently to stay within. Diets, to the extent that they look to bring one's body beneath that range, do not work.

There are questions that naturally arise for a theory such as this: Is this bad news for those whose weight range is higher, perhaps considered within the range of obesity? What *is* an unhealthy body, then, if it is not a fat body that could be thin? Though BMI is often appealed to as a standard for what a healthy weight must be, its merits are seriously deficient. Ancel Keys, of the starvation experiments, popularized the use of BMI with the help of insurance companies who wanted a convenient metric by which to adjudicate the health of a person. The trouble is that BMI is merely a calculation of weight in relation to height without any regard to the *kind* of weight it is considering. Keys developed BMI from the ideas of a Belgian mathematician named Adolphe Quetelet (1796–1874), who himself based his standardized ratios on what he took an "average man" to be—namely, Europeans with whom he came into contact.[70] Keys praised Quetelet's ideas and recommended the

67. Kolata, *Rethinking Thin*, 117.
68. Kolata, *Rethinking Thin*, 118.
69. Kolata, *Rethinking Thin*, 118–19.
70. Manne, *Unshrinking*, 67–68.

BMI as a reliable method for measuring health in a famous 1972 paper. BMI, however, fails to consider whether someone's weight is attributable to fat or to muscle mass or bone mineral density, leading it to consistently classify black women as having the highest BMI on average. That claim, however, achieves little more than telling us that black women from the twentieth and twenty-first centuries are not European males from the nineteenth century. What it does not do, despite its widespread medical usage, is reliably indicate health.

If BMI is an inadequate measure of health, is obesity possibly a better one? In fact, it is not—or at least, it is not provable through empirical methods that obesity is the cause of bad health. Part of the reason for that has to do with the difficulty of designing an experiment to prove the claim (it would require taking non-obese people and making them obese, or vice versa, and that, as we have seen, is remarkably difficult to do). But when studies have been conducted that measure weight loss from obesity, such as the 2013 study published in the *New England Journal of Medicine*,[71] they found only minimal health benefits from weight loss. Some studies establish a relationship between fat and health, but they do so on the basis of *waist circumference*, or where one's body is widest, and not on weight alone. A high waist circumference is linked to health problems since fat is gathered around organs in the abdomen, whereas a low waist circumference indicates that fat is located in the hips and thighs, which is unrelated to health problems. Traci Mann clarifies the difference helpfully:

> Waist circumference is of course related to obesity, but it is also importantly different from it. There are many obese people with a relatively low waist circumference, as well as non-obese people with a high waist circumference (imagine a skinny guy with a beer belly). Studies have carefully teased out the effects of your weight and your waist circumference on health, and they show that waist circumference is what matters. A higher waist circumference leads to a higher risk of mortality, *regardless of your weight*. In fact, the people with the highest risk of mortality in one study were people who were at a "healthy" weight but who had a high waist circumference. People who were obese but had a low waist circumference had the lowest death rate. So what matters is how your weight is distributed on your body, rather than how much weight there is.[72]

71. Look AHEAD Research Group, "Cardiovascular Effects of Intensive Lifestyle Intervention in Type 2 Diabetes," *New England Journal of Medicine* 369, no. 2 (2013): 145–54.

72. Mann, *Secrets from the Eating Lab*, 78–79 (emphasis added).

It is misleading, then, to say that *obesity* causes health problems. Rather, it is the distribution of weight resulting in a high waist circumference that is associated with health risks. Even if it could be shown that obesity *as such* is the cause of health issues, we would be faced with the problem that obesity has no direct behavioral cause. When he studied 1,660 individuals designed to represent a population of 100,000, Albert Stunkard found that obese people did not display greater tendencies toward psychiatric pathologies than non-obese individuals (where such pathologies would account for a failure of self-control).[73] Stunkard discerned that there are no characteristic behaviors of obese people that account for their obesity, which would make it a highly impracticable indicator for poor health. We would be telling individuals that they are at a weight perilous to their health, but we would also be saying that they probably did not do anything to cause this, and that they cannot do anything to fix it. Why is it that obesity simpliciter has been claimed to be the cause of bad health of epidemic proportions? There are political forces at play, as there usually are,[74] but we can also consider the difficulty such scientifically nuanced claims face in being publicly communicated. We can be sure of this, however: It is possible to have a relatively high set weight range and be perfectly healthy.

As far as reliable weight-related markers for bad health go, only two have solid backing: weight cycling, or the constant relapse from one's diet target weight back into one's set range, and whether one is economically poor. Studies have shown that those who remain at a constant obese weight are at a lower risk of death than those who start obese, lose weight, and gain it back.[75] Kolata describes the story of Mary Frances Neely, who at age forty-five claims to have lost a total of six or seven hundred pounds in her adult life from a series of diets. Neely would lose eighty pounds, then gain it back, then lose over one hundred pounds, then gain it back. It was not for want of effort that she could not keep it off. Neely would meticulously structure her life to lose weight, including replacing large dishes in her home with small ones. Tragically, Neely's original weight would be less of a harm to her than

73. Kolata, *Rethinking Thin*, 91–93.

74. For accounts of the politics behind the so-called obesity epidemic, see J. Eric Oliver, *Fat Politics: The Real Story Behind America's Obesity Epidemic* (Oxford University Press, 2006); Paul Campos, *The Obesity Myth: Why America's Obsession with Weight Is Hazardous to Your Health* (Gotham, 2004).

75. See Mann, *Secrets from the Eating Lab*, 64. See also Manne, *Unshrinking*, 53.

the endless diets that diet culture has pressured her to take on.[76] Moreover, the same study conducted by Stunkard showing that obese individuals showed no differences in their behaviors *did* show a correlation between obesity and social class.[77] Yet, being poor is bad for one's health for reasons far broader than one's fatness, and poverty's correlation with fatness is very likely due to inaccessibility of food that is often within reach only for the rich.[78] In short, if we want to know what unhealthy bodies look like, we should probably look to the bodies of the poor and of those constantly crushed by the pressure once again to lose the weight they have regained. Both of these, however, have explanations that extend far beyond the mere choice between calories. Poverty, in particular, has far more to do with the structural harms poor people have faced.

Diet culture claims that weight loss is a matter of free choice between intrinsically good and intrinsically bad foods. Eat enough of the good kind and avoid enough of the bad kind, and you will have the body you desire. In this section I have tried to show that this is not the case. We have far less control over our weight than we think: Our bodies have a natural weight range that is biologically very difficult to live beyond. There is an irony here. As we saw in chapter 2, there are some Christians who say that sexed bodies are fixed realities, and if conflict should arise between bodies and gender identities, we should prioritize the sexed body over the gender identity. These same Christians also host weight-loss groups in their churches and fail to challenge the diet culture that tries to push beyond a biological limitation that is just as fixed as they take one's sex to be. This is a serious inconsistency that needs to be redressed. While Christian weight-loss groups are not the only ones guilty of such inconsistency, their inconsistency testifies once again to the divide often separating the theological commitments we claim to have and the theological guidelines by which we actually live.

In the end, the fundamental premise of diet culture is false. We do not have the control over our weight that diet culture promises because we each have a genetically set weight range, and diets do not work for that reason. There is also a theological problem with diet culture, and it has to do with its construal of the intrinsic goodness or badness of food.

---

76. Kolata, *Rethinking Thin*, 166–67.

77. Kolata, *Rethinking Thin*, 92.

78. For an early discussion of this, see Amartya Sen, *Poverty and Famines: An Essay on Entitlement and Deprivation* (Oxford University Press, 1983).

Food Is Not Intrinsically Good or Bad, and Being Fat Is Not the Sin of Gluttony: The Second Objection

Caloric Pelagianism, as we have seen, depends on the classification of some foods as intrinsically good and others as intrinsically bad. As Bringle, quoted above, says, "We categorize some foods (carrots and celery, low-fat cottage cheese) as intrinsically good, our allies against the law of our members; others (chocolate, cookies, ice cream, fried anything) are intrinsically wicked, our sworn foes."[79] The successful dieter wields her will to avoid the latter and cling to the former. If she does so, she loses weight and has the body she desires. These are the "Syns" that Hannah Bacon described, and we must use our free choice to abstain from them and lose unwanted weight. Failing to do so, moreover, implicates one in the sin of gluttony. This is the featured sin once theological concepts migrate to diet culture. Gluttony "has become an affront to prevailing standards of beauty and health rather than an offense against God, the wages of sin have changed and now involve a version of hell on earth: the pity, contempt, and distaste of one's fellow mortals."[80] We have already seen how many in the Christian tradition mark gluttony as the first sin, and this narrow focus on gluttony has migrated into diet culture and has become synonymous with overeating. As one First Place participant said, "I think the moral issue is we're kind of denying God when we allow our overeating to take the place of God. . . . The gluttony. The gluttony. It says in there [the Bible] you know you shouldn't be a glutton. And I was being a glutton and I am."[81] Diet culture sees sin as an intrinsic property of the food we should avoid and sees our avoidance as a choice of our unbound wills, lest we become gluttons. This is caloric Pelagianism, and both of its foundational claims are wrong.

In the introduction, I argued that it is theologically unviable to see sin as inherent within creatures. I suggested that this was a helpful way to find conceptual space between the claim that gender must be reduced to a list of roles and properties that apply in all times and all places and the claim that gender can be reduced to its cultural particularity. There are too many gendered goods for either option. But if, with Augustine, we maintain that "sin consists *not in the things themselves*, but in the unlawful *use* of them,"[82] then our moral

79. Bringle, "Confessions of a Glutton." See further Bringle, *God of Thinness*, 147.

80. Francine Prose, *Gluttony: The Seven Deadly Sins* (Oxford University Press, 2003), 5.

81. Gerber, *Seeking the Straight and Narrow*, 29.

82. Augustine, *The Literal Meaning of Genesis*, in *On Genesis*, trans. Edmund Hill, The Works of Saint Augustine: A Translation for the 21st Century 1/13 (New City, 2002), 1.1.13.

attention is turned to the quality of our use rather than to the objects of use themselves. This is Augustine's way of balancing two apparently incompatible claims in the Christian confession: first, that God has made everything that exists and cannot be implicated in making something evil, which means that all creatures must be good; and second, that sin has affected all of creation. Augustine's solution, usually articulated in response to the Manichees, is to affirm the goodness of creation and to construe sin as a privation. This has the result of both liberating and constricting our moral agency: We are liberated because nothing can be said to be evil on account of its intrinsic properties (it is the Lord who has made it), and we are constricted because everything has the potential to become twisted and warped into sin by our use. Yet the sin lies not in the object itself but in our use of it. As 1 Timothy 4:4–5 claims, "Everything created by God is good, and nothing is to be rejected, provided it is received with thanksgiving; for it is sanctified by God's word and by prayer."[83]

Importantly, Augustine connected such insights to food: "It makes no difference at all what foods you take to support the needs of the body, provided that in the sorts of foods you are in harmony with those among whom you have to live."[84] Or again, after reaffirming his firm belief in the goodness of creation, Augustine says, "It is not unclean food I fear, but rather unclean desires."[85] Food, by virtue of being a creature, is good. It may be counterintuitive to say it, but Cheetos, fast food, desserts, and other foods forbidden to diets are *good*. They can be used in such a way that they generate sin, of course, and there may be sinful use baked into their production. But this can be the case for low-fat foods too. They may be creations of production processes that are necessarily problematic, but that is a claim about use, not about the intrinsic qualities of the food. Claims that *some* foods are intrinsically bad require a revision to a central conviction regarding creation, and they also run the risk of elitist bias with regard to who can achieve moral excellence in this life.[86] For instance, when Norman Wirzba states that "fast food does not

83. I have defended this reading in "'Sin Consists Not in the Things Themselves, but in the Unlawful Use of Them': An Approach to the Moral Analysis of Contextual Goods," in *Receiving Redemption: Explorations in Constructive Dogmatics*, ed. Fred Sanders and Uche Anizor (Zondervan Academic, 2026), 108–24.

84. Augustine, *Questions on the Gospels*, in *The New Testament I and II*, The Works of Saint Augustine: A Translation for the 21st Century 1/15 and 1/16 (New City, 2014), 2.11.

85. Augustine, *Confessions* 10.46, trans. Carolyn Hammond, Loeb Classical Library 27 (Harvard University Press, 2016), 149.

86. For another argument that food ethics must be contextually evaluated, but one that draws on an Aristotelean mean and virtue ethics, see Christina Van Dyke, "Manly Meat and

facilitate or encourage contemplation, nor does it promote an affectionate regard for what is eaten," he mistakes the food itself for the manner in which it is eaten.[87] There are problems related to fast food (and Wirzba perceptively names them), but they are not with the food itself (fast food *can* promote affection for what is eaten, such as when my daughter chooses it for her special birthday dinner). Its wrongness lies in the uses involved in producing it and the disaffection that *can* be cultivated by the pace at which it is delivered. But the claim that fast food *itself* is morally problematic forgets that use must be our moral focus. And it forgets that the majority of people who are eating fast food—namely, the poor—would be set at a significant moral disadvantage through no fault of their own.

It is important to remember here that Christianity has no specific food prohibitions.[88] When Peter was "hungry and wanted something to eat" (Acts 10:10), God presented to him a variety of foods that Peter considered "profane or unclean" (10:14). God's response is decisive: "What God has made clean, you must not call profane" (10:15). Such episodes emphasize God's extension of hospitality apart from social divisions, including dietary practices.[89] Food is implicated in sin when we eat it wrongfully, not when it is too fattening, a carbohydrate, or a dessert.[90] As Bringle rightly affirms, "Sin lies in a *manner* of consumption, not in consumption itself."[91] Or again, as Paul Griffiths

---

Gendered Eating: Correcting Imbalance and Seeking Virtue," in *Philosophy Comes to Dinner: Arguments on the Ethics of Eating*, ed. Andrew Chignell, Terence Cuneo, and Matthew C. Halteman (Routledge, 2016).

87. Wirzba, *Food and Faith*, 243.

88. According to Bringle, in the Bible, we do not meet "a dogmatics of diet. . . . Christianity has no laws of kosher, proscribes no specific foods, no specific abstinence. Rather, what we meet in Christian Scripture is a remarkable balance in attitudes toward eating. Put briefly, this balance affirms that food is good—but is not a supreme good; and that care taken with food is important—but not of paramount importance" (*God of Thinness*, 57).

89. See Joshua W. Jipp, *Reading Acts* (Cascade Books, 2018), 79–80.

90. This is not to say that extrinsic reasons do not exist for refraining from eating certain foods. For instance, we might refrain from food on the basis of cultural prohibitions (such as when Americans do not eat horse meat) or prohibitions on account of love for another (such as Paul's recommendation in Romans 14:15). It seems to me that dietary restrictions given under the law fall under some kind of extrinsic prohibition when taken canonically: It is not a prohibition on account of the intrinsic properties of the food but a prohibition on the basis of what God wants for Israel. Those specifications, however, do not identify intrinsic properties of the food consumed; rather, they provide extrinsic reasons for dietary avoidance on other grounds. Thank you to Joshua Jipp, Michelle Knight, and Madison Pierce for helping me think through this issue.

91. Bringle, *God of Thinness*, 63.

states, "Save the eucharist, there is no properly Christian diet."[92] For Christians, food is neither intrinsically good nor bad; rather, the manner by which we eat is what must be evaluated. So, when *does* a Christian eat wrongfully? For an answer, we need to revisit the sin of gluttony.

Like modesty in the previous chapter, gluttony has been altered by its migration into a non-Christian paradigm. Gluttony is now understood to be the same as overeating and identifiable by the result of overeating: fatness. The glutton overeats and is therefore fat. But this not at all what the historical understanding of this vice actually means. Rebecca DeYoung, in her treatment of the vices, asks, "What if the label of gluttony doesn't first apply to overeating and being overweight, or forgoing the diet for the doughnuts? What if your extra pounds won't be enough to tip the scales of judgment further toward sin? Can health-food eaters, the skim-milk latte crowd, and the gourmands be as gluttonous as the junk-food junkies?"[93] In fact, this is precisely the conclusion we reach when we examine traditional understandings of gluttony. For instance, Gregory the Great, whose *Moralia in Job* provided one of the most systematic treatments of the seven capital vices, maintains, "It is not the food, but the desire that is in fault" (concurring with our denial of food's intrinsic moral value). The desire for food, moreover, can "tempt us in five ways."[94] As Gregory's account of the vices grew in popularity, a slogan developed to summarize his identification of the five manifestations of glutinous desire: eating "too daintily, too sumptuously, too hastily, too greedily, too much." Or, in DeYoung's updated wording: "eating *fastidiously*, *ravenously*, *excessively*, *sumptuously*, and *hastily*."[95] Gluttony, then, is when Christians approach their food with disordered loves, and this can happen in various ways. Eating too much is one of them, but so is paying too much fastidious attention to what is consumed, which is precisely what a modern diet requires. The counting of points—or worse, "Syns"—is as paradigmatic an instance of gluttony as overeating.

Gluttony, as a result, is quite broad. We might be gluttons if we eat too much, but we might also be gluttons if we rush to food without regard for our neighbor who is hungry. Or we might be gluttons if we become so obsessed with our meals that we have no gratitude for them. Or we might be gluttons

92. Paul Griffiths, *Christian Flesh* (Stanford University Press, 2018), 105.

93. Rebecca Konyndyk DeYoung, *Glittering Vices: A New Look at the Seven Deadly Sins and Their Remedies*, 2nd ed. (Brazos, 2020), 164.

94. Gregory the Great, *Morals on the Book of Job*, trans. J. F. D. Rivington and J. Rivington (John Henry Parker, 1844), 964 (30.60).

95. DeYoung, *Glittering Vices*, 166. Helpfully, her translation yields the acronym FRESH.

if we gulp a meal in the car as we drive to work. Or we might be gluttons when we make food only to post it to social media. It does not matter *what* we are eating; what matters is *how*. Thus Bringle: "The sinfulness of gluttony does not inhere in the substance of the food itself, which is good."[96] We are gluttonous, in short, if our loves terminate on the food without recognizing it as God's gift.[97] When we are hungry, we stretch ourselves toward some end for our eating.[98] Gluttonous eating misdirects eating from its proper ends: enjoyment of God, love of neighbor, and love of self. Diet culture, with its cruel condemnation, does not help us to avoid gluttony; it promotes and systematizes it.

Diet culture's understanding of sin, the doctrine that serves as the source of so much guilt, shame, and embarrassment for so many women, is errant in both of its claims. It claims that certain foods are intrinsically good while others are intrinsically bad. By means of an unbound will, women must choose the good foods to acquire and retain a body that conforms to impossible standards. If they should fail to do so and become fat, they are gluttonous. So says diet culture and its caloric Pelagianism. But it is wrong in every move it has made. Creatures are not intrinsically evil. A Christian doctrine of creation, with its affirmation of God's universal creation of all that is, does not tolerate such a Manichean claim. Foods are not intrinsically bad; our loves for them can lead us to use them badly, but that is not due to the food. When our loves for food are disordered, we are gluttonous. But gluttony is a broad category, and most of us are gluttons, perhaps even regularly. This raises a question: Can we be free of sinful eating? Is our free choice one inevitably mired in death?

The Freedom to Eat: Body "Okayness" and the Compassion We Owe to One Another

There is one final element of diet culture that needs to be addressed, and it shall serve as the basis of this concluding constructive section. Diet culture

96. Bringle, *God of Thinness*, 76.

97. Thus Griffiths: "Gluttons are, rather, those whose appetites for food and drink are recursive: they eat and drink only to eat and drink; the meaning of their eating and drinking is given solely by the acts themselves, remembered from the past and anticipated in the future" (*Christian Flesh*, 114).

98. Augustine, *On the Advantage of Fasting* 1.

paints a picture of an unbound will able to choose between good and bad foods. But are we really so free with regard to our eating? We have already seen how many dieters deny this when they describe their experience with losing weight: "It must be that free will, when it comes to eating, is an illusion," says one dieter interviewed by Kolata.[99] Cole Kazdin's account of her struggles with diet culture and eating disorders illustrates this powerfully. She notes how "eating disorders can provide a false sense of power and control, even though the feeling around food is total absence of control," and even though she *knew* the number on the scale was "just a number, not your worth," she found that such a phrase "wasn't really true outside of my bathroom."[100] She discloses, "Even before I had an official eating disorder, I'd had such a disordered relationship with food and my body. Dieting, body dissatisfaction—all of it. I'm not sure who I am without it. I don't know if it feels that way because it's been going on for so long, or if it's something fundamental about me."[101] It is here, I want to suggest, that a recovered doctrine of sin and its impact on our wills serves as an aid to the difficulties we encounter with food. Kazdin is right: The challenges she continues to feel *are* due to something that has been going on for a long time—since humanity's inception. But while the doctrine of original sin can help us understand why we continue to feel so bound by the behaviors we know harm us, it should—if used correctly—also encourage us to show compassion to one another.

Bringle also reaches for the language of sin to describe her experience with compulsive eating. While she is emphatic that being fat is not a sin and that diet culture's moralization of food is wrongheaded, she confesses, "I *know* I am doing something self-destructive. . . . I do recognize in my own experience that habits of compulsive eating (and of compulsive non-eating) stand as signs of a fundamental brokenness and alienation. I recognize that feeding myself with frantic mouthfuls of food can be a way of swallowing down emotions and seeking to flee some uncomfortable truth about myself. I recognize that obsessing about calories consumed or expended can be a way of worshipping the cultural 'god of thinness,' deflecting my devotion from the One True God."[102] So, while we ought to deny diet culture's calorically Pelagian understanding of the will and sin, we must also replace it with an improved doctrine

99. Kolata, *Rethinking Thin*, 155.
100. Kazdin, *What's Eating Us*, 7, 75, 100.
101. Kazdin, *What's Eating Us*, 123.
102. Bringle, *God of Thinness*, 15.

of sin that is both much more familiar to the Christian confession and fosters much more compassion. We saw that caloric Pelagianism's account of sin yields guilt, shame, and self-destruction. I hope now to show that Christian anti-Pelagianism yields compassion, grace, and, ultimately, "body okayness."

Throughout this book, I have operated with a broad theology of death, one that defines death as more than the end of biological life. Death is the sum total of all that has corrupted creation, including a breakdown of the friendship we have with our bodies. Death, in short, is the chief representative of original sin. Recognizing this broad definition of death in Christian theology, Norman Wirzba reminds us that eating is always embroiled in death: "Eating is the daily reminder of creaturely mortality. We eat to live, knowing that without food we will starve and die. But to eat we must also kill, realizing that without the deaths of others—microbes, insects, plants, animals—we can have no food. . . . No matter how much or how well we eat, our biological life, as well as the lives of others, will come to a mortal end."[103] Eating, of any kind, requires death. What we must account for, then, is the death that we carry within us and that encircles us as we approach the dinner plate.

If death is what Christian theology claims it is, then we cannot be the agents of free choice that diet culture claims we are. There are some complex theological and philosophical issues that need to be addressed in that assertion (and I suspect those who comment on weight loss and freedom do not intend to invoke those issues),[104] but for our purposes it suffices to say that death significantly affects our ability to choose rightly. Jesse Couenhoven summarizes Augustine's views here well: "To be a sinner, Augustine believed, is to be at odds with oneself, trapped by a twisted second nature, original sin, that undermines the good for which human nature was created. He found the agency of sinners lacking in significant respects, and he displayed a good deal of compassion for sinners, among whom he located himself. . . . Such . . . is the life of a sinner. It is a life of such severely diminished agency that it is properly thought of as akin to being tied down."[105] Being at odds with oneself, lacking agency, feeling trapped—these are terms similar to the ones

103. Wirzba, *Food and Faith*, 156–57.

104. I am particularly persuaded by the argument for "Augustinian compatibilism" developed by Jesse Couenhoven. See Jesse Couenhoven, "Augustinian Compatibilism," in *Stricken by Sin, Cured by Christ: Agency, Necessity, and Culpability in Augustinian Theology* (Oxford University Press, 2013).

105. Jesse Couenhoven, "Augustine of Hippo," in *The Routledge Companion to Free Will*, ed. Kevin Timpe et al. (Routledge, 2017), 254.

used by Kazdin and Bringle. It is not so much that they are committing sins as that they are held in its grasp, tied down by it. What is the response to such a tragic state of affairs? If diet culture and caloric Pelagianism condemn such experiences with a hell on earth, what is Christianity's remedy?

If we consider how God has responded to our sin, we see that the remedy is *compassion*. Just as God has been merciful to us as sinners, so we must be merciful to one another. Framed with the doctrine of original sin, recognition of our mutual weakness and frailty ought to generate a response of humane compassion. This is precisely how Augustine intended his doctrine of original sin to function. Critiquing the Stoic rejection of compassion, Augustine says, "For what is compassion but a kind of fellow-feeling in our hearts for the misery of another that compels us to come to his aid if we can? And this emotion is in full accord with reason when we show compassion in ways that keep justice unimpaired, as when we give to the poor or forgive the penitent."[106] When faced with someone confined and brought low by the devastation of sin and death, we must respond with compassion, thought Augustine. Just as God responded to our state of sin with compassion, so we respond to the plight of others with compassion.

If our experiences with food are associated with sin and death far more than they are with a fully liberated will, what is a compassionate response? What does compassion look like when we are held by caloric Pelagianism's grasp? It must be a compassion shown to oneself, to one's body, in the effort to say that though our bodies are still being redeemed, they are *our* bodies, objects of a difficult love that requires constant care. I want to claim that compassion looks like *body okayness*, which is the term Traci Mann uses in lieu of *body positivity*. She writes, in line with the claims I have made about the difficulty of making friends with our body, "Perhaps loving your body is something to strive for, but all we really need to do is respect our bodies, appreciate them, and be generally okay with them."[107] Body okayness is an appropriate posture for human beings living during the saeculum and still grappling with the lingering effects of death, carrying about with us bodies crying out for our compassion and love. "Feeling good about your body is a tall order," writes Kazdin, pointing out an Instagram ad for a shapewear

106. Augustine, *City of God*, trans. William Babcock, ed. Boniface Ramsey, The Works of Saint Augustine: A Translation for the 21st Century, 1/6 and 1/7 (New City, 2012–13), 9.5.

107. Mann, *Secrets from the Eating Lab*, 167.

brand made to help women look smaller while claiming to be body positive.[108] Such claims show that perfect friendship with our bodies, as argued above, is a resurrection promise. In the meantime, for this earthly pilgrimage, perhaps body okayness will do.

There is a danger to ignoring the effects of original sin and encouraging an overly optimistic body-positivity message. Just as *toxic positivity* has emerged as a misguided response to the complexity of this life, it has also been the case, as studies have shown, that many women experience toxic body positivity. When pressure is placed on them, largely from advertisements and other exploitative sources, to display a confidence in their body that they are not ready to have, such is the outcome.[109] Such messages, they say, circumvent a woman's agency in *cultivating* body positivity through the difficult challenges such a task poses. Put in a theological register, hasty claims to body positivity attempt to get at resurrection without cultivating friendship with the body during the saeculum. And in a world where brands rush in to commodify messages intended to be positive, a suspicious eye toward such optimistic goals seems wise.

This is why thinkers like Traci Mann, Cole Kazdin, Kate Manne, and others opt for something less ambitious but much more merciful. Body okayness recognizes that these are *our* bodies, not decorations to be evaluated by others.[110] It says to one's body, "Okay, you are not easy to love, but you've also brought me so much joy. We've got a long road together, and we will receive God's promises together. Tell me what you need to be loved well, and I will love you well." It means being okay with a fat body, but also being okay with not being okay with one's body every day, knowing that self-doubt will always creep in. It expects failure, knowing that death's impact is still felt, and it stretches to celebrate victories, knowing that doing so is often much harder than focusing on failure. Body okayness recognizes that food is a blessed gift, meant to be loved in God, to be shared with neighbors, and to anticipate the blessed feast we will have when we see God face-to-face.

We can eat fast food, but we can also take small steps in hope, such as eating some more vegetables. When practicing body okayness, whatever we

108. Kazdin, *What's Eating Us*, 98–100.

109. See Lisa Legault and Anise Sago, "When Body Positivity Falls Flat: Divergent Effects of Body Acceptance Messages That Support vs. Undermine Basic Psychological Needs," *Body Image* 41 (June 2022): 225–38.

110. Manne, *Unshrinking*, 195.

eat, we do so in love for God, neighbor, enemy, and ourselves. Body okayness is neither complacent in its moral striving nor compulsive in its strictures. It promotes effort even while it promotes forgiveness, and setting goals while recognizing that we can do nothing on our own. It encourages savoring the taste of food without allowing such delight to terminate on itself. It suggests staying away from scales. It is merciful.

In a world of restricted freedom, sin, and death, body okayness is a helpful placeholder until the fulfillment of Christ's promises is reached. It is a posture of befriending one's body in compassion, love, and patience.

Conclusion

"It makes no difference at all what foods you take to support the needs of the body, provided that in the sorts of foods you are in harmony with those among whom you have to live."[111] This was Augustine's advice, and it has turned out to be the opposite message of diet culture, which I have taken as the focus of the descriptive task of this chapter. Diet culture claims that if we control what we eat—intrinsically good foods over intrinsically bad foods—we will have the bodies that we desire, and it assures us that such control is fully within our remit to exercise. I have called this set of ideas "caloric Pelagianism," and it is present both in non-Christian weight-loss groups and in Christian ones. It has as its hallmark a doctrine of sin that does nothing but overwhelm and destroy those over whom it exercises its dominion. Finally, diet culture has set women in particular in its sights, utilizing shifting beauty norms to place onerous pressures on them to conform.

I have argued that both of diet culture's fundamental claims are false. We do not get the bodies we want by dieting. Biologically speaking, our bodies have naturally set weight ranges that we cannot live beyond unless we make it our full-time jobs to do so. Attempts to do so, moreover, trigger metabolic responses that regulate our bodies back to their natural ranges, and having a higher weight range is not a determination of death. Rather, obesity and BMI are poor markers of health; while there are markers of health we can look to, they are not numbers on scales. Additionally, we cannot make sin an intrinsic feature of food. All foods, by virtue of being creatures, are good. Sin occurs in *how* we eat, not *what* we eat. We saw this

111. Augustine, *Questions on the Gospels* 2.11.

with the traditional doctrine of gluttony, which is starkly juxtaposed to diet culture's bowdlerized version.

Finally, I sought to reclaim a place for sin in these discussions. This was the culmination of my normative task. We cannot escape the grasp of death when we eat—eating *requires* death—so we must figure in the pressures of sin and death when we eat. This is not an optimistic view of freedom, but I have sought to show that it is one that summons a response of compassion. Diet culture tolerates no compassion, but Christians must be known for compassion. The merciful response to our bodies is cultivating "body okayness," which is more clear-eyed about death than body positivity and so is a crucial element in cultivating friendship with our bodies. It is not optimistic, but hopefully it is compassionate. As we take food into our bodies as gifts of God, body okayness creates the space we need to respond to our food with gratitude and in community. Whether we are eating a leafy salad, chicken nuggets, or something else, our uses of food and our cultivation of body okayness can aid us in our pilgrimage to God and our anticipation of the glory of the resurrection.

6

Just *Friends* or *Just* Friends?

Gender in Dating Relationships

What I'm saying is—and this is not a come-on in any way, shape or form—is that men and women can't be friends because the sex part always gets in the way.

—Harry Burns, *When Harry Met Sally*[1]

If Souls no Sexes have, for Men t'exclude
Women from Friendship's vast capacity,
Is a Design injurious or rude,
Only maintain'd by partial tyranny.
Love is allow'd to us and Innocence,
And noblest Friendships do proceed from thence.

—Katherine Philips, 1631–64[2]

Sexes make no difference, since in souls there is none; and they are the subjects of friendship.

—William Penn, 1693[3]

1. *When Harry Met Sally*, directed by Rob Reiner (Columbia Pictures, 1989).
2. "Poems by the most deservedly admired Mrs. Katherine Philips, the matchless Orinda; to which is added Monsieur Corneille's Pompey & Horace, tragedies; with several other translations out of French," *Early English Books Online 2* (University of Michigan Library, Digital Collections), 95.
3. William Penn, *Some Fruits of Solitude* (1693; repr., F. Sowle, 1718), 26. https://upload.wikimedia.org/wikipedia/commons/f/f4/Some_fruits_of_solitude_%28IA_somefruitsofsoli00penniala%29.pdf.

There is a popular trope in contemporary literature and film referred to as *friends to lovers*. The typical flow of this kind of story begins with two people who are "just friends" and interact in "strictly platonic" ways. Perhaps they are coworkers who bond over having to cope with a miserable boss, or perhaps they grew up as childhood friends in the same neighborhood. They are, as the saying goes, firmly in the "friend zone," and remaining in the friend zone means that no romantic developments will occur. But, after the introduction of some unforeseen changes of perspective, these friends become "more than friends"—they become lovers. When Harry meets Sally in the eponymous film, they go from enemies to begrudging friends. Their friendship grows over a period of time, eventually graduating into a marriage. The point of the film, it seems, is that friends cannot be lovers simultaneously; if two people are friends, they cannot be lovers, and vice versa. Undergirding this common trope is a conviction about the incompatibility of friendship and dating.

The subject of this chapter is how gender should be understood in relation to contemporary practices of dating. I suggest that a theological conception of friendship can help. Contrary to the friends-to-lovers trope, I will assume, with the majority of the Christian tradition, that marriage is a type of friendship. If that is the case, then dating is also plausibly a type of friendship. I will argue that friendships ought to aspire to certain virtues and that the virtue of specific importance for dating is trust. This is because dating is in a descriptively bad place, with daters from many different contexts describing their experiences as unsafe and depleting. My normative recommendation will be that, having seen dating as a type of friendship, we practice and test out trusting relationships. Trust brings together safety, friendship, and love, so if trust successfully characterizes a friendship, it will be safe. First, we need to understand friendship and dating descriptively. I begin with a theological description of friendship and its relevant virtues, with special attention to how friendships have been understood between women and men. Then I describe contemporary dating, which is shot through with feelings of shame, a lack of safety, and emptiness. The final section develops a normative account of dating where the central virtue that ought to be pursued by partners is trust and trustworthiness, for trust brings together love, friendship, and safety. The outcome will be an approach to friendship and dating wherein friendship is the primary form human love takes when virtuously shown to persons, and it is the necessary place for trust to grow.

Friendship: Love Shown to Persons

Both in *Gender as Love* and in the introductory chapter of this book, I argue that love is natural to human beings. Part of what it means to be human is to have a capacity to love.[4] Here we might usefully begin with a distinction between *nonpersonal* objects of love and *personal* objects of love. We love persons differently than we love objects. This does not mean that our love for persons is necessarily *better* than nonpersonal love; it only means that it is *different*. Persons (whether human, animal, or divine) summon us to a different set of responsibilities than nonpersons do. In this chapter our focus will be on personal love, and we can give it further definition by noting that there are *good* or *virtuous* ways to love persons and *bad* or *vicious* ways to love them. The latter, a direct product of the introduction of sin into the world, works to dominate, destroy, and possess the beloved. With Augustine, I have previously called this the *libido dominandi*, the "lust for domination"—or we may simply refer to it as hatred.[5] Such is vicious personal love.

What is virtuous personal love? Virtuous love shown toward persons is friendship. Christian reflection on friendship has regularly revolved around two biblical texts that lend themselves to this claim. John 15:13, the most commonly cited of these, has Jesus stating, "No one has greater love than this, to lay down one's life for one's friends." Additionally, Proverbs 17:17 affirms that "a friend loves at all times," and from these two texts, Christians have affirmed that friendship is the ideal shape of Christian love shown to persons. For instance, Ambrose inquires, "For what is a friend but a partner in love?"[6] Augustine similarly asserts, "Where there is love, there is friendship."[7] In the twelfth century, Aelred of Rievaulx wrote one of the most developed treatises on Christian friendship available and made love its defining characteristic: "What is true of charity, I surely do not hesitate to grant to friendship. . . . The fountain and source of friendship is love. There can be no love without

4. See, in particular, Fellipe do Vale, *Gender as Love: A Theological Account of Human Identity, Embodied Desire, and Our Social Worlds* (Baker Academic, 2023), chap. 4.

5. Do Vale, *Gender as Love*, 135.

6. Ambrose, *De officiis* 3.134; English translation from Ivor J. Davidson, trans. and ed., *Ambrose: De Officiis; Edited with an Introduction, Translation, and Commentary*, 2 vols. (Oxford University Press, 2001–2), 3.134.

7. Augustine, *De sermone Domini in monte* 1.11.31 (my trans.). The Latin word here translated as "love" is *benevolentia*, which is often translated as "benevolence." "Love" is a justifiable translation because, for Augustine, benevolence is one of the most important desires that compose love.

friendship, but friendship without love is impossible. . . . Friendship is founded on love."[8] For much of the Christian tradition, when Christians love other persons rightly, they form friendships with them.[9]

Contrary to this generalized priority of friendship is a common notion that women and men cannot and should not be friends because, in the immortalized words of Harry Burns, "the sex part always gets in the way." This is likely the first question raised in the minds of those who are thinking about the gendered implications of friendship. It turns out that this resistance to friendships with persons of other genders is hardly new, and the church has not been immune to it. An edict of Honorius and Theodosius II from 420 warned against such friendships on account of the rumors that could arise about sexual activities: "Although [depravity] does not penetrate into this association and friendship, rumor contaminates and the addition of the other sex affords occasion for evil morals."[10] It is clear that for both Harry Burns and Emperor Theodosius II, men and women should not be friends because of the possibility, whether actual or rumored, of sex. This sensibility has now become the assumed norm, so much so that contemporary author Aimee Byrd writes, "Over time, I learned that much of the conservative church believes the 'Billy Crystal Rule' taught by Burns."[11] Friendships, so it came to be accepted in much of the Christian tradition, were designed for persons of the same gender.

However, as we have seen throughout this book, stated theology and practiced theology do not always overlap, and normative prescriptions do not always describe concrete situations. So, alongside this resistance to friendships

8. Aelred, *De spirituali amicitia* 1:70, 3:2, 3:128; English translation from Aelred of Rievaulx, *Spiritual Friendship*, ed. Marsha L. Dutton, trans. Lawrence C. Braceland (Cistercian Publications, 2010).

9. There is classical precedent for this. Cicero, whose *De amicitia* served as a chief influence for authors like Aelred, makes an observation Aelred will later repeat: "It is love [*amor*] from which the word 'friendship' [*amicitia*] comes, and this is the origin of goodwill" (Cicero, *De amicitia* §26; English translation from Marcus Tullius Cicero, *How to Be a Friend: An Ancient Guide to True Friendship*, trans. Philip Freeman [Princeton University Press, 2018]). See Aelred, *De spirituali amicitia* 1.19. Aristotle, similarly, connects friendship with love: "Friendship seems to consist more in loving than in being loved" (*Nicomachean Ethics*, rev. ed., trans. Roger Crisp, Cambridge Texts in the History of Philosophy [Cambridge University Press, 2014], 1159a.28). The association of friendship with love, therefore, not only has warrant from the Bible and Christian tradition; it also seems to be axiomatic for the classical philosophical discussion.

10. "Letter of Honorius and Theodosius on Clerical Cohabitation and on Delation About Rapists of Consecrated Virgins, 420," in *Roman State and Christian Church: A Collection of Legal Documents to A.D. 503*, vol. 2, ed. P. R. Coleman-Norton (SPCK, 1966), 612.

11. Aimee Byrd, *Why Can't We Be Friends? Avoidance Is Not Purity* (P&R, 2018), 23.

between women and men there developed another theological trajectory resulting in deep, edifying, and spiritually fruitful friendships between women and men, most of whom were nonnegotiably committed to celibacy. According to the classical philosophical literature on friendship, in order to have a friendship the two friends must enjoy equality in some form. So Aristotle, whose writing on friendship has exercised an enormous influence on subsequent reflection, makes equality central to his threefold division of friendship: "So there are three kinds of friendship, and in all of them there is a sense in which friendship is said to be in accordance with equality."[12] Ordinarily, such equality could not obtain between men and women in antiquity. But certain eschatological developments throughout the early church opened new avenues of partial equality between women and men that allowed for friendships to blossom.

Rosemary Rader, in her treatment of these developments, summarizes them nicely: "Heterosexual friendship was one of the early Christians' subjective responses to the reconciliatory emphasis of their new world view, a 'new heaven and earth.' The notion of the Christians' 'oneness in Christ,' exemplified in Jesus' recorded acceptance of and empathy with his followers and friends (man, woman, slave, free, rich, poor, Jew, Gentile) paved the way for an irruption of those boundaries which normally restricted communication between people."[13] As Rader's quotation describes, many early Christians drew from varied theological sources (such as Gal. 3:28, a developing admiration of the martyrs, and the privileging of celibacy) to establish an equality sufficient for friendship between men and women. This happened *despite* gender; it was *as if* the martyrs or celibate monastics were not gendered at all because of their spiritual superiority. For instance, in his oration for his sister Gorgonia, Gregory of Nazianzus praises her piety by showing how it made her femininity irrelevant: "O nature of woman overcoming that of man in the common struggle for salvation, and demonstrating that the distinction between male and female is one of body not of soul!"[14] These Christians affirmed that gender was not a property of the soul

12. Aristotle, *Eudemian Ethics*, trans. Brad Inwood and Raphael Woolf, Cambridge Texts in the History of Philosophy (Cambridge University Press, 2013), 1238b.15–16.

13. Rosemary Rader, *Breaking Boundaries: Male/Female Friendship in Early Christian Communities* (Paulist Press, 1983), 43.

14. Gregory of Nazianzus, *Oration 8*, in vol. 7 of *Nicene and Post-Nicene Fathers of the Christian Church*, 2nd series (Eerdmans, 1986), §14. For the Cappadocian Fathers (Gregory of Nazianzus and his contemporaries Gregory of Nyssa and Basil of Caesarea), gender was *actually* removed eschatologically. While that makes the equality of persons more obvious through

and, therefore, it would not carry the same evaluative weight in the eschaton that it did in their time and place in history. As they practiced resurrection in their day, they anticipated the eschatological blessings of equality would break in. The life to come began in their day-to-day lives as new and surprising social bonds formed—specifically, friendships between women and men whose sanctity outweighed any bias that, in their day, was wrongly attributed to gender.

There are numerous such examples of friendships between women and men.[15] Famously, the practice of *syneisaktism*, or "spiritual marriage," began in the early church and may have continued until as late as the Middle Ages. In it, "celibate men and women vowed their lives to God and lived together for mutual support and encouragement." Even though they were subjected to rumors and suspicion, practitioners saw themselves as engaging in "the means toward the attainment of a personal state of perfection" that awaited them eschatologically.[16] Men and women became friends without benefits for the sake of the greater benefit of sampling eschatological beatitude. Or we can also look to the letters of theologians like Chrysostom and Jerome, who, despite their infelicitous comments about them, had rich friendships with women.[17] Chrysostom wrote letters to Olympias from exile in a "natural, sometimes coaxing, teasing, almost playful style," letters whose "general tone is one of warm affection for someone who was a friend, mutual advisor, and defender of his policies and actions."[18] Jerome, similarly, is famous for his friendship with Paula, and he also expanded his network of friendships with

the erasure of gender, this equality is still compatible with the weaker claim that gender is not erased but is detached from how one measures worth. I have argued for this latter claim in Fellipe do Vale, "Cappadocian or Augustinian? Adjudicating Debates on Gender in the Resurrection," *International Journal of Systematic Theology* 21, no. 2 (2019): 182–98; Fellipe do Vale, *Gender as Love: A Theological Account of Human Identity, Embodied Desire, and Our Social Worlds* (Baker Academic, 2023); and Fellipe do Vale, "Gender Identity: To Infinity and Beyond," *Pro Ecclesia* 32, no. 1 (2023): 24–46.

15. For a more recent example, consider Cassandra A. Good, *Founding Friendships: Friendships Between Men and Women in the Early American Republic* (Oxford University Press, 2015). In ecclesial history, see the life of Katherine Philips, one of whose poems I have used as an epigraph for this chapter, and the practice of the Quaker William Penn. In particular, see Linda Ford, "William Penn's Views on Women: Subjects of Friendship," *Quaker History* 72, no. 2 (1983): 75–102.

16. Rader, *Breaking Boundaries*, 62, 65.

17. For an analysis of this seemingly incompatible state of affairs, see Elizabeth A. Clark, *Jerome, Chrysostom, and Friends: Essays and Translations*, Studies in Women and Religion (Edwin Mellen, 1982). That Jerome and Chrysostom were quite bluntly sexist in their normative claims while developing descriptively deep friendships with women should come as no surprise to readers of this book by this point.

18. Rader, *Breaking Boundaries*, 98.

women to others living in celibate communities like Marcella, Principia, and Eustochium. Defending his friendships with women, Jerome writes,

> The unbelieving reader may perhaps laugh at me for dwelling so long on the praises of mere women; yet if he will but remember how holy women followed our Lord and Saviour and ministered to Him of their substance, and how the three Marys stood before the cross and especially how Mary Magdalen—called the tower from the earnestness and glow of her faith—was privileged to see the rising Christ first of all before the very apostles, he will convict himself of pride sooner than me of folly. *For we judge of people's virtue not by their sex but by their character*, and hold those to be worthy of the highest glory who have renounced both rank and wealth.[19]

Jerome's confidence in forming friendships with women came from his observation of the life of Christ, who was himself the friend of women. This led Jerome to conclude that sex and gender were not the most relevant points of consideration when forming friendships. While this did not translate to his normative theology, his christological convictions "provided him with the motivation and spirit to work, pray, study, and correspond with women friends whom he considered equal and even superior in regard to ascetic prowess."[20] As eminent counterexamples to Harry Burns, we can witness friendships of equality between women and men in the Christian tradition where the sex part did not get in the way. In fact, a commitment to celibacy opened the doors for such friendships.

At the same time, it was not as though the early church thought that friendships and sex were *incompatible*. In fact, marriage—the proper place for sex, in their eyes—was a *species* of friendship. Augustine, for instance, saw both sex and marriage as activities suitable for a certain type of friendship. Addressing the friendship of the married life, he writes, "Marriage and sleeping together, are necessary for friendship."[21] Centuries later, Thomas Aquinas continues the association between marriage, friendship, and sex: "There seems to be the greatest friendship between husband and wife: for

19. Jerome, *Letter 127*, in vol. 6 of *Nicene and Post-Nicene Fathers of the Christian Church*, 2nd series (Eerdmans, 1986), §5 (emphasis added).

20. Rader, *Breaking Boundaries*, 108–9.

21. Augustine, *De bono coniugali* ("The Excellence of Marriage"), in *Marriage and Virginity*, trans. Ray Kearney, The Works of Saint Augustine: A Translation for the 21st Century 1/9 (New City, 1999), 9.9.

they are made one not only in the act of carnal intercourse, which even among dumb animals causes an agreeable fellowship, but also as partners in the whole intercourse of daily life."[22] Finally, the most superlative statement of marriage's place within friendship likely comes from the Anglican spiritual theologian Jeremy Taylor, who in 1657 wrote the following in his influential treatise on friendship: "Marriage is the Queen of friendships, in which there is a communication of all that can be communicated by friendship: and it being made sacred by vows and love, by bodies and souls, by interest and custome, by religion and by laws, by common counsels, and common fortunes; it is the principal in the kind of friendship, and the measure of all the rest."[23] So central was friendship's role in marriage that many saw the best outcome of marriage as a celibate friendship between two people who had enjoyed a lifetime together raising children.[24]

When we look at the church's history to see whether women and men can be friends, therefore, we get a complex answer. We can discern both resistance and affirmation, but we must immediately ask another question: *What kind of friendship is in mind?* A friendship shared between persons committed to celibacy? A friendship between two persons committed to one another in marriage? Burns's confusions about sex in friendship comes from a failure to discern friendship in all of its varieties. The point often missed is that friendships vary, so the key is attending to what makes them different and when one style of friendship is more appropriate to one occasion than another. Friendships between women and men *must* exist, but that is not the interesting question. What is far more important to discern is the nature of friendship, what virtues pertain to different types of friendship, and how these reflections shed light on the different relationships that can exist between women and men. What remains true, however, is that virtuous human love shown to persons is friendship, and since friendships can differ

22. Thomas Aquinas, *Summa contra gentiles* 3.123; English translation from Thomas Aquinas, *Summa Contra Gentiles, Books III & IV*, trans. Laurence Shapcote, Aquinas Institute Latin/English Edition of the Works of St. Thomas Aquinas 11 (Emmaus Academic, 2018).

23. Jeremy Taylor, *A Discourse of the Nature, Offices, and Measures of Friendship with Rules of Conducting It, Written in Answer to a Letter from the Most Ingenious and Vertuous M. K. P. by J. T.* (London, 1657), 72, https://name.umdl.umich.edu/A63784.0001.001.

24. Paulinus of Nola, for instance, writes in a letter to Aper and Amanda, "See how you remain the married couple you were, yet not coupled as you were. You are yourselves yet not yourselves. Now you know each other, as you know Christ, apart from the flesh" (*Letters of St. Paulinus of Nola*, trans. P. G. Walsh II, Ancient Christian Writers 36 [Longmans, Green, 1967], 237).

in their types, friendship is seen as a capacious concept for thinking through good personal relationships.

As historical reflection on the varieties of friendship continued, different claims were made about which kinds of friendship were *best*. Aristotle thought that friendships based on virtue were paradigmatic.[25] Similarly, Cicero thought that the best friendships could occur only between two virtuous persons: "Friendship is not possible except between good people."[26] It is from these considerations about what kind of friendship is best that Aelred develops his particular notion of "spiritual friendship." He begins in agreement with Cicero that "friendship cannot exist among the wicked."[27] From there, he distinguishes between "carnal," "worldly," and "spiritual" friendships.[28] Whereas carnal friendships form out of sin and worldly friendship out of personal advantage, spiritual friendship, "which we call true, . . . is born of a similarity in life, morals, and pursuits, that is, it is a mutual conformity in matters human and divine united with benevolence and charity."[29] For Aelred, such conformity is Christocentric from beginning to end: "For what more sublime can be said of friendship, what more true, what more profitable, than that it ought to, and is proved to, begin in Christ, continue in Christ, and be perfected in Christ?"[30] As friends love one another in a spiritual friendship, they will develop the traits that make them more and more Christlike, making spiritual friendship one of the final steps toward moral perfection.

While important concerns have been raised about this selective and virtue-focused construal of friendship (and I am sympathetic with them),[31] it is

25. Aristotle, *Eudemian Ethics* 1236a.17, 1238a.32. See also Aristotle, *Nicomachean Ethics* 1155b.19.

26. Cicero, *De amicitia* §18; see also §20: "Without virtue friendship is not able to exist"; §48: "Virtue holds friendship together"; §74: "Good people can't be friends with bad or bad with good"; and §100: "Virtue creates and preserves friendships."

27. Aelred, *De spirituali amicitia* 2.36. When asked, "What, then, has friendship to do with us, who are not good?," Aelred shifts the goalposts: "We call a man 'good' who according to the limits of our mortality" lives in virtue (2.42–43). The tension between friendships based on virtue and the sheer absence of virtuous people is not addressed by Aelred, which reveals a limitation in his model of friendship.

28. Aelred, *De spirituali amicitia* 1.38.

29. Aelred, *De spirituali amicitia* 1.45–46. Here Aelred is adapting Cicero's definition of friendship: "Friendship is nothing other than agreement with goodwill and affection between people about all things divine and human" (§39).

30. Aelred, *De spirituali amicitia* 1.10.

31. For instance, see Oliver O'Donovan, *Entering into Rest*, vol. 3, *Ethics as Theology* (Eerdmans, 2017), 141: Classical friendship "had an ambivalent, even disdainful view of 'vulgar friendship,' and an elitist and restrictive idea of 'true friendship.'" Emphasizing virtue too

important to see friendship as oriented toward growing in virtuous Christ-likeness. The virtue that I would like to emphasize in this chapter—for reasons that will be clear in the next section—is *trust*. In the final section, I will clarify the relationship that trust has with love and safety. For now, however, notice its relationship to friendship. Trudy Govier, in her analysis of friendship, puts the matter succinctly: "Trust is certainly possible, and actual, outside friendship. But friendship is not possible without trust."[32] Friendship is the appropriate place for intimacy, and for intimacy not to be betrayed requires a successful relationship of trust. Our friends are the ones we share our hearts with, the core element of vulnerability and intimacy, and we rely on them not to betray our most intimate feelings. Such a belief in the dependability of a friend—that friend's commitment to being reliable—is the central dynamic of trust. The notion to glean here is that friendship is the place where vulnerability is safe because it is enmeshed in a relationship of trust: "We feel safe and secure with our friends. We have a confident expectation that good, not harm, will come to us from this relationship; friends are people we trust. These positive expectations are based on our sense of the friends' integrity and genuine affection."[33] As we develop a friendship, we see evidence of a friend's trustworthiness and become, slowly, willing to place ourselves in a position of potential harm, knowing that they will not take advantage of it. Good friendships require trust, in short, because of the potential for harm associated with vulnerability. We are vulnerable when we are intimate with others and open our hearts to them. Doing so can make us liable to harm; when our hearts are in the wrong hands, and when we are being harmed, we are not safe. Safety is inversely related to the likelihood of harm; the safer we are, the less we are at risk of being harmed.[34] As we go deeper into a relationship, we learn who will not harm us, and they gain our trust. This happens most fittingly in a friendship. Without the trust of friendship,

much, in short, ignores how friendships can be based not on virtue but on its pursuit, on the forgiveness of sins, and on shared weakness. If it is true that great love follows great forgiveness (Luke 7:47), then we can envisage strong friendship based around vulnerability about and forgiveness of wrongs done.

32. Trudy Govier, *Dilemmas of Trust* (McGill-Queen's University Press, 1998), 21.

33. Govier, *Dilemmas of Trust*, 32.

34. This is not uncontroversial. For a challenge to this definition of safety, and for an argument that the pursuit of safety has been overemphasized, see Jeremy Lundgren, *The Pursuit of Safety: A Theology of Danger, Risk, and Security*, Studies in Christian Doctrine and Scripture (IVP Academic, 2024). I think we can take Lundgren's recommendations for a properly theological acceptance of risk without abandoning safety altogether. Additionally, Lundgren's emphasis is not on interpersonal relationships of safety, making his arguments slightly less applicable in this case.

vulnerability becomes an unwelcome and unsafe risk.[35] It is good to hold this in mind when we go on to discuss dating, for as we shall see, a lack of safety is precisely what dating suffers from presently. To anticipate the argument, we ought to focus our efforts on cultivating trust in dating friendships, for only then will the vulnerability of dating not bring about harm. Trust is necessary to friendship because of the vulnerability involved in loving another person.

I have tried to describe theological trajectories of friendship in this section according to which friendship is what rightly ordered Christian love looks like when shown to persons. When we love persons well, we befriend them. Different accounts of the best kind of friendship have been given, and most of them center on virtue. While many different moral characteristics will be needed for friendship, I have tried to highlight *trust* for the purposes of this chapter. Friendships, because they expose vulnerability, must be characterized by trust. This, I hope, lays the theological groundwork for understanding dating. In what follows, I will describe contemporary dating practices with an emphasis on the fears, insecurities, and vulnerabilities they summon in their participants. Discerning this will shed theological light on a gendered good that makes up so much of the lived experience of contemporary people looking to form deep romantic bonds with other persons, bonds that require trust.

The Pressures of Dating

The purpose of this section and the next is to understand dating relationships and then to provide a theological analysis of them. So, first, what is dating as it is practiced these days? At its most basic level, the concern of dating is one of *criterion*. Daters today ask themselves, "What partner shall I choose, and how will I know if I have found the best one?" Social psychologists have referred to such patterns of thought as "relational maximization," according to which individuals look for the *best* partner in terms of satisfaction, investment, and commitment, and not merely a *satisfactory* one.[36] Both relational maximizers

35. Govier states this well: "Trusting our friends means that we can feel relaxed with them. We are at ease. We are willing to let ourselves be vulnerable. In the context of friendship, trust means that we expect affection, loyalty, and dependability; we feel confident and relaxed; we interpret what the friend says and does in a positive way; we can accept our own vulnerability" (*Dilemmas of Trust*, 32).

36. See Alan C. Mikkelson and Perry M. Pauley, "Maximizing Relationship Possibilities: Relational Maximization in Romantic Relationships," *Journal of Social Psychology* 153, no. 4 (2013): 467–85.

and relational satisficers employ a series of criteria to judge whether to be just satisfied or maximally fulfilled; in either case, daters are attempting to discern, with the wisdom available to them, whether they have found "the one" (or the closest approximation of "the one"). The criteria applied in dating, since it is a practice of relational maximization, is applied in the effort to find the most optimal partner.

The history of dating bears this out. In her fascinating history of personal newspaper ads, Francesca Beauman shows how those looking for love would articulate a series of desired traits for potential suitors in what might be seen as a precursor to modern dating apps like Tinder, Match, Hinge, or Bumble. These traits evolved over time, and many of them were colorful and said something about the dater. Thus, one personal ad from 1851 from a woman named Ada states, "My husband must be from twenty to thirty; good sense preferred to good looks; and no simpering fool, who imagines a lady taken off her feet by his smiles, no uneducated ape in lavender kids and yellow stick, no mature dandy, such as promenade for smiles of silly girls and impudent stares, no mustached baboon, need apply, as no one will please me but a sensible, educated gentleman who appreciates domestic happiness by the possession of one heart."[37] Ada listed her criteria for a suitable mate in the hopes that such a man would respond (sans mustache). Thus would begin the courtship, the precursor to modern dating,[38] and Ada and her companion would determine whether their criteria were met and next steps could be taken. Some ads focused on personality and appearance, whereas others would appeal to higher attributes, such as the couple who lived in "perfect equality . . . as two friends."[39] As they sat down to pen their personal ads (just as many people today sit down to create their Tinder profiles) these women and men had to think of what traits would compose their criteria for the maximally satisfactory partner.

Where did these criteria come from? Dating qualifications from the nineteenth century to today are shaped by at least three forces: context, personal identity, and common objects of love. Context might be the most important here. Beauman shows how ads changed according to where they were published. As American westward expansion proceeded, criteria shifted to

37. Francesca Beauman, *Matrimony, Inc.: From Personal Ads to Swiping Right, a Story of America Looking for Love* (Pegasus Books, 2020), 53.
38. For a helpful history of dating, see Beth L. Bailey, *From Front Porch to Back Seat: Courtship in Twentieth-Century America* (Johns Hopkins University Press, 1988).
39. Beauman, *Matrimony, Inc.*, 54.

partners who could work a field and could tolerate an intense winter. As one journalist for the *Dubuque Iowa News* recounted in 1838, "So anxious are our settlers for wives that they never ask a single lady her age. All they require is *teeth*."[40] Or again, once the suffrage movement gained traction after the Seneca Falls Convention, women began to advertise for men who were willing to have equitable relationships, especially in the home.[41] Whether it is economic, political, or even aesthetic, context shapes how daters look for their mates.

Racialized contexts also matter, particularly in today's online dating marketplace. As Christian Rudder, one of the founders of OkCupid, confessed, "When you're looking at how two American strangers behave in a romantic context, race is the ultimate confounding factor."[42] As a result, contemporary dating apps operate with algorithms that reflect racial bias. That is the observation made by sociologist Apryl Williams: "There is indeed explicit racial bias in online dating platforms—both in the algorithms that are used in sorting and within the personal dating ethos of dating app users. . . . Dating platforms automate sexual racism through the use of racialized algorithmic sorting and ranking systems."[43] The algorithms in question work as a mass voting competition; the more positive responses a user receives (right swipes on Tinder, for instance), the higher they are registered within the app.[44] They will then "protect" these higher-ranked users from lower-ranked ones, for if the most desirable users are bombarded with requests from the least desirable ones, they will leave the app.

The algorithms of dating apps not only use user responses to rank and sort matches; they also use trackable features like common friends and interests on social media, grade level of the writing on their bios, IQ, and facial-recognition algorithms.[45] The last of these explicitly takes into account racial categorizations. Regarding the facial signals they will collect, Match Group's official patent states, "Implicit signals may also include facial recognition algorithms to detect ethnicity, hair color, eye color, etc. of profiles that [users

40. Beauman, *Matrimony, Inc.*, 80.

41. Beauman, *Matrimony, Inc.*, 78–79.

42. Christian Rudder, *Dataclysm: Who We Are (When We Think No One's Looking)* (Crown, 2014), 99.

43. Apryl Williams, *Not My Type: Automating Sexual Racism in Online Dating* (Stanford University Press, 2024), 24.

44. Williams, *Not My Type*, 50–51.

45. Williams, *Not My Type*, 59, 66.

have] expressed interest in."[46] In simpler terms, the proprietary algorithms of dating apps look at their users' faces to detect both their ethnicity and the ethnicity of those to whom they respond positively, effectively encoding racial bias in their programming. The resulting ranking of racial attractiveness is predictable: "Asian men rated Black women as 20 percent less attractive than other women, Latino men rated Black women as 18 percent less attractive than other women, and White men rated Black women as 17 percent less attractive than other women."[47] Black women, according to the algorithm used by dating apps, should be read as the least valued and desired category of user. Context, including the contexts from which racial biases arise, inform the criteria used for selecting dating partners.

Second, our attempts to communicate personal identity also shape these criteria. Beauman notes how vegetarians wanted to find vegetarian partners and how persons of one weight range wanted to find partners of a similar weight range.[48] In a touching example from 1903, a "young man" with "moderate circumstances" who had "a glass eye" sought "the acquaintance of a young girl who also [had] a glass eye," so that she would not bring up his glass eye should they enter into a marital disagreement.[49] It was an important feature of their personal identity that these individuals were vegetarians, or were of a certain weight, or had a glass eye; they wanted to find someone who would see them for who they were. From that comes a desire to share common objects of love. Intuitively, if something is important to an individual, they want their significant others to share that object of importance and recognize its worth. So, in an example from 1834, a white man who was "a friend of equal rights" wanted to "bear testimony against prejudice by marrying a Colored Woman . . . (entirely or chiefly of African descent), who would be willing to endure the insults and reproaches that would be heaped upon her for being the partner of a white man."[50] Setting aside the problematic elements of reducing a romantic partner to her race, this man wanted to share something he cared deeply about with another who would be a collaborator for its advancement. Conversely, ads appeared in which the opposite was put on display: "No abolitionists need apply."[51] Whether in favor of abolition or

46. Quoted in Williams, *Not My Type*, 63.
47. Williams, *Not My Type*, 8.
48. Beauman, *Matrimony, Inc.*, 97, 117.
49. Quoted in Beauman, *Matrimony, Inc.*, 153.
50. Quoted in Beauman, *Matrimony, Inc.*, 32.
51. Quoted in Beauman, *Matrimony, Inc.*, 95.

against it, those who sought love used their dating profiles to advance and share the things they cared most deeply about.

So, dating is a matter of discerning criteria about what partners will be best for us. Those criteria come from several sources, including context, personal identity, and shared objects of love. Together, they inform us who is *best* for us, and not merely good or suitable. Yet it is also descriptively the case that contemporary dating is in a very bad place; daters have had a very difficult time identifying their criteria, sticking to them, and finding a partner in whom they see the best. Because of the vulnerability, difficulty, and rejection involved—in short, because of the *pressure* of dating—current dating feels unsafe. Sociologist Ellen Lamont discovered this when she studied daters in the Bay Area of San Francisco. These were "highly educated, professional-track young adults," those one might expect "to be at the vanguard of progressive beliefs."[52] While the narratives they held about the principles of dating reflected those progressive beliefs, Lamont found that their practice did not: "By clinging to traditional courtship scripts, young adults are unwittingly undermining the gender revolution they say they embrace. . . . Despite the expressed desire for egalitarian relationships, they tend to form long-term relationships that mirror the patterns of gender difference established during courtship."[53] While these Bay Area daters described themselves according to one narrative, their practices adhered to something different altogether. In the words of a magazine article, "You're a feminist . . . so why don't you date like one?"[54] The women she studied, for instance, wanted a balanced work life, an equitable distribution of housework and childcare, and to feel empowered and independent; but in practice, they "expect men to ask and pay for the first date, confirm the exclusivity of the relationship, and propose marriage."[55] Though these women would in principle reject many of the following courtship traditions, in practice most wanted men to define the relationship for them, to pay for their dates, to propose marriage, and, once married, they wanted to take their husband's last name.[56] Men, by contrast, were quick to identify themselves as feminists and to distance themselves

52. Ellen Lamont, *The Mating Game: How Gender Still Shapes How We Date* (University of California Press, 2020), 14.

53. Lamont, *Mating Game*, 17–18.

54. Arielle Pardes, "You're a Feminist . . . So Why Don't You Date Like One?," *Women's Health*, April 4, 2014.

55. Lamont, *Mating Game*, 54.

56. See Lamont, *Mating Game*, 61, 60, 66, 71, respectively.

from what they saw as stereotypically misogynistic men; yet they "remained very much committed to certain privileges they claim in their relationships."[57] They were quick to allow their partners to work significantly longer hours at work while still bearing the bulk of the household responsibilities, claiming that women are simply more interested in such chores.[58] Lamont concludes, "While heterosexual women and men assert that they want egalitarian relationships, they tend to cling to the idea of gendered preferences and skills."[59] Ultimately, whereas one would expect to see new and creative practices of dating emerge among these progressive partners, one ends up finding the very same courtship practices their parents and grandparents would recognize.

What is the cause of the inconsistency? Overwhelmingly, respondents testified to the pressure that dating put on them. Many were worried about rejection or being perceived as weak, or they were simply uncertain about how to proceed with dating.[60] Daters generally felt no safety or trust and found dating relationships to be hazy and obscure. To demystify this obscurity, women and men reached for the last set of dating norms they knew to be stable—namely, the putatively antiquated ones they claimed to reject. As Lamont summarizes, "Dating can be confusing and fraught with emotions. But dating norms provide a script that men and women can comfortably follow to ensure they are relating to each other in the expected ways, thereby lessening the tensions that go along with getting to know someone new. The possibility of a misstep that may take you off the other person's radar decreases."[61] While the narratives were new, dating practices, even dating practices in the most "progressive" spaces, remained the same. They may have talked the talk, but they walked a very different walk, all due to severe pressure generated by an absence of trust and safety.

This pressure and subsequent insecurity are even more apparent in hookup culture on university campuses. The years spent in university, so the popular story goes, are ones of sexual liberty and exploration for students, full of

---

57. Lamont, *Mating Game*, 80.

58. See Lamont, *Mating Game*, 143: "That preferences might be the result of gender socialization was not considered."

59. Lamont, *Mating Game*, 170. What's more, these daters explained their behaviors by an appeal to gender biological essentialism. As one of the respondents stated, "It's just partly biological. In animals, the guy always flashes. The male bird always flashes his colors—his feathers or something—to go after what he wants" (55). This is not what one would expect to hear among young Bay Area professionals.

60. See Lamont, *Mating Game*, 81, 84, 85.

61. Lamont, *Mating Game*, 176.

endless partners and reckless abandon. What actually ends up happening is that a context is created that produces relationships that leave their participants feeling hollow and dissatisfied. In her study of hookup culture on American university campuses, sociologist Lisa Wade cites students who describe their sexual experiences as "traumatic" and "very difficult to handle."[62] Female students, in particular, were caught by conflicting pressures: "Clingy, desperate, and needy are extremely effective insults, invoking all the things that students don't want to be: weak, insecure, unable to control one's emotions, and powerless to separate sex from feelings."[63] Though they did their best to avoid such insults, most college women testify to having exactly these feelings. University men were not exempt, either. Thus Wade: "One male student hooked up with three women in a row, only to be treated with indifference afterward. 'I am depressed, frustrated, and feel unrespected and worthless to the opposite sex,' he wrote dejectedly."[64] Hookup culture largely left students feeling vulnerable and unable to cultivate genuine emotional connection. As one female student lamented, "I would love to have meaningful sex with people I respect. . . . I think it could be like, you make me feel optimistic or you make me feel alive, or *you make me feel safe*."[65] Though hookup culture is the only precursor most young college students have for a world of relationships later in life, they come away feeling disrespected, distrustful, and unsafe. Because hookups are meant to be meaningless, they leave their participants feeling empty: "Hookup culture isn't carefree; it's care-less."[66]

Because Christian colleges and universities often explicitly reject hookup culture, Christians might be feeling a sense of superiority at this point. We should not. Christians participate in their fair share of hookup culture (even within Christian colleges),[67] and when they opt out, they develop their own version of cultural compulsion that turns dating into a withering force of

62. Lisa Wade, *American Hookup: The New Culture of Sex on Campus* (Norton, 2017), 15.

63. Wade, *American Hookup*, 139.

64. Wade, *American Hookup*, 144.

65. Wade, *American Hookup*, 156 (emphasis added).

66. Wade, *American Hookup*, 142. For a similar conclusion about the adverse effects of hookup culture, see Donna Freitas, *The End of Sex: How Hookup Culture Is Leaving a Generation Unhappy, Sexually Unfulfilled, and Confused About Intimacy* (Basic Books, 2013); Jennifer Beste, *College Hookup Culture and Christian Ethics: The Lives and Longings of Emerging Adults* (Oxford University Press, 2018).

67. Wade makes an alarming claim: "Men who attend church are actually more likely to hook up than non-religious men" (*American Hookup*, 97). For further analysis of this phenomenon, see Donna Freitas, *Sex and the Soul: Juggling Sexuality, Spirituality, Romance, and Religion on America's College Campuses* (Oxford University Press, 2008). For the prevalence of hookup

pressure and anxiety: *ring by spring*. This is the notion that a successful dating relationship must result in a marriage proposal by the spring of a college student's senior year. Undergirding it is the notion that dating and marriage are inseparably linked. It is not enough that dating *ideally* results in marriage; rather, *dating is only morally permissible if it results in marriage*, such that any dating relationships that fail to attain to this standard are deemed failures. Stacy Keogh George identified this assumption in her study of dating in Christian colleges: "Dating was only acceptable if the result was engagement."[68] Because marriage is not just ideal but also necessary, "romantic relationships are taken seriously very quickly," with the result that "dating becomes an extremely high-risk activity."[69] Daters on evangelical campuses described their experiences in exactly the same way that Bay Area daters and hookup-culture participants did: They felt pressure. One student said that dating in a Christian college "results in this weird *pressure* to feel committed to someone that you just went on a date with." Another explained, "Men are afraid to ask out a girl because there is *pressure* to marry that person right away."[70] In fact, observes George, "*pressure* was the most often described word in their responses" when students were asked to define *ring by spring*. The "repetition of words like 'pressure' and 'fear' and sentiments of individual failure and unworthiness occupied most of the open-ended responses."[71] The need to get a ring by spring piled pressure onto these students to think of dating with an outsized seriousness and to take steps they did not feel fully safe taking.

The "best-case scenario" occurs when a student actually gets a ring by spring. For those who do not, a general sense of failure, shame, and worthlessness accompanies their diploma (especially if the student in question is a woman).[72] One student admitted, "I feel so unworthy and unwanted. I am so afraid I'm going to be alone forever."[73] Or, again, one woman who graduated

culture on Catholic campuses, see Jason King, *Faith with Benefits: Hookup Culture on Catholic Campuses* (Oxford University Press, 2017).

68. Stacy Keogh George, *Ring by Spring: Dating and Relationship Cultures at Christian Colleges* (Cascade Books, 2019), 84. For a similar study that came to the same conclusion, see Dana M. Malone, *From Single to Serious: Relationships, Gender, and Sexuality on American Evangelical Campuses* (Rutgers University Press, 2018).

69. George, *Ring by Spring*, 83.

70. George, *Ring by Spring*, 25, 33 (emphasis added).

71. George, *Ring by Spring*, 44, 39.

72. See George, *Ring by Spring*, 24: "The reality is that the consequences of these strict dating rituals result in feelings of failures and worthlessness in the long run for those who graduate without a partner."

73. George, *Ring by Spring*, 74.

without marrying confessed, "I felt a bit vulnerable, disappointed, and like I had done something wrong. I felt even embarrassed."[74] The point here is not that happy and enduring marriages do not come about on Christian college campuses; many do. Rather, the point is that the culture in which these relationships form can stand in the way of safe decision-making, at best, and leave those who do not succeed according to its rules feeling dangerously vulnerable and unworthy, at worst.

Whichever way we look, then, dating is not doing well. Daters in the Bay Area are lost, anxious, and confused; daters in hookup culture feel empty and dejected; daters in Christian colleges feel rejected and as though they have failed. All these feelings are attributed to one repeated theme: pressure. Dating puts pressure on people by requiring a set of criteria that yields maximal returns; the one we choose must be the best, and while *best* can hold different meanings, the goal of the criteria is the same. Such pressure makes even successful dating relationships feel unsafe, scary, and tenuous. This is not a suitable environment in which to discern whether someone has found the best partner possible according to the criteria that matter most to them. Even then, those criteria might come polluted by problematic contexts, like overtly racialized standards and methods for finding a date. This, descriptively, seems to be the plight of those who go on dates in the twenty-first century.

This is not how things ought to be, normatively. How might Christians, who aspire to have their friendships characterized by trust in Christ, seek to practice something better? In the next section, I will combine the reflections on friendship and dating so far to propose a normative theology of dating and friendship aimed at safety. To practice safe dating, I will argue, friendships need to display trust. Trust is what brings love, friendship, and safety together.

Friends and Their Benefits: Safe Dating

At this juncture, a few normative theological alternatives are available. One possible route is to take a *regulative* approach to dating: Sort out the relevant rules one considers to be most important for finding the best partner, and do your best to stick to them. This is a well-worn approach, with books like *The Rules* and *He's Just Not That Into You* telling daters who feel lost how to go

74. George, *Ring by Spring*, 37.

about things.[75] More recently, and from a theological angle, Boston College professor Kerry Cronin assigns her students to go on dates for class credit, and she gives them detailed rules for how to go about it, such as forbidding them to ask for a date over the phone and spending at least sixty minutes and at most ninety minutes together.[76] When students were given these rules, they testified to feeling safer and more confident in their dating. Yet, as Ellen Lamont showed above, *having rules* and *living by them* are very different endeavors. Daters seem to continue to fall beneath their own standards, no matter how clear and useful their parameters are. Once again, we are left with the risks outlined in the previous section.

Perhaps we give up on dating altogether. We may not be so foolish as to kiss it goodbye only to regret it afterward, but maybe we simply concede that dating cannot secure a healthy long-term relationship and that the real work begins after the commitment has been made. This seems to be Stanley Hauerwas's view, captured in what he calls "Hauerwas' Law."[77] Against the assumption "that there is someone right for us to marry and that if we look closely enough we will find the right person," Hauerwas states, "We always marry the wrong person. We never know whom to marry; we just think we do. Or even if we first marry the right person, just give it a while and he or she will change. For marriage, being what it is, means we aren't the same person after we have entered it. The primary problem morally is learning how to love and care for this stranger to whom you find yourself married."[78] While his law might give the impression that Hauerwas does not think any criteria should be applied to dating, it is actually not quite so strong. In his own memoir he points to significant criteria of attraction and compatibility he considered when it came to his marriage with Paula.[79] All the same, "Hauerwas' Law"

75. See Ellen Fein and Sherrie Schneider, *The Rules: Time-Tested Secrets for Capturing the Heart of Mr. Right* (Warner Books, 1995); Greg Behrendt and Liz Tuccillo, *He's Just Not That into You: The No-Excuses Truth to Understanding Guys* (Simon & Schuster, 2007).

76. See Molly Cahill, "I Went on a Date in College for Extra Credit: What It Taught Me About Love and Worthiness Was Priceless," *America Magazine*, February 14, 2021, https://www.americamagazine.org/faith/2021/02/14/dating-assignment-kerry-cronin-boston-college-valentine-239961/.

77. He refers to it as such in Stanley Hauerwas, "Sex and Politics: Bertrand Russell and 'Human Sexuality,'" *Christian Century*, April 19, 1978, 422.

78. Stanley Hauerwas, *A Community of Character: Toward a Constructive Christian Social Ethic* (University of Notre Dame Press, 1981), 172.

79. See Stanley Hauerwas, *Hannah's Child: A Theologian's Memoir* (Eerdmans, 2010), 212–13: "One of the things that attracted me to Paula was the dedication she brings to her work. . . . She was a 'strong woman.'" Hauerwas himself notes the oddity of claims like this:

can suggest, as Rebecca Leong summarizes, that "it is what one does within marriage (rather than any practices or choices before marriage) . . . that matters most for the survival and thriving of the marital relationship."[80] As a corrective, I think Hauerwas's statement is suggestive. It is probably true that people change so much throughout the course of a marriage that even if one were able to maximize one's partner selection, such maximalization would simply be invalidated with time. "Hauerwas' Law" is a powerful reminder that relational maximization is a mistaken notion. We should not be looking for the *best* one, let alone *the* one. Even if we found such a person, their perfect features would alter with time. And yet, as Hauerwas's own practice shows, his law is not meant to abolish *any* criteria for dating. He rightly rejects relational maximalism, but we are still uncertain as to what might replace it.

Perhaps we can opt for a more virtue-oriented approach. Instead of specifying rules about how dating should go, we can identify the kind of people *we* should be, and having done so, we can have greater confidence in our dating.[81] In what is probably the most developed theological engagement with dating available, Rebecca Leong commends such a virtue-oriented approach. Her argument is that if dating is directed by the four cardinal virtues—prudence, courage, temperance, and justice, with an overarching calibration by love—then it will enable daters to flourish and image God in their relationship. Thus, prudent daters will know the difference between a "good catch" and a "good fit," courageous daters will endure difficult times with honesty and transparency while knowing when to walk away even when it is hard, temperate daters will exercise self-control when it comes to physical intimacy and know the proper place for sexual attraction, and just daters will give to each other what is due, disclosing all the relevant facts necessary for long-term commitment.[82] Finally, daters who love rightly will be intolerant of abuse and exploitation, and they will seek to order their loves to their love for God.[83] A virtue-oriented approach will provide the flexibility needed to guide daters in all their various

"Of course, I was the guy who had argued that love was an insufficient basis for a couple to think that they should be married. I continued to think that I was right about that, but I was also sure that Paula and I should be married" (210).

80. Rebecca Leong, *Living More Human(e)ly? Towards Better Approaches to Dating and Couple Relationships in Contemporary Anglo-American Contexts* (Pickwick, 2025), 31.

81. See, e.g., Jason King and Donna Freitas, "Sex, Time, and Meaning: A Theology of Dating," *Horizons* 30, no. 1 (2003): 36.

82. Leong, *Living More Human(e)ly?*, 247–54.

83. Leong, *Living More Human(e)ly?*, 256–58.

contexts and life stages, but it remains fairly distant from concrete practice. There are many ways, for instance, temperance *could* be exercised in a dating relationship, but its successful practice (as virtue ethicists themselves will tell us) will require constant practice and refinement over time. Must I go on as many dates as it takes before I am temperate? How do these virtues, timeless and imitative of divinity as they are, connect to the actual stresses of dating? Additionally, focusing only on personal virtue does not guarantee that the relationship is working toward safety. I may be a virtuous person, but if my partner does not share my commitment to virtue, I may, for that reason, still experience great harm in the relationship.

My suggestion here is that we adopt as many approaches as we can use to our benefit; none of the above recommendations is incompatible with any other approach. If it is helpful to have clear-cut rules for dating and its stages, then we ought to use them. We also ought not to approach dating as the attempt to find the maximally perfect "one," recognizing that the task of loving a constantly changing person is *itself* constantly changing and is therefore never finished. Virtues also matter for dating, both for figuring out what kind of dater to be and also for deciding what sort of person to look for. While none of these approaches suffice on their own, the complex world of dating will require us to summon every tool at our disposal. Oddly missing from all these options, however, is any direct and explicit mention of the pressure and lack of safety we saw in the experiences of daters in the last section. Pressure, peril, and feelings of worthlessness are the most descriptively salient parts of dating, and some theological guidance is needed there. What I will attempt to provide, then, to this diverse and growing body of theological resources on dating, is an articulation of what dating ought to be if it is going to address the pressure and experiences of failure and lack of safety. For that, I suggest, we need to focus on trust in dating.

What does it look like to date another person and feel safe? I think it looks like cultivating trust. Much has been written of late on the nature of trust, and what has been said shows that trust helpfully joins together the three themes under consideration in this chapter: safety, friendship, and love. We have already seen in the work of Trudy Govier that trust is necessary for friendship. Because friendship is virtuous love shown to persons, trust must also have something to say about love. When I trust another person, I share myself with them and care about them; my confidence in their ability not to harm me when I do so is one way I believe in them and attach myself to them. Because of this, ethicist Stephen Darwall states, "Trust is a form of love."[84] He draws on the work of theologian Knud Eijler Løgstrup, who saw a deep connection between trust and love.[85] When love is shown to a person, a certain vulnerability to harm is introduced, and when we rely on those we love not to harm us, we trust them.[86] This is the natural point of connection between trust, love, and safety. For a great many of those who write on trust, the difference between merely relying on someone and trusting them is accepted vulnerability. Thus Annette Baier affirms, "Trust, then, . . . is accepted vulnerability to another's possible but not expected ill will (or lack of goodwill) toward one."[87] The distinctive feature of trust, for Baier and others, is our willingness to be in a position of potential harm on the basis of our belief that the other person will not take advantage of it. Because of that, trust brings about safety: "Without trust, what matters to me would be unsafe."[88] In short, trust highlights that aspect of a relationship of love where vulnerability is accepted, an act we would do only with our friends. Because we believe they will not harm us, we trust them, and if that belief turns out to be true, we have a safe relationship.

Dating relationships, then, must aim to develop trust for the sake of safety. How might this work? I want to conclude that safe trust is found when we, with sufficient evidence, move from trusting another person with respect to external objects to trusting them in a deep, personal way. Thomas Simpson, in a recent treatment of the ethics of trust, develops a view according to which trust is believing and accepting that a friend has made a commitment to you.[89] Correspondingly, the trusted person is *trustworthy* if they possess "the disposition

---

84. Stephen Darwall, *The Heart and Its Attitudes* (Oxford University Press, 2024), 98.

85. See, especially, Knud Eijler Løgstrup, *The Ethical Demand*, trans. Bjørn Rabjerg and Robert Stern, Selected Works of K. E. Løgstrup (Oxford University Press, 2020).

86. This is beautifully articulated in Lorraine Hansberry's *A Raisin in the Sun*, where Mama tells Walter, "I ain't never stop trusting you. Like I ain't never stop loving you" (*A Raisin in the Sun* [Bloomsbury, 2021], 81).

87. Annette Baier, "Trust and Antitrust," in *Moral Prejudices: Essays on Ethics* (Harvard University Press, 1994), 99.

88. Baier, "Trust and Antitrust," 95. Elsewhere, Baier says, "Any adequate account of trust must cover those cases where there is no particular task we allocate to the trusted, but merely feel safe when moving among them, as well as cases where a definite task is allocated" ("What Is Trust?," in *Reading Onora O'Neill*, ed. David Archard et al. [Routledge, 2013], 179).

89. Thomas Simpson, *Trust: A Philosophical Study* (Oxford University Press, 2023), 112: "'Believing a speaker' or 'trusting a speaker' is the compound act of accepting a speaker's commitment to oneself and taking them to make that commitment felicitously—sincerely and from a position of knowledge."

to acknowledge one's commitments appropriately and to act in light of them," something that requires competence and motivation.[90] More simply, I trust you if I believe and accept that you will follow through on your commitments (where doing so keeps me safe from harm), and you are trustworthy if you have acknowledged that commitment and go on to carry it out. Trust, additionally, can take either two-place or three-place forms. A three-place form of trust is one where I trust you with *something*. So, if I ask my neighbor to keep an eye on my house while I travel, I have entered into a three-place trust relation. A two-place form of trust is one where the trust is directed to *a person*. It makes sense to say "I trust you" without specifying any particular object, and this might be understood as a claim about you as a person. Simpson claims that, in proper circumstances, two-place trust grounds three-place trust.[91] I will trust my neighbor with my house because, at least to some degree, I trust my neighbor. My neighbor's trustworthiness can be understood with respect to individual acts (she will check to see if I have received any packages), or it may be a claim about her as a person (she has a trustworthy character because she tends to fulfill all her obligations).[92] Two-place trust relationships often require trusting those with a trustworthy character, while three-place relationships require trustworthiness with respect to performing individual acts. Let us bring these elements together: Trust is a relationship where one accepts that the other person will come through on their commitments, making them trustworthy. Their trustworthiness can describe their dependability to perform a certain action, or it can describe their character. When we trust someone to do something (e.g., to look after our home while we're away), we have a three-place trust relationship, which requires their trustworthiness in relation to actions. When I trust a person (e.g., when I trust my neighbor), that person and I have a two-place trust relationship, which requires trustworthiness as a trait of their character. Simpson's original contribution is that two-place trust relationships often ground three-place trust relationships: "I trust my neighbor; that's why I trust her to look after my house while I am away."

There are times, however, when three-place trust grounds a special kind of deep two-place trust.[93] Trust is deep when it is strong, when it is resilient

90. Simpson, *Trust*, 58; see also 68.

91. See Simpson, *Trust*, 102, 121.

92. Simpson, *Trust*, 50.

93. On the ways trust can be deep, see Michael Pace, "The Strength of Faith and Trust," *International Journal for Philosophy of Religion* 81, no. 1 (2017): 135–50.

and durable in the face of distress, when the one trusting has a high degree of confidence in the one trusted and is therefore prepared to entrust to them matters that involve high degrees of risk.[94] We arrive at deep trust when we have experienced a person's trustworthy actions over a long period of time, when diverse circumstances present themselves, and they consistently come through. We enter into many three-place trust relationships with them, and these relationships mount up evidence for their trustworthiness as a character trait, bringing us to a place of deep trust. So, after trusting my neighbor with my house, I may ask her to take care of my pet while I am gone. After that, I may take her up on her offer to walk my daughter to school. When enough of these interactions happen, I may divulge to her some difficulties I am experiencing at work and the consequences they are having on my mental health, and I would trust her to respond well to that information. There is no clear threshold here, but eventually I may reach a point where I can simply say, "I deeply trust my neighbor." Perhaps I would "trust her with my life," or I can say that she possesses a robustly trustworthy character. She and I have a deep two-place trust relationship built from several successful three-place trust interactions.

This, to conclude, is the goal of trust in dating. Daters will begin their relationships by engaging in a variety of three-place trust interactions. They may arrange to meet at a café and trust each other to show up on time. From there, they may come to trust each other to respect their boundaries. They might leave their phones unlocked on the table, trusting that their date will not snoop through it. Each may come to trust the other to meet their friends, and their friends may make decisions about the trustworthiness of the new partner—decisions that corroborate their friend's growing trust in their new partner or that cast that trust into doubt. The point is this: A dating relationship will, ideally, be a place where three-place trust relationships can be tested out for their safety and love. As they develop, a deep, two-place trust can grow. And a deep, loving, two-place trust relationship with a friend is the safest place one can be.

It is important to note that many dating relationships are not like this. In fact, many *marriages* are not like this either. This is a normative proposal about what dating *should* be like given a description of the way things are now. Importantly, I think, it helps illuminate many of the complexities latent

94. Simpson, *Trust*, 157.

in romantic relationships. I think a deep-trust relationship is what we look for, for example, when we ask what sexual consent should amount to. Consent, that elusive ingredient missing from so many sexual encounters, has been difficult to make sense of, with some feminist theorists suggesting that we should abandon the concept altogether.[95] Sexual consent, however, is trust applied to sexual relationships; apart from relationships of trust, consent makes no sense. And while I have focused on the emotional and affective forms of harm that dating can bring about, there is also a very physical form of harm of which daters need to be aware. Sexual assault is probably the most prevalent form of harm in relationships (especially for women), and daters need to test relationships and search for evidence that an individual is truly trustworthy enough to have another person put their life and body in a position of vulnerability with them. Thus, this account of trust for dating would go a long way toward making sense of some of the most pressing issues in the ethics of relationships.

Daters have told us that they are unsafe. They feel vulnerable, rejected, and abandoned. Their relationships are superficial and devoid of care, and they want to know what it would mean to be in a safe relationship. I think many things are necessary, but if we want to know how to have friendship, love, and safety in our relationships, we must look to establishing trust. Dating relationships, I have argued, must be contexts in which three-place trust relationships are tested and evidence is gathered in order to determine whether a partner is trustworthy in both act and character. With time, a deep-trust relationship will hopefully come about. When it does, we will know the safety of another.

Conclusion

Friendships, love, safety, trust, and dating—we have considered a complex web of topics, matters deeply pressing to ordinary gendered people. Today, it is quite difficult to avoid dating if one lives in a place where it is a live option. Christian ethics must take dating into consideration, and I have attempted to

95. On an influential case for the problems with consent, see Catherine A. MacKinnon, "Sexuality, Pornography, and Method: Pleasure Under Patriarchy," *Ethics* 99, no. 2 (1989): 314–46. For a constructive account of consent that responds to these concerns, see Manon Garcia, *The Joy of Consent: A Philosophy of Good Sex* (Belknap, 2023). I have tried to develop an account for consent based on the above considerations of trust in "A Theological Account of Consent to Sex: Reciprocal Trust" (forthcoming).

give a descriptive and normative account of it. My account hinges on the claim that dating is a species of friendship, with friendship being the category of virtuous love when it is shown to persons. Friendships are the place for trust to blossom, and a relationship of trust and trustworthiness is the crucial missing ingredient when a lack of safety is felt. For many daters, safety *is* lacking. Whether they engage in traditional dating scripts despite their progressive beliefs, participate in hookup culture with a feeling of hollow disappointment, or aspire to a ring by spring on a Christian college campus, they do not enjoy safety. I have argued that, along with an array of other theological tools like rules, rejection of relational maximalism, and the pursuit of virtue, we need to build trust. Trust brings together love, friendship, and safety, and deep trust should be the goal of daters who wish for something different. With a deep-trust relationship, dating is no longer subject to painful vulnerability. In a deep-trust relationship, vulnerability is a joy.

Conclusion

Compassion, Love, and Death

> All good men will . . . avoid compassion; for it's the fault of a paltry spirit that collapses at the impression of other people's woes. Accordingly, it's most familiar to all the worst people: old or foolish women, whom even the most noxious types move with their tears—they'd stage a prison break, given the chance.
>
> —Seneca, *On Clemency*[1]

> Hear the Apostle when he endeavors to commend to us the mercy of Him who for our sake became weak so that He might gather His chickens under His wings, instructing other disciples who, from lack of strength had arisen to a certain strength, so that they too might show compassion for the weakness of their weaker brethren since He had come down to our weakness from heavenly strength. The Apostle says: "Have this mind in you which was also in Christ Jesus." "Consider it an honor," he says, "to imitate the Son of God in compassion for his little ones."
>
> —Augustine, "Sermon 264"[2]

We have thought about politics and the nature of history as understood by men. We have considered how difficult it is to make friends with our bodies and the complexities introduced by trans

1. In *Anger, Mercy, Revenge*, by Lucius Annaeus Seneca, trans. Robert A. Kaster and Martha C. Nussbaum (University of Chicago Press, 2010), 173. In this quote, for clarity, "compassion" was substituted for "pity." Both terms mean roughly the same thing, depending on the context.

2. In *Sermons on Liturgical Seasons*, by Augustine, trans. Mary Sarah Muldowney, Fathers of the Church 38 (Catholic University of America Press, 1959), 398–99 (slightly altered for clarity).

identities. We have recognized the marketing that pervasively surrounds us. We have looked at the clothes we put on. We have appraised the food we eat. And we have tried to understand the dates we go on and the friends we make. Though certainly not exhaustive, these are the elements of many of our gendered days. In response to the otherworldliness often characterizing theologies of gender today, the chapters in this book have sought to place gender back where it belongs: in the world, amid the cares of ordinary people who have ordinary yet terribly important lives to live.

The above chapters have attended to two tasks: the descriptive and the normative. While they have not followed any particular conceptual or chronological order, each chapter has described the topic in question and looked to make normative recommendations for how to handle it. The theological tools used to make these normative recommendations have been an appeal to the eschatological nature of humanity and a focus on the moral importance of love, particularly as the latter plays a key role in the formation of social identities and in providing a contextually flexible framework for evaluating gendered goods despite their differences across time and place. Put together, I have argued, love and eschatology yield compassion. As we consider human weakness in the face of death before the completion of all things in Christ, our primary moral response to ourselves and one another should be loving care and compassion.

While I have said quite a bit about love and eschatology, I have not made clear what I mean by compassion. Having seen how compassion should be shown in different contexts throughout the chapters of this book, we can now see what it is in itself. For those who will consider other topics in gender and theology, my recommendation is that they do so compassionately, and I hope to have done so up to this point. But what is compassion, and what does it require of us? In this conclusion, I will give an account of the virtue of compassion that has been in the background in the previous chapters. Hopefully, the account will coalesce the normative claims of this book into a summative moral recommendation. I will argue that compassion is what love looks like when it is directed to those suffering during the time before the last things (what I have called the *saeculum*), a time when all of humanity is mired in death. This death brings us to a place of common vulnerability, weakness, sorrow, and complexity; compassion is the Christlike response to those who, like us, walk in death.

Eschatology Plus Love Equals Compassion

Many who have reflected on compassion have begun with Aristotle's definition in the *Rhetoric*. For Aristotle, compassion "may be defined as a feeling of pain at an apparent evil, destructive or painful, which befalls one who does not deserve it, and which we might expect to befall ourselves or some friend of ours, and moreover to befall us soon."[3] Aristotle defines compassion as a feeling or emotion that consists of three necessary parts: (1) we perceive someone suffering in a serious way (i.e., *seriousness*) (2) for something they are not guilty of (i.e., *nonculpability*) (3) that we can imagine ourselves facing (i.e., *solidarity*). So, compassion has often been seen as a feeling directed at serious, underserved, and potentially mutual suffering.[4] In relation to these three criteria, however, Christians have some important modifications to make. As Robert Roberts has argued, "Christianity does have a distinctive kind of compassion, both as an emotion and as a virtue."[5] Christian compassion generates some distinctively theological pressures that alter Aristotle's three conditions in fairly important ways.

Before attending to the three criteria, we must assert that, theologically, compassion is not merely an emotion; it is a form of love. As Roberts states, "Compassion is a form of love based in the fellowship of suffering and deficiency," which makes it "a form of neighbor-love."[6] Intrinsic to compassion is caring about someone and identifying with that care. We witness their plight, it becomes important to us, and we do not regret this orientation of our hearts. When we care about something, I have previously argued, we love it.[7] Since compassion is a type of care for the frail, vulnerable, and suffering, it is a type of love, one that is directed toward neighbors.

There is a unique way Christians confess that humanity suffers seriously, which is the first criterion. While we readily acknowledge that serious suffering

3. Aristotle, *Rhetoric* 1385b.13–16; ET from Aristotle, "Rhetoric," in *The Complete Works of Aristotle*, ed. Jonathan Barnes, vol. 2, Bollingen Series 71.2 (Princeton University Press, 1984), 2152–269.

4. For a discussion of compassion in this tradition, see Martha C. Nussbaum, *Upheavals of Thought: The Intelligence of Emotions* (Cambridge University Press, 2001), part 2.

5. Robert C. Roberts, *Attention to Virtues: An Affective Grammar* (Cambridge University Press, 2025), 69. In this section, I am heavily indebted to Roberts's account of compassion in this book and in his previous work.

6. Robert C. Roberts, *Spiritual Emotions: A Psychology of Christian Virtues* (Eerdmans, 2007), 180.

7. Fellipe do Vale, *Gender as Love: A Theological Account of Human Identity, Embodied Desire, and Our Social Worlds* (Baker Academic, 2023), 158–61.

exists, we make a further claim: All people on pilgrimage to God suffer on account of that pilgrimage. That pilgrimage, whose end point is the consummated kingdom of God, is characterized throughout by death. Nussbaum, Roberts, and others have shown that how one understands evil and suffering significantly shapes how one understands compassion.[8] Christians confess that our alienation from God is a unique form of suffering that serves as a category for all other suffering. Augustine puts it powerfully:

> The troubles of our pilgrimage. This very fact that we are not yet home with God, that we are tossed about amid temptations and vexations, that we cannot be free from fear—all of this is tribulation. This is not the security promised to us. Any of us who have not discovered this tribulation that dogs our pilgrimage are not under pressure to return to our homeland. . . . We are confronted by miserable people to whom we show mercy, and the misery of the miserable arouses compassion in us. . . . It is easy enough for a sick person to recognize that he or she is wretched: but when you are in good health, ask yourself whether you are miserable because you are not yet with God.[9]

All kinds of miserable sufferings can serve as grounds for compassion. Enveloping them all is a story about how human beings are estranged from the source of all good, how sin has corrupted and tarnished all that we enjoy, and how any experience of health and peace we know now is restrained by its incompleteness and liability to fail. Because we have not arrived home from pilgrimage, because our promised eschatological state is still ahead of us, our lives are characterized by pain and suffering.

There is another way to see this. Nussbaum observes, "Implicit in pity itself is a conception of human flourishing, the best one the pitier is able to form."[10] Our compassion, demonstrates Nussbaum, depends on our ability to measure up someone's current state against what it would mean for them to flourish. In the introduction, I argued that a person's true self, the self that thrives and flourishes, is a person's eschatological self. It is only when

8. Roberts, *Attention to Virtues*, 70: One's "concept of evil radically affects their concept of compassion." See also Nussbaum, *Upheavals of Thought*, 357.

9. Augustine, *Expositions on the Psalms, 33–50*, trans. Maria Boulding, The Works of Saint Augustine: A Translation for the 21st Century 3/16 (New City, 2000), 401.

10. Martha Nussbaum, "Compassion: The Basic Social Emotion," *Social Philosophy and Policy* 13, no. 1 (1996): 33. As above, *pity* and *compassion* name the same virtue, though with different connotations.

we are resurrected that death is defeated and we see God face-to-face (1 John 3:2). Or we can say with Saint Paul that we have not "already reached the goal," or telos, of our lives. Instead, we must be "straining forward to what lies ahead," pressing on "toward the goal" of the "heavenly call of God in Christ Jesus" (Phil. 3:12–14). No human beings, prior to their resurrection, can say that they flourish. Until then, there is always cause for compassion. Most people, in the words of Daniel Lee Hill, are "carrying on": "At times, it seems to me, the best we can do in a postlapsum world is to strive to carry on and encourage one another to do the same."[11] This is a world devastated, hurting, and weeping tears of what could have been in the light of the way things are supposed to be. None of us flourish, though we have been promised flourishing one day. This distance between the world as it is and the world as it should be, our lives as they are and our lives as they should be, is not bridged in the saeculum. This contrast supplies the contextual ground for the serious suffering all of us face simply on account of the fact that we have not yet arrived at home.

Compassion requires serious suffering, and Christians understand that serious suffering as an eschatological tension. The second of Aristotle's conditions for compassion is that those suffering cannot be culpable for their suffering. If they are the cause of their own suffering, so goes the thinking of Aristotle, they cannot be pitied. Christian compassion, by contrast, makes the opposite claim. Christian Scripture directly links compassion to the effects of sin and death. In fact, Christian compassion in its most characteristic form directly requires a prior judgment of sinfulness. Psalm 78, after observing that Israel's "heart was not steadfast toward" God and that "they were not true to his covenant," says, "Yet he, being compassionate, forgave their iniquity, and did not destroy them. . . . He remembered that they were but flesh, a wind that passes and does not come again" (78:37–39). God's compassion takes into full account the prior sinfulness of the pitied; indeed, taking that sinfulness into account is a prior condition of God's compassion. Similarly, Psalm 103 illustrates how "a father has compassion for his children, so the Lord has compassion for those who fear him" by making reference to our sin: "He does not deal with us according to our sins, nor repay us according to our iniquities. For as the heavens are high above the earth, so great is his steadfast

11. Daniel Lee Hill, *Bearing Witness: What the Church Can Learn from Early Abolitionists* (Baker Academic, 2025), 84n86.

love toward those who fear him; as far as the east is from the west, so far he removes our transgressions from us" (103:10–13). Finally, the prodigal son's father "saw him and was filled with compassion; he ran and put his arms around him and kissed him" when he recognized his son's confession of sin "against heaven and before" him (Luke 15:20–21). Rather than claiming that compassion is incompatible with sin, Christianity makes the opposite claim: Compassion is the proper response to sin.

The reason Christians can say that sin is not an obstacle to compassion but a ground for compassion has to do with the nature of forgiveness. Roberts notes, "In the Christian tradition compassion and forgiveness are closely associated: compassion is frequently a motivation for forgiveness, and forgiveness clears the way for compassion. . . . The gospel itself is a story of God's compassionate forgiveness of the human race. All have sinned and fallen short of the glory of God. The world is not divided into forgivers and forgiven; every forgiver needs forgiveness."[12] In Aristotle's day, forgiveness was not given a prominent social position, which would have been necessary for compassionate action.[13] A Christian account of compassion can draw upon forgiveness, by contrast, because it must be christological in its emphasis: Because Christ has forgiven us out of his compassion, we too must be compassionate and forgiving toward both ourselves and others. This was Augustine's exhortation quoted in the second epigraph to this conclusion: We must "imitate the Son of God in compassion." Susan Wessel captures his idea nicely: "For Christians, the highest ideal is to feel the same compassion Christ felt for the weakest of the weak and imitate the divine compassion."[14] Christ is the one who forgives sin out of compassion. He grants "the forgiveness of their sins" by the "tender compassion of our God" (Luke 1:77–78, alt.).[15] Since we are called to imitate Christ, we too must direct our compassion toward sinners.

A worry arises here: This claim makes sense for those who *suffer* from sin at the hands of evildoers, but does it apply to those who commit the sins? Can we show compassion to the wicked and evil? I think the answer here is yes, but with important clarifications. First, we must say that an evildoer's

12. Roberts, *Attention to Virtues*, 73–74.

13. For the argument that forgiveness was not available then, see David Konstan, *Before Forgiveness: The Origins of a Moral Idea* (Cambridge University Press, 2010).

14. Susan Wessel, *On Compassion, Healing, Suffering, and the Purpose of the Emotional Life*, Reading Augustine (Bloomsbury Academic, 2020), 75.

15. "Compassion" here translates the Greek word *eleous*, the same word Aristotle uses. I have altered the NRSV's "mercy" to "compassion" on account of this.

disposition to do evil deeds is *pitiable*. Their inability to do good and resist the forces of death is a weakness on their part, a weakness that does a great deal of damage. Just as a broken part in a car's engine can do great damage to those who ride in the car, the brokenness of the evildoer can wound. Yet that brokenness is not a great strength of theirs; it is a pitiable and lamentable aspect of who they are, a flaw of character from which they suffer. Roberts observes, "It takes resoluteness and a bit of empathetic insight to see through the façade of strength and boasting and arrogance and wealth and power and intelligence to see one who is in trouble, one of God's lost sheep."[16] Second, the compassion I show to evildoers may appropriately take different forms. I can show compassion on account of someone's weakness and suffering from a flawed character and think that they need to be kept apart from the people they might harm. We can have resources removed from them to keep them from doing damage and have them removed from leadership positions. All of these responses are compatible with compassion; in fact, compassion might even ensure that they are carried out appropriately. We can stage a revolution that ousts a leader and yet, if we lack compassion, impose a cruel regime in its place. A right perception of the weakness of human beings can guard against this. Finally, Christian eschatology puts us in the awkward place of saying that no one is inescapably lost in this life. It is potentially and hopefully true of all evildoers that they will come to the end of their ways and repent.[17] They should not be kept within arm's reach of the vulnerable before they change for the better, but compassionate care is always possible alongside their potential and actual repentance.

So, unlike Aristotle, Christians must make a prior judgment of the sinfulness of those on whom they will have compassion. That prior judgment, moreover, must be made of ourselves as well. Compassion, on Aristotle's third condition, requires *solidarity* with the one being shown compassion. Nussbaum comments, "The point seems to be that the pain of another will be an object of my concern only if I acknowledge some sort of community between myself and the other, understanding what it might be for me to face such pain."[18] Without this, I would be indifferent to the suffering of the other. I must have solidarity with the one to whom I am showing compassion. This

16. Roberts, *Spiritual Emotions*, 193–94.

17. This is one way, though not the only way, to read the character arc of Zacchaeus, the rich tax collector who committed himself to make reparations for those he defrauded (Luke 19:1–10).

18. Nussbaum, "Compassion," 35.

is not, to be clear, the same thing as empathy, where empathy is understood to be "*the act of coming to experience the world as you think someone else does*."[19] Neuroscientists Tania Singer and Olga Klimecki emphasize the difference between empathy and compassion: "In contrast to empathy, compassion does not mean sharing the suffering of the other: rather, it is characterized by feelings of warmth, concern and care for the other, as well as a strong motivation to improve the other's wellbeing. Compassion is feeling *for* and empathy is feeling *with* the other."[20] Although compassion requires some kind of solidarity with the person at whom it is aimed, that solidarity does not need to be empathy (though it could be).[21] In fact, there are theological resources for solidarity that do not directly appeal to empathy.

Christians do not need to imagine themselves in the plight of another because, in a real sense, they are in the same plight. For much of the Christian tradition, suffering and sin are neither optional nor avoidable: "In the world you face suffering [*thlipsin*]" (John 16:33, alt.). Given that original sin is a universal property of all unglorified humanity, and original sin both makes our lives miserable and necessarily means that we will make the lives of others miserable, it is untenable to assume that anyone can avoid suffering. We all, in one way or another, limp and stumble on our way to God. In discussing Augustine's view on the matter, Wessel captures the idea well: "In the light of Adam's guilt, feelings of remorse, sorrow, and pain—what Augustine would have called *dolor* and *miseria*—were intrinsic to the examined Christian life. The question was not whether to feel remorse, sorrow, and pain, but how to contextualize and give legitimacy to such feelings in a well-lived, morally rich existence."[22] Ideally, then, we would have a storehouse of sorrows from which to draw when it comes time to be compassionate. When I see the misery of others, I know something of what it is like to be miserable, and I draw upon those resources to be a compassionate consolation. Augustine is clear: "So long as we bear the weakness of this life, . . . we certainly would not be living

19. Paul Bloom, *Against Empathy: The Case for Rational Compassion* (Bodley Head, 2016), 16.

20. Tania Singer and Olga M. Klimecki, "Empathy and Compassion," *Current Biology* 24, no. 18 (September 2014): R875.

21. Paul Bloom makes the stronger claim that the solidarity required for compassion actually could not be empathy, given empathy's selective tendencies and the possibility of expressing empathy with vicious emotions. See Bloom, *Against Empathy*. My argument does not depend on Bloom being incorrect; if he is correct, the alternative avenues for solidarity that I mention will suffice.

22. Wessel, *On Compassion, Healing, Suffering*, 7.

rightly if we did not feel these emotions at all. . . . For so long as we are in this place of misery, to live entirely without pain—as one of this world's men of letters saw and said—comes only at the high price of an inhuman mind and unfeeling body."[23] To have no analogue for the suffering of another in one's own heart is to deaden one's heart or to be in ignorance of one's own true state.

Roberts's account of compassion highlights this helpfully. When it comes to solidarity, he affirms, "*the sufferer and I have a common vulnerability*."[24] We both bear the corruption of death, and I can recognize in my object of compassion the same ailment that plagues me. Like Nussbaum, Roberts argues that there is an important sense in which we must do serious self-examination to detect how our own hearts are broken and liable to break the hearts of others: "Suffering can become the basis of compassion only if the person in some way comes to an acceptance of it. If I dissociate myself from my own death, sufferings, sins, and inadequacies—denying that they are really part of me and part of my condition in this life—then it is natural that I will keep my emotional distance from sufferers."[25] It is from a deep familiarity with our own tears that we can cry with others. A stance of superiority or distance fails to peel back the layers to uncover the underlying sadness that afflicts every sin-struck heart. Or, in the words of Saint Paul, Christ "consoles us in all our affliction, so that we may be able to console those who are in any affliction with the consolation with which we ourselves are consoled by God. For just as the sufferings of Christ are abundant for us, so also our consolation is abundant through Christ" (2 Cor. 1:4–5). Paul describes a cascading dynamic when it comes to making it through miserable times. Divine sustenance enables Paul to sustain those to whom he ministers. Roberts summarizes the self-awareness necessary for compassion:

> [The process of becoming transparent to myself] forces me to come to terms with my vulnerability and weakness; I come to know viscerally and steadily that I am destined for death and subject to moral failure, and in one way or another I become reconciled to this fact. I get an emotionally clear view of myself in my darker aspect, and thus lay the groundwork for seeing as fellows those who

---

23. Augustine, *City of God*, trans. William Babcock, ed. Boniface Ramsey, The Works of Saint Augustine: A Translation for the 21st Century 1/6 and 1/7 (New City, 2012–13), 14.9.

24. Roberts, *Attention to Virtues*, 74.

25. Roberts, *Spiritual Emotions*, 183.

> are walking through the valley of the shadow of death. . . . The experience of suffering, finitude, and dysfunction is needed in the development of compassion; in addition one needs an acceptance of these as a part of one's identity.[26]

Compassion begins when I have taken true stock of myself and see the sorrow within. Drawing from that, I can show solidarity to those who are sorrowful before me. This is compassionate solidarity.

It is plainly true, however, that not all suffering is the same. I write this as my toddler son undergoes leukemia treatment. Many loving and well-intentioned people have been hesitant to tell me how their lives are difficult after they have asked me about mine. While they are insecure about comparison and complaining, this often has the effect of isolating that person from me. They feel as though their suffering is meager when placed alongside mine, but this often undermines their compassion. While suffering exists on a wide spectrum, Roberts reminds us that we can "stretch" our self-concepts by picking up "analogues of weakness" and using them as "points of departure, to see commonalities between [the sufferer] and her weak neighbor."[27] Under the biblical command to "rejoice with those who rejoice, weep with those who weep" (Rom. 12:15), Christians need to find the space between flattening all suffering into trivialities ("I know just how you feel!") and isolating the sufferer from any commensurate sharing ("I can't imagine how you feel!"). That middle space is the solidarity that comes from stretching ourselves to see that the cause of our misery is shared, even when its expressions are not. This is the sense of compassion that I hope shines through the discussion of trans identities in chapter 2, above; in a way, that chapter can be summarized as a call to a deep sense of theological solidarity for the sake of compassion.

Compassion was helpfully analyzed by Aristotle as an emotion that involves three components: a perception of serious suffering, a lack of culpability for that suffering, and a solidarity shared with the sufferer. Christian compassion, I have argued, modulates this analysis. Compassion is not merely an emotion but a form of love brought forth by the fact that the love of God has been poured into our hearts by the Holy Spirit (Rom. 5:5). Serious suffering has occurred among all of humanity because no human being is their true self. A true self is a flourishing, eschatological self, and our pilgrimage toward that end means that we all endure serious hardship and heartache. Human

26. Roberts, *Spiritual Emotions*, 184.
27. Roberts, *Spiritual Emotions*, 188.

beings are meant to be so much more than what we are, and this is a serious fault. Against Aristotle, Christian compassion embraces the sin of the one being shown compassion, not least because compassion is an avenue for and consequence of forgiveness. And finally, Christian solidarity means that we recognize sin in ourselves too, stretching our own experiences of suffering and propensity to harm and turning them into occasions for solidarity with others. This does not require our suffering to be identical in proportion or breadth to someone else's, but it does require an ability to weep with those who weep.

The Road Traveled and the Road Ahead

My hope is that the above elaboration of compassion is not foreign to those who have read the previous chapters of this book. Hopefully it is a recognizable distillation of the normative moral parameters I have offered throughout. Love and eschatology, our two normative guides, yield compassion. So, with respect to politics, I have tried to point out how aggrieved men failed in their compassion, opting to generate enemies rather than to see the saeculum as a complex time when all suffer deeply. Even so, I have suggested that we show compassion to these misguided men, recognizing genuine pains at their losses and recommending broad-based community organizing as a resource, especially when they can partner up with surprising allies who have similar grievances. I have also tried to show that the source of the conflict between our bodies and our gender identities is the death that characterizes our common plight, recommending that our task now is to cultivate friendship with our bodies, showing compassion to one another as we struggle to do so together in solidarity. Marketing, I have argued, creates a deadly environment where we do not choose what gendered goods are placed before us, and compassion requires that we all find creative ways to redirect those goods. I have also put forward a theological account of modesty with respect to gendered clothing, one according to which modesty is the compassionate recognition that our worth is attributable not to our outward displays but to our identity in Christ. As we wait for the eschatological revelation of Christ, we clothe ourselves in this compassionate modesty. Gender and food requires, I have argued (in distinction from diet culture's caloric Pelagianism), a compassionate *body okayness*, where we know that our bodies will not be fully lovable but that they nonetheless require our compassionate care. Showing compassion to one's own body may be the hardest moral task recommended in this book, for we each "carry around in our body the death of Jesus"—a defeated death, to be sure, but a painful one all the same (2 Cor. 4:10 NIV). Finally, I have suggested that safe dating requires the cultivation of trust so that vulnerability can be shown without damage being done. Compassion recognizes the vulnerability of all those whom we date, presuming their weakness and being careful with it.

With these tools, finally, we can see how the topics left untreated in this book can be analyzed. We could have addressed, for instance, gender and education: For so many years, equitable education was not available to girls, and much of the early feminist movement was concerned with making it available. How should we think today about the growing rates of girls entering STEM fields? Is this progress? To the degree that it represents the overcoming of a previous obstacle, surely it is. But does it come at the cost of other forms of knowledge important for human development?[28] Or again, we may have treated not just dating but also marriages and families, and there is a lot to mention in relation to what an ideal family should look like and how historical forces have made gender factors far too weighty in the social formation of families.[29] Finally, though it was often mentioned in relation to the topics covered in this book, we could have explicitly considered race in its connections with gender.[30] Race, like gender, is an identity that organizes social goods. Yet, unlike gender, race's dogmatic location within the biblical story depends on the domination of others, a domination introduced by sin. As Jonathan Tran, Willie Jennings, Brian Bantum, and others have argued, race is dependent on death: It is a way of structuring our worlds so that some may be dominated and exploited by others, often painfully and cruelly.[31] So, whereas something remains of gender after the eschatological healing of all

28. The key figure here is Mary Wollstonecraft. See Emily Dumler-Winckler, *Modern Virtue: Mary Wollstonecraft and a Tradition of Dissent* (Oxford University Press, 2022).

29. See, for instance, Emily Hunter McGowin, *Quivering Families: The Quiverfull Movement and Evangelical Theology of the Family* (Fortress, 2018); and Emily Hunter McGowin, *Households of Faith: Practicing Family in the Kingdom of God* (IVP Academic, 2025); on parenthood, see Amy Laura Hall, *Conceiving Parenthood: American Protestantism and the Spirit of Reproduction* (Eerdmans, 2008).

30. For important theological reflections on gender and race, see Kelly Brown Douglas, *Sexuality and the Black Church: A Womanist Perspective* (Orbis Books, 1999); and Delores S. Williams, *Sisters in the Wilderness: The Challenge of Womanist God*, 20th anniversary ed. (Orbis Books, 2013).

31. See, crucially, Brian Bantum, *The Death of Race: Building a New Christianity in a Racial World* (Fortress, 2016); Willie James Jennings, *The Christian Imagination: Theology and the Origins of Race* (Yale University Press, 2011); Jonathan Tran, *Asian Americans and the Spirit of Racial Capitalism* (Oxford University Press, 2021).

wounds and the undoing of all unjust social systems, nothing will remain of race apart from its scars and lacerations.[32] How might these differences, while being recognized, illuminate the points of commonality between gender and race? The gamble I make in this book, though space and time have not allowed direct treatment of these other topics, is that they *could* be discussed in much the same way that the above chapters have discussed politics, bodies, food, and so on.

In *Gender as Love*, I argued that gender is the appropriation of cultural goods pertaining to the sexed body through our loves, by means of which the sexed body is socially manifested in something like an identity.[33] In this book, I have examined some representative cultural goods that I have judged to be very relevant to the lives of ordinary gendered people to help us discern how to love them well. I conclude now by saying that loving gendered goods well and loving them compassionately are the same task. Compassion is what love looks like in the time before the completion of all things. With it, we can live our theologies of gender in a complicated world torn apart by death and its associates. In its presence, we can love with the love of Christ, empowered by the Spirit, thereby resisting death until Christ returns. How, then, should we love our gendered world? Compassionately.

32. See the theologically insightful account by Daniel Lee Hill, "The End of Race? Racial Identity and the Resurrection of the Body," *Pro Ecclesia* 32, nos. 1–2 (2023): 47–72.

33. See do Vale, *Gender as Love*, 143.

Acknowledgments

I wish I had the presence of mind and memory to thank all those who have supported me and cared for me during the writing of this book. I can write about compassion only because I have been shown compassion in occasions both great and small.

This book began during a sabbatical generously granted to me by Trinity Evangelical Divinity School, and I am grateful to Dean David Pao and my colleagues in the systematic theology department—Kevin Vanhoozer, Kimberley Kroll, Michael Sleasman, and Harold Netland—for allowing me such a luxury, especially during a difficult time at the institution.

I had opportunities to share these ideas at a variety of conferences and presentations, and I am grateful to those who invited me and to those who attended and offered insight. I presented portions of chapter 1 to those in attendance at the Calvin University Healthy Dialogue Series on election night in 2024, and I am grateful to Noah Toly and Jodi VanWingerden for their hospitality. The same material was also shared at the 2025 Political Theologies for a Democratic Common Life conference at New College, Oxford University, and I am thankful to those who attended and to Luke Bretherton and Marietta van der Tol for the opportunity. Material from chapter 5 was presented as a keynote at the 2026 annual meeting of the American Scientific Affiliation; thank you to Janel Curry for the invitation.

Many people read and offered generous feedback on various parts of the book, and I thank them for their care and time. Daniel Lee Hill is an ever-present conversation partner and has shaped my thought in more ways than he knows; friends like him are difficult to find, and he reminds me of what is valuable in life and in the work we do. Matt Jenson, likewise, read many of these words, offered crucial book recommendations, and was a consistent source of emotional intelligence. The "Fronds"—Ty Kieser, Gayle Doornbos, and Sam Keithley—gave me insightful feedback and provided an unfailingly caring and encouraging theological community for me. Madison Pierce, Joshua Jipp, and Michelle Knight were key helps in moments when I needed insight on biblical materials, and they are all splendid friends in their own right. Anna Gissing first believed in this project and was a source of insight and encouragement; Dustyn Keepers, who took over as editor after Anna, also clarified and strengthened the work. Alex DeMarco's keen editorial eye made what I wrote so much cleaner and easier to read. Thank you to these individuals and any others I have not mentioned.

This book was completed as my two-year-old son underwent leukemia treatment, some of it at his bedside when he was critically ill. I imagine this shaped my writing in ways I cannot fully appreciate, and it is important to acknowledge Oscar here. I am grateful he is still with us and for how he makes me aware of my heart. Eliza, my daughter, exemplified fortitude and love throughout the treatment, and I admire her for how she endured a confusing and difficult time. The people listed in the previous paragraph also prayed for us and were sources of compassion, making a scary time not feel so lonely. In addition to them, Jamie, Becky, Sam, and Pippa Davies deserve special mention. You welcomed us to a new environment when we were at our worst, and you made us feel like family. Peter and Sue Hatton, likewise, took amazing care of us, and the church communities of St. Edyth's and Highgrove did not hesitate to show genuine Christian care. My colleagues and students at Trinity College, Bristol, were understanding and supportive when their new lecturer started work quite frayed at the edges. The medical staff at Bristol Royal Hospital for Children also deserve thanks. In very tangible ways, all of these people made this work possible.

I have dedicated this book to my wife, Karla. The year in which the latter part of this book was written was laden with trouble—a cancer diagnosis, an intercontinental move, not knowing when safety and stability might be felt again, and a dismantling of our sense of self. Through it all, I am so grateful for you. You have taught me what I know about compassion, friendship, and trust, and you know me better than anyone else. That is no easy task. Thank you for your courage, support, and belief, for weeping with me and rejoicing with me, and for being a constant when everything else felt unstable. With you I feel safe.

Lent, 2026

Index